Reconceptualizing
Social Policy

INTRODUCING SOCIAL POLICY
Series Editor: David Gladstone

Published titles

Reconceptualizing Social Policy

Sociological Perspectives on Contemporary Social Policy

AMANDA COFFEY

Open University Press

Open University Press
McGraw-Hill Education
McGraw-Hill House
Shoppenhangers Road
Maidenhead
Berkshire
England
SL6 2QL

email: enquiries@openup.co.uk
world wide web: www.openup.co.uk

and Two Penn Plaza, New York, NY 10121–2289, USA

First published 2004

A catalogue record of this book is available from the British Library

ISBN 0 335 20629 8 (pb)   0 335 20630 1 (hb)

Library of Congress Cataloging-in-Publication Data
CIP data applied for

Typeset by RefineCatch Ltd, Bungay, Suffolk
Printed in the UK by Bell & Bain Ltd, Glasgow

Contents

Series Editor's Foreword

Welcome to the fifth volume in the Introducing Social Policy series. The series itself is designed to provide a range of well informed texts on a wide variety of topics that fall within the ambit of social policy studies.

Although primarily designed with undergraduate social policy students in mind, it is hoped that the series – and individual titles within it – will have a wider appeal to students in other social science disciplines and to those engaged on professional and post-qualifying courses in health care and social welfare.

The aim throughout the planning of the series has been to produce a series of texts that both reflect and contribute to contemporary thinking and scholarship, and which present their discussion in a readable and easily accessible format.

Amanda Coffey has produced an innovative, well informed and, at times, provocative discussion of the ways in which sociological perspectives can be used to explore, describe and analyse contemporary social policy.

After two chapters exploring the historical traditions and contemporary 'turns' in sociological theorizing – such as postmodernism and feminism – she then addresses themes that are – or are fast becoming – part of the discourse of studies in Social Policy: citizenship and identity; equality and difference; the ways in which social policy practices and processes focus upon bodies in terms of potential, function and needs; and the value of space and time as a means of examining everyday social settings. In each and all of these substantive discussions, Amanda Coffey contributes to the development of theorizing and firmly anchors her discussion across a wide range of policies, practice and experience.

This lucid and clearly written account will thus have its appeal to a wide variety of students and their teachers. It informs. It challenges long-held assumptions. It urges a reconfiguration of the subject and its research techniques, strongly advocating an approach that is both more open and accepting of newer perspectives. But, in addition, it also encourages the reader not only to study Social Policy but to critically engage with the techniques of social research. For Coffey, the research activity is an integral activity of what it is to 'do' Social Policy.

The two final chapters in which she explores the subject's 'research capacity building task' is another of her important messages. Her image and exploration of 'researchers engaging with and in people's lives – sharing their experiences, fears, hopes, concerns and problems' makes this a timely and very welcome addition to the Introducing Social Policy series.

David Gladstone, University of Bristol.

Acknowledgements

I am grateful to Justin Vaughan and Miriam Selwyn (both formally of Open University Press) for all of their support during the writing of this book. I am also grateful to Mark Barratt of McGraw Hill/Open University Press for seeing the project through to completion. I would especially like to acknowledge David Gladstone for inviting me to write the book, and for being a most supportive series editor. Chapter 4 of the book draws on research undertaken with Tom Hall and Howard Williamson, and funded by the Economic and Social Research Council (grant number R000236673). I would like to acknowledge the continued support of my colleagues in the Cardiff School of Social Sciences – especially Tom Hall, Jonathan Scourfield, Rob Evans, Emma Renold, Paul Atkinson and Sara Delamont. I would also like to take this opportunity to thank Pete, Kath, Paul, Nell, Debbie and Martin for being such brilliant friends, and to whom I owe a special debt. Finally, all my love and thanks to Julian.

chapter one

Introduction

Explorations and opportunities

This book undertakes a sociological exploration of contemporary social policy. It considers some of the ways in which sociological theories, frameworks, concepts and ideas can be used to make sense of – and in some instances rethink – the worlds and work of social policy. The book does not claim to be a definitive text on the relationships between sociology and social policy. Nor is it a comprehensive and systematic sociological analysis of a distinctive field of study. Rather the aim of the volume is to explore the *potential* of applying and drawing upon sociological perspectives as part of a broader project of social policy analysis.

To an extent, making the distinction between social policy and sociology – as fields of study or as intellectual disciplines – is in itself arbitrary. There is certainly a considerable degree of overlap between the two. The subject matter and preoccupations of social policy – such as relationships between the State and the individual; the identification, explanation and amelioration of social problems; social justice and (in)equalities – have also long been associated with sociological analyses. The establishment and development of social policy as an academic discipline was in itself set within an interdisciplinary context – and appropriately drew upon the scholarship of sociologists as well as political scientists, economists and philosophers. Many contemporary scholars of social policy continue to work with/in sociological discourses, and would position themselves as working across and between the disciplines of social policy and sociology.

Equally, many students of social policy will, of necessity and opportunity, visit similar intellectual spaces – across and between the two disciplines. It is difficult to learn and teach about social policy without at least some recourse to sociological research and ideas. Moreover, many social policy degree schemes and programmes of study are located within interdisciplinary social science schools and faculties.

Many of these complex and longstanding relationships between sociology and social policy are often taken for granted, and certainly rarely made an explicit focus for discussion and analysis. Thus this volume aims to go some way to addressing that gap, by recognizing and exploring the sociology *within* social policy. This then is a not a matter of undermining social policy as a field of study or as an academic discipline in its own right, but rather an opportunity to build upon longstanding intellectual friendships between the disciplines, and perhaps, also, to forge some new friendships along the way.

The (re)definition of social policy

Social policy is not an easy arena or discipline to define, as Alcock, Payne and Sullivan (2004: 1) note: 'Social policy as an academic field of study is one of those curious items, rather like an elephant, which we recognise when we see it, but which is notoriously difficult to describe.' There are at least three different ways of attempting a definition of or for social policy, all of which have been subject to some revision in recent times.

Firstly, social policy has conventionally been used as a term to denote a set of policies and practices concerned with promoting social welfare and well-being. This definition has most usually been associated with the provision of social welfare through institutions of the State. However, the growth of more plural economies of welfare has prompted a recognition that social policies can be made, enacted and implemented within and outside the auspices of the State.

A second definition of social policy builds directly upon this initial understanding, and recognizes social policy as a distinctive field of study. The conventional study of social policy has been concerned with the Welfare State and its main social services (health, housing, education, social security and personal social services). But this demarcation only goes some of the way towards recognizing arenas for social policy, and hence for social policy analysis. At its broadest, social policy could incorporate all government policy that has, by definition, a social dimension. More specifically there are a range of policies – for example, concerned with the family and with the labour market – that might not be explicitly identified as distinctively social policies, but which do, nevertheless, have social welfare implications. Moreover, the recognition that well-being is also promoted and hindered from outside as well as from within the State (through, for instance, the family, the voluntary sector and the private market) extends the scope of social policy as a diverse series of arenas or fields of study.

A third definition of social policy is in part encapsulated within this, and is concerned with social policy as a distinctive academic discipline – not only with a (re)defined subject matter and empirical agenda, but also with its own theoretical and conceptual frameworks. As Twigg (2002) notes, social policy as an intellectual discipline emerged out of a particular historical moment (of the post-war welfare states) and built a theoretical and conceptual base from the assumptions that underpinned that moment. Like other social science disciplines, social policy has been keen to mark out its theoretical spaces and analytical frameworks. And as with other disciplines, these spaces and frameworks have been challenged and reshaped by broader theoretical developments, such as those associated with feminism, postmodernism and poststructuralism. For example, the pursuit of all-encompassing theoretical explanations has been 'troubled' by calls to diversity, difference, partiality and the local. Thus, alongside other social science discourses, the discourses of social policy have been increasingly subjected to critical scrutiny.

Hence, there have been 'shifts in the contours and orientation of social policy' (Lewis 2000: 1), and thus social policy has been and remains difficult to define in any simple sense. As noted above, there have been a number of changes within the (inter)disciplinary field and subject of social policy in recent decades. These have partly occurred as responses to wider social changes and transformations, which have shifted the theoretical, empirical, political, economic and social landscapes within which contemporary social policy is located. Social policy has been reconceptualized – both in terms of 'what counts as social policy', and in terms of the tools for social policy analysis. It is no longer desirable, or indeed possible, to define social policy in terms of a narrow understanding of social welfare or social services. Such understandings have been disrupted, not least by neoliberal and other challenges to the very idea of the welfare state. There has been an increasing recognition of the multiple and plural routes to and of social welfare and well-being. Moreover, in so far as it ever was, it is no longer appropriate to view social policies in isolation from other forms of social organization and social structure. For example, the changes to family life and the domestic spheres more generally, and the restructuring of employment and labour markets, have had profound impacts on the agendas for and experiences of social policy. The arenas of social policy have also broadened in other ways. It is difficult to sustain a simple national view of social policy in the face of increased global communications, and the processes of globalization more generally. There are a range of international and transnational settings for social policy-making, implementation and experiences, which interconnect with national processes and practices. There has also been increasing reflection on the ways in which our experiences of, and interactions with, other spheres of social life – for example, the arts, popular culture, consumption, leisure and travel – have social policy dimensions, not least in terms of the promotion or hindrance of well-being.

In general, then, it is possible to identify fundamental shifts in what might be considered the sphere(s) of social policy. There are certainly increasingly expansive opportunities for thinking about the empirical and theoretical projects of social policy, as well as its field and subject matter. That is not to say that social policy as an academic discipline is necessarily teeming with new ideas, interests and understandings. Indeed, some commentators have remained rather cautious of such theoretical or empirical expansions, and their consequences for the distinctiveness and underpinning aims of the discipline (Taylor Gooby 1994; Carter 1998). And it remains a matter of debate as to how far contemporary students of social policy are (or should be) exposed to these shifts in focus, orientation or explanation. Nevertheless, by taking a more holistic, and a less essentialist, view of social policy it is possible to expand the social policy horizon in analytically useful and important ways (Twigg 2002; Alcock *et al.* 2004).

Such an approach fits well with the application of sociological perspectives, which to a greater or lesser extent have been subject to the same shifts, developments and transformations. Thus the definition of social policy that is used in this book implicitly adopts a more dynamic and holistic approach than perhaps some social policy commentators would wish. While the institutions and social welfare practices of the State remain an important dimension, these are set within wider contexts of social policy provision and experience. Social policy actors thus include statutory policy-makers, welfare practitioners and recipients, but also others who are involved in providing and consuming social policy, or those who are implicated or reconstructed with/in social policy discourses. The same general approach is also adopted for the intellectual discipline of social policy, both recognizing its historical-theoretical basis and its broader contribution within (inter-disciplinary) social science.

Aims and themes

The main agenda of this book is to draw upon sociological perspectives and analyses in order to expand upon, rethink and challenge contemporary understandings of social policy. The book considers the everyday experiences, arenas and sites of social policy, as well as the empirical and intellectual development of the academic discipline. The book is concerned with using sociology as a set of frameworks and tools for thinking with and thinking about, rather than providing an exhaustive critical sociological commentary on social policy. Interwoven throughout the book are a number of overarching and interconnected sociological themes. These do not map directly onto individual chapters, but rather are ideas that are recurrent within and across chapter demarcations.

Identities and biographies

The book is concerned with exploring the ways in which identities are shaped by and in turn help to shape social policy processes and experiences. This recognizes the ways in which personal and social identities are negotiated and fluid, rather than fixed and static, and the ways in which selves, lives and social policy are connected and interwoven. Throughout the book, therefore, are examples of the ways in which auto/biographies are constructed and reconstructed through and by everyday social policy. Social policy is thus reconceptualized as experiential, embodied, temporal and spatial, through which lives are lived, remembered and retold.

Experiences and lived realities

There is also a related focus within the book on the everyday lived realities of social policy. The book explores the ways in which everyday social policy is defined, negotiated and accomplished. This theme underpins discussions of concepts such as citizenship and equal opportunities, but is also explored through investigations of some of the mundane and ordinary aspects of social policy – such as familiar social institutions, understanding social policy as work, and managing and coping. Hence the book is concerned to show the impact that social policy processes, interventions and outcomes have on individuals and social groups, and the ways in which social (policy) actors make sense of their lived experiences.

Discourses and representations

Contemporary developments in social theory have placed an increased emphasis on discourse – the language, texts, signs and symbols that underpin everyday social life and through which social life is constructed and accomplished. There are a number of competing (or indeed complementary) discourses of social policy, including policy analysis, as well as professional and practitioner discourses. A theme running through the book is the ways in which these various discursive practices underpin the practice and the intellectual project of social policy, and the ways in which alternative discourses can disrupt taken-for-granted assumptions. More generally, there is a concern throughout the volume with the (re)presentation of social policy. That is, the ways in which social policy is and can be (re)presented – through discourses, narratives, and empirical and professional projects.

It is perhaps appropriate to say something at this point about other (sociological) themes or topics that are implicit within the text. Of course, the way in which this book is organized is only one possible way of addressing complex relationships between social policy and sociology. There are a number of core topics that could equally have been used to organize the text – social categories such as socio-economic class, gender, ethnicity or age; or key concepts such as power, bureaucracy or the State. Indeed, it would be difficult to write a text on 'sociological perspectives' without reference to such fundamental topics. (It could equally be argued that it would be almost impossible to write a text on social policy without recourse to the very same topics and themes.) Hence these themes are present within the book, and while not a central organizing principle, do provide some points of continuity between and across individual chapters.

Organization and structure

The book is thematically organized to reflect a range of ways in which sociological perspectives can be utilized to explore, describe and analyse social policy. The first two substantive chapters consider some of the possible relationships between sociological theory and social policy. Chapter 2 begins by offering some working definitions of sociology, and provides a brief history of classic sociological thought. This provides a theoretical and conceptual framework for exploring how we might think sociologically about social policy. Chapter 3 continues this discussion through an examination of contemporary developments in sociological theory. Sociology has engaged in a range of 'critical conversations' in recent years, with intellectual movements such as feminism and postmodernism. The implications of these conversations for sociology, and for sociological perspectives on social policy, are explored in this chapter. This includes a consideration of the impact of feminism on the discipline and practice of social policy, and an exploration of the seeming reluctance on the part of the discipline of social policy to engage with postmodernist discourses.

Chapters 4 and 5 provide more specific examples of the ways in which sociological perspectives can help to reconceptualize social policy principles, theoretical frameworks and underlying assumptions. Chapter 4 explores historical and contemporary discourses of citizenship and identity. The contributions of sociology to the ways in which citizenship is redefined, enacted and experienced are explored, and set within a social policy context. Transitions to adulthood and citizenship education are two of the main empirical examples discussed in this chapter. Chapter 5 takes the concepts of equality and difference as its main focus, and explores the rhetorics and realities of equality of opportunity with/in social policy. The chapter draws upon sociological and feminist articulations of equality, diversity and difference, and considers some of the implications of the new politics of difference for social policy.

The last four chapters of the book place greater emphasis on the everyday experiences of social policy and the ways in which these experiences are researched and represented. Chapters 6 and 7 consider some contemporary sociological themes and their implications for making sense of social policy. Chapter 6 draws upon sociological explorations of the body and the embodiment of social life. The chapter explores some of the reasons why social policy analysts have not been overly keen to engage in the development of an embodied perspective, before going on to explore the various kinds of body work, body organization and body talk that take place within social policy arenas. Chapter 7 is concerned with the spatial and temporal dimensions of social policy, and draws upon sociological understandings of time and space. Thus this chapter explores the times of and for social policy, and the spaces through which and in which social policy is accomplished. The temporal rhythm of social exclusion is used as a specific example, and aspects of identity construction and consumption are also explored.

The book concludes with two chapters that address methodological and epistemological issues. Chapter 8 specifically focuses on the researching of social policy. It notes the strong empirical tradition of the discipline, and the simultaneous lack of critical attention to methodological concerns. This chapter is also practically focused, and provides an overview of the range of research strategies that are available to the social policy researcher, together with examples of these strategies in action. The chapter ends with a brief consideration of methodological developments that might make a difference to the ways in which social policy research is conceptualized. These developments are expanded upon and consolidated in the final chapter of the book. Chapter 9 considers crises, innovations and experiments within sociological research, and explores some of their possible implications for the discipline of social policy. The chapter includes discussions of writing and representation, the role of auto/biography, and undertaking research in technological and digital times. The chapter ends with some brief comments about research capacity-building within social policy

In summary, *Reconceptualizing Social Policy* considers the theorization, conceptualization, experiencing, researching and representing of social policy. These help to give the book a logical internal structure, and provide some explicit links within and between the chapters. Each chapter can also be read on an individual basis, and this inevitably leads to a small amount of necessary repetition. To ease navigation and readability, each chapter has an introduction that clearly identifies its main themes, contexts, aims and structure. Where cognate issues and themes are discussed, appropriate references have also been made across and between chapters.

Further reading

Lewis, G., Gewirtz, S. and Clarke, J. (eds) (2000) *Rethinking Social Policy*. London: Sage. An excellent edited collection that considers the implications for social policy of contemporary intellectual and political shifts. The contributors show how the discipline of social policy can be, and is being, expanded and reworked through new disciplinary, theoretical and substantive analyses.

Townsend, P. (1975) *Sociology and Social Policy*. London: Allen Lane. This classic text considers some of the historical and intellectual continuities between social policy and sociology. While now rather dated, it remains an important contribution to our understanding of the relationships between the two disciplines.

Sociological Theory and Thinking

Introduction

Sociology can be a difficult discipline to define, not least because its subject matter is varied and wide-ranging. Sociological investigations and analyses encompass a wide spectrum of issues, topics and contexts – including, for example, the local and the global; individual social encounters and structural responses to social change; the management of social organizations and institutions; and individual lives, biographies and experiences. Giddens (1997: 2) has described sociology as a 'dazzling and compelling enterprise'. Partly this is a recognition of its broad scope, but this also refers to the sociological enterprise, and what sociology sets out to do – that is to understand 'the subtle yet complex and profound ways in which our individual lives reflect the contexts of our social experience' (Giddens 1997: 3). One way of defining sociology therefore is in the way(s) in which it sets out to consider, describe and make sense of the relationships between individual lives and social contexts. Developing the sociological imagination (see Mills 1959), is hence concerned with understanding the larger social (cultural, economic and historical) 'scene' or 'stage' in which individual lives take place and are 'performed' (Goffman 1959). Within such a general working definition it thus becomes possible to envisage what sociologists 'think' about, regardless of their particular theoretical postionings. While there are a range of theoretical perspectives that have shaped, and continue to shape, the discipline of sociology, there is a common focus on illuminating the processes and patterns that give shape to, and are shaped by, society. Sociological thinking in this sense, then, is concerned with 'seeing' the social, and exploring the links between the social (society) and the individual.

There is an extent to which all of the chapters in this book are about developing the sociological imagination and thinking sociologically; 'seeing' the social and reflecting upon the ways in which this shapes, and is shaped by, individual experiences. The book as a whole is about developing a socio-logical imagination *about* social policy; exploring the ways in which so-ciological ideas and perspectives can be used to illuminate the processes, patterns and experiences of social policy. It is perhaps unhelpful, therefore, to distinguish too readily between those chapters that focus primarily on 'theory' or 'ideas' and those that concentrate on more substantive or empirical areas. All the chapters in the book are about developing and using sociological theories and ideas. However, it is important to develop some understanding of the historical and contemporary contexts of sociology, and the ways in which different sociological perspectives have emerged and developed. Contemporary sociological work draws upon a range of differ-ent theoretical perspectives, and these various positionings have different, though often complementary, implications for the sociological study of social policy. This chapter and Chapter 3 have both been written with this in mind.

This chapter provides a brief introduction to (what are often described as) classic sociological perspectives and theoretical positionings. These include functionalist, Marxist and interactionist perspectives. The aim of the chap-ter is not to provide a comprehensive or critical reading of sociological theory. This is beyond the scope of this volume. Many of the introductory sociology texts already have accessible chapters on sociological theory and the history of the discipline (see, for example, Macionis and Plummer 2002; Fulcher and Scott 2003) and there are also more detailed and critical social theory texts (see, for example, Craib 1997). Rather this chapter explores some of the ways in which 'classic' or 'conventional' sociological theory and perspectives might relate to, and be used in, analyses of social policy. The first sections briefly outline the historical development of soci-ology, and introduce the main (conventional) schools of sociological thought. The chapter then goes on to explore how it might be possible to think sociologically about social policy.

Thinking sociologically

Sociology as an academic discipline has historically been characterized by a range of different theoretical positionings and frameworks. For the purposes of this chapter (and indeed this volume) it is perhaps unhelpful to think of these necessarily as oppositional or mutually exclusive perspectives. This does not deny that different sociologists can have different and/or opposing understandings of the social world, or that some theoretical positions can be more persuasive than others. It is, however, important to recognize that all social theories can be viewed as particular and situated, and that social theories can be used in combination with one another. More generally, in order to draw upon sociological perspectives, it is not necessary to align oneself to any one particular sociological school of thought or theoretical position. Rather it is possible to think about sociological ideas as a toolbox of theoretical, methodological and analytical resources on which one can variously draw.

At a very general level, sociological theory, in its many different guises, has a common objective: to try to describe, understand and explain the social world. Sociological work subjects social processes, institutions and phenomena to systematic analyses. From these analyses come theories or 'ideas' about how the social world works. C. Wright Mills (1959) coined the phrase the 'sociological imagination' to capture this process of thinking sociologically about the social world. Mills put forward the position that sociology (and sociological thought) has the capacity to transform personal problems into public and political issues. This illuminates a key aspect of sociological work – the way in which it allows us to move from individual experiences to collective understandings of the social world, and to explore the interconnections between the two. So to 'think' sociologically is to critically examine relationships between the collective and the individual; to explore the ways in which the biographical and the social are intertwined; and to study the particular in order to explore general patterns and processes. The specific frameworks that are drawn upon in order to undertake these tasks, and the analytical and methodological strategies that are employed, are part of what distinguishes different social theorists and schools of sociological thought. There are a range of theoretical and methodological influences that have scaffolded the development of sociology as a discipline, and serve to underpin contemporary sociological analyses. The levels of analyses, choice of social processes, institutions and phenomena to be studied, and strategies of social investigation used to substantiate theoretical work, can all provide points of comparison and contrast between sociologists. In turn, these are informed by different traditions, theoretical frameworks and social theorists. One way of making sense of these complementary theoretical perspectives is by considering the historical development of sociology as an academic discipline.

A brief history of sociology

The beginnings of the contemporary discipline of sociology are often located within the context of the Enlightenment of the 1800s, and associated with (male) scholars who were concerned with attempting to establish a 'science of society'. For example, the German philosopher and social thinker G.W.F. Hegel recognized historical shifts that were taking place in society (even then) – from the local to the global, and the associated growth of political and social institutions – and began to theorize about the relationships between culture, social organization and social action. The actual term 'sociology' is usually credited to Auguste Comte, a French social philosopher. Writing in the first half of the nineteenth century, he coined the term 'sociology' to characterize his developing ideas about the study and understanding of society – and used it to describe a kind of 'social physics' (Giddens 1997). Comte developed and advocated a view that we should be 'scientific' in method in order to understand society. This drew directly on a positivist view of (social) science, and advocated the study of directly observable phenomena, and the systematic identification of connections or patterns in those observations. Hegel and Comte were among a group of social thinkers who developed ideas that societies can be characterized as complex systems and social structures, with 'observable' laws, interdependencies and institutions, and within which individuals are embedded. In some quite fundamental ways these ideas remain at the heart of sociological investigation and theorization.

From these nineteenth-century beginnings has developed what is often referred to as the 'grand narrative(s) of sociology', and with this the identification of classical schools of sociological thought. This particular story of sociology is one with which many students of sociology will be familiar. The grand narrative(s) usually revolves around a rather small group of men (often just three) who all theorized about society during the latter decades of the nineteenth and early decades of the twentieth centuries. Of course, contemporary understandings challenge the idea that there is ever only one 'story' to be told, and recognize that all narratives are constructed in order to reproduce a particular version of social reality (see Chapter 3 for a more detailed discussion of contemporary theoretical perspectives). Thus in rehearsing some aspects of the grand narrative here, the intention is not to represent this story of sociology as the only story that can be told. Nor is it to privilege this story above all others. But, within the context of this particular book, it is perhaps helpful to indicate some of the different approaches that were developed in order to theorize about and seek to understand the social world. For example, Karl Marx, Émile Durkheim and Max Weber (often referred to, some would say controversially, as the founding fathers of sociology) presented different ways of seeing and understanding the social world, and emphasized complementary aspects of the social. (It is, of course, impossible to give a full account of, or do justice to, the ideas of these (or indeed other) social theorists within the confines of this chapter. See Craib 1997 for a good overview; also see Eadie 2001 and Delamont 2003 for feminist critiques of the grand narrative(s) of sociology.)

The work of German scholar Karl Marx will be familiar to those within and outwith the discipline of sociology. Marx articulated a view of society that drew upon the concepts of power, class and inequality. Marx concerned himself with attempting to understand the development of capitalist societies, and in particular with the ways in which the relations of labour and capital operated in order to reproduce inequalities – the mainstay of capitalism. Marx's contribution to the development of social theory and sociological theorizing has been significant. Marxism, as a body of ideas, has been appropriated, developed and adapted in a number of different ways (including, for example, by feminist and postcolonial scholars). Marxist sociology developed as a particular school of sociological thought during the mid-twentieth century. Moreover, many of the ideas of Marx have informed sociology more generally. For example, the concept of social reproduction, often associated with Marxist theorization, has been widely adopted and used within sociology. Also attempting to map, explain and indeed prompt social change, as Marx was concerned to do, underpins many contemporary articulations of sociology.

While Marx was an economic, philosophical and social commentator of the nineteenth century (rather than a sociologist *per se*), Émile Durkheim is often credited with establishing sociology as a scientific discipline, taking forward the vision of Comte. Durkheim, a French philosopher, became one of the first professors of sociology, in the early twentieth century. His sociological studies sought to systematically link the individual to the collective – through the observance of 'social facts'. Social facts were defined by Durkheim as those aspects of social life that give shape and context to individual lives. These facts are, by definition, things that can be studied – and might include social institutions and other structures within which collective action and representation takes place. Durkheim developed an analysis of the ways in which societies are functionally organized in order to maintain social order and social solidarity. Durkheim observed a high degree of specialization or division of labour within modern society – whereby there was a clear differentiation of tasks (including social, legal, political and economic functions). According to Durkheim, this social organization was based on a specialization of function, and built upon reciprocity, trust, shared norms and common values. Thus Durkheim was able to consider how society is patterned and ordered (through this functional differentiation or specialization), and how the individual relates to the collective or the social. Durkheim also considered the (undesirable) consequences of this order or solidarity breaking down, which he described through his concept of 'anomie'.

Both Marx and Durkheim were concerned with social structure, and with how society operated and was organized. As such both of these scholars worked at a macro level. Max Weber, a German contemporary of Durkheim, was also interested in the structure and organization of society. Indeed, he wrote extensively on the nature of bureaucracy, and was primarily concerned with the nature and exercising of power and authority. However, Weber was also keen to recognize the significance of social action (and indeed social interaction), and argued that social action rather than social structure should be the analytical starting point for sociological work. Hence Weber reflected upon the ways in which social actors interpret and make sense of social worlds, and how social action can have real and symbolic value. This prompted the beginnings of an understanding that it is possible to have different meanings and interpretations of social reality (and hence society). Weber developed a conceptual tool of 'ideal types' in order to explore this phenomenon. The development of ideal types was not an attempt to categorize society (and individuals within society) in any definitive sense. Rather, it presented a way of exploring the variety of social experience, meaning and action through the construction of possible types (or ideals).

These brief sketches of Marx, Durkheim and Weber do a considerable disservice to their lifetimes of scholarly work. Certainly no reader of this book should take these brief synopses as any kind of definitive guide to their work, or to the historical and theoretical development of the discipline of sociology. They are presented here to provide a 'gentle' introduction to some of the ideas and concepts significant in the development of sociology; and more particularly to illustrate the ways in which 'sociology' has always encompassed a variety of perspectives and frameworks. For our purposes it is certainly more helpful to think of the ways in which these perspectives, frameworks and understandings might complement, rather than fight, one another. For example, structure and action are themselves complementary ways of viewing the social world, and many contemporary sociological perspectives would draw on both. Early scholars of 'sociology', such as Marx, Weber and Durkheim, were all engaged in theoretical projects aimed at understanding complex social realities. They were all writing of, and in, changing economic, political and social times, and developing their ideas in relation to present and future transformations. In the next section of this chapter, some of their legacies are outlined in terms of the schools of sociological thought that developed during the twentieth century.

Consensus, conflict and interaction

It is possible to categorize or describe the development of modern sociological theory in a number of different ways. For example, different sociological canons have developed on different continents and in different countries. It is possible to make distinctions between American and European sociology, and between German, French and British traditions. There is a rich cast list to be acknowledged in addition to those individuals already mentioned in this chapter, all of whom have contributed, in some way, to the development of the discipline – such as Robert Merton, Talcott Parsons, Erving Goffman and Michel Foucault. While some of these, for example Foucault, would not necessarily identify themselves as sociologists, their ideas and theoretical frameworks have become part of the stock in trade of sociology. More recently, scholars such as Pierre Bourdieu, Basil Bernstein and Ulrich Beck have consolidated and expanded this sociological landscape (Bourdieu 1990; Beck 1992; Bernstein 2003). Of course, it is also important to recognize that the grand narrative of sociology has in itself been a 'malestream' story. Feminist scholars have sought to make visible the significant contribution of women to the founding and development of sociology, and in doing so have both critiqued and developed sociological theory (see Deegan 1988; Delamont 2003; also see Wise and Stanley 2003 for a review of feminist sociology). Recent articulations of social theory, such as postmodernism and poststructuralism, have also presented new challenges for sociology (see Chapter 3 of this volume). Any summary of the scope and diversity of sociology, and particularly of sociological theory, cannot do justice to these contributions, or the multiple sociological perspectives that have emerged as a result. However, acknowledging this rich diversity is important in its own right. Moreover, it is empowering in that it provides a range of theoretical backdrops from which to develop sociological analyses and insights.

A rather conventional way of distinguishing between main schools of sociological thought is to map the ideas of social theorists (such as Marx, Weber and Durkheim) onto the sociological perspectives and approaches that developed over the course of the last century. This is an imprecise science, and any mapping can only be a broad approximation. However, such an approach can be used to consider the contrasts and complementarity of different sociological frameworks, and thus is a useful exercise to undertake. Moreover, these distinctions or bodies of work are often presented as the cornerstones of sociology in introductory texts, and hence may well be familiar to readers already. For example, some of the legacies of Durkheim's work include functionalist and structuralist approaches to sociology. As Delamont (2003) has argued, there are at least two Durkheimian traditions in contemporary sociology – the North American version of positivist social science developed by Parsons, and the Gallic version of structuralism that has been carried forward by scholars such as Lévi-Strauss and Bourdieu. The distinction between these two is significant, given that they have led to rather different bodies of empirical and theoretical work. However, and relevant for our purposes here, the structural-functionalist schools share some common elements. These include: a focus on the normative frameworks and social structures of society; a recognition of complex divisions of labour and social positions; an emphasis on social order and social rules; a consideration of the ways in which social functions are differentiated (and social norms learned and reinforced) in order to promote stability and solidarity. Hence these sets of sociological perspectives continue and develop macro-analyses of society. These analyses recognize social complexity. Moreover, they are concerned with the ways in which society is organized, and achieves order and stability through consensus.

As with all social theoretical frameworks, structural functionalism (in all its various guises) is subject to critique. However, it is important, at this stage, not to set up unhelpful dichotomies between different schools of thought. Our theoretical choices or preferences do not have to be characterized in terms of either/or, and indeed many sociologists would reject any requirement to align themselves with any one theoretical school or perspective, preferring instead to draw on a range of theoretical resources. However, it is worth noting that structural functionalism adopts a macro perspective to the study of social life and social organization, and in so doing, structure is perhaps prioritized over experience and action. Further, while these theoretical perspectives are predicated on the recognition (and indeed the inevitability) of social difference, this is not the same as problematizing social inequalities. Structural-functionalist perspectives have thus been critiqued in terms of their capacity to square social justice concerns with societies reliant upon significant social differentiation and inequality.

By contrast, the sociological work that has drawn upon and developed Marxist theoretical perspectives has placed much more emphasis upon social inequalities and the need for social transformation. To an extent such perspectives also recognize complex divisions of labour and social positionings, but theorize these within frameworks of power, inequality and conflict. Hence there are recurrent concerns – with the ways in which resources are distributed; the ways in which power and authority are reinforced and reproduced; and the unequal relations between different groups within society. From these positions, the social world is hence conceptualized, not so much in terms of shared values and social solidarity, but in terms of struggle and transformation – to retain, gain or overthrow power. Hence this range of theories (that might include, for example, neo-Marxism, feminist Marxism and some postcolonial theories, among others) is concerned with identifying the conditions that might bring about social change and the elimination of inequalities. Like structural-functional perspectives, these so-called conflict theories continue a macro analysis of the social world, whereby individuals are subsumed within understandings of collective structures and collective action. There are other similarities that could be explored. For example, an ironic contrast can be drawn between *socialization* into the shared norms and values of society (order through consensus) and the *reproduction* of existing relations of inequality (order through coercion). Both of these positions could be articulated in terms of the maintenance of certain kinds of societal 'order', through processes of learning and assimilation.

By contrast, interactionist theories, in very general terms, are primarily concerned with the social encounters and interactions of everyday life; with the construction of everyday knowledge and the enactment of the mundane and the ordinary. Hence interactionist perspectives concern themselves more with the micro order of society. To an extent, therefore, interactionist perspectives build upon the earlier sociological work on social action, as they emphasize the real and symbolic value of everyday interactions between social actors. Interactionist work within sociology has drawn upon a range of theoretical influences, and as with other 'schools' or 'traditions', there is considerable variety in application and form. Indeed, it can be argued that interactionist ideas have been associated with, and have informed the development of, a variety of contemporary theoretical and methodological work (Atkinson and Housley 2003). The development of interactionist sociology was closely associated with the development of sociology at the University of Chicago in the 1920s and 1930s and, among other things, informed a set of methodological commitments (based on qualitative fieldwork). Sociologists working within an interactionist framework have had a sustained interest in the ways in which individuals and social groups experience the social world, and how, through social interaction of various kinds, societies, identities and 'realities' are socially constructed. Within this there has been a recurrent focus on meanings, signs and symbols, and an understanding of social worlds and social identities as the outcomes or products of social processes and interactions, located with/in particular places and specific times. Erving Goffman (1959) was a key figure within the development of interactionism – not least through his work on social identities and the self. One of his contributions was the development of the metaphor of everyday social life as theatre or drama. Adopting a dramaturgical analysis enables us to think of the social world as a 'stage', and people as 'actors' and 'audiences'. Thus it becomes possible to understand the ways in which social actors present and represent their 'characters' or social identities (referred to by Goffman as managing the 'personal front'). It also enables social worlds to be conceptualized in terms of 'frontstage' (public/visible) and 'backstage' (private/'behind the scenes'); to consider the relationships between these different settings and sets of activities; and to think about the ways in which social identities and the self are managed and constructed on and off these different 'stages'.

In keeping with the other comments in this chapter, it is not the intention here to either defend or damn particular sociological perspectives or theoretical schools. Arguably interactionism has had a considerable impact on the development of sociology, and while often not recognized in quite such explicit terms, 'many of the key ideas of interactionism have become part of the contemporary mainstream of sociological thought' (Atkinson and Housley 2003: x). For example, ideas around identity management, the construction of the self, relationships between the person and the organization – as well as a commitment to qualitative methods of inquiry – have been developed and 'claimed' by many contemporary scholars. At the same time, a criticism that can be levelled at interactionist perspectives in the round is that broader calls to social structure can be obscured. Nevertheless such perspectives are useful in thinking about the ways in which social worlds and social identities are experienced, understood, constructed and represented through everyday social processes situated in particular places and times.

The sociological perspectives that have been outlined within this chapter of course only tell a partial story and recount a partial history of the intellectual development of the discipline. There are other histories and other stories to be told, some of which are outlined in the next chapter (for example, the development of feminist sociology, and the influence of postmodernism). However, the distinctions that have been made in this chapter often form the starting point of 'conventional' introductions to sociology, and in that sense might be thought of as the classic perspectives and legacies of some of the early contributions to sociological understanding. It has not been the intention within this chapter to provide a comprehensive review of these different perspectives or schools of sociological thought. Nor is this chapter an appropriate forum for detailed or sustained critiques of any or each of them. Nor, incidentally, does any inclusion or exclusion mean an unreflective adherence to the conventional story of sociology. Rather, the purpose of this brief overview has been to indicate something of the range of theoretical frameworks available for sociological thinking and analysis.

In a short chapter of this kind it is impossible to do justice to the richness of these theoretical perspectives. (Indeed, whole volumes can be and have been written on each.) But it is possible to begin to see the differences and value of each – for example, concerns with structure, action and interaction; or the ways in which social change is managed and understood. As was indicated earlier, it is perhaps more helpful to think of different sociological traditions or theories as complementary rather than oppositional, certainly in terms of the potential they offer for describing and explaining the social world. That is not to say that as individuals we will not be persuaded by or drawn to some sociological perspectives more than others, or that as social researchers we might find them more or less helpful in terms of the questions they help us to pose about social life or the social world, and the guidance they offer for sociological investigation. Most importantly however, sociological theories – and the ideas, concepts and methodologies that are associated with them – are tools to help us think. Even if we choose to critique or reject one theoretical perspective or another, they will still have served this purpose of making us think imaginatively and critically about the social world.

In the remainder of this chapter, attention is turned to the ways in which it might be possible to think sociologically about social policy. This draws explicitly and implicitly on the range of sociological perspectives that have been outlined thus far, as well as beginning to consider the wider applications of sociological theorizing for making sense of contemporary social policy. To an extent this is the intention of this book as a whole – to provide sociological perspectives on social policy. However, in order to set the scene for the chapters that follow, it is a useful exercise to explore the general theoretical contributions that sociology can bring to an understanding of social policy arenas and domains.

Thinking sociologically about social policy

The variety of theoretical, and indeed methodological, approaches within sociology provide a rich framework for analysing social policy. Both individually and collectively, different sociological perspectives have the potential to contribute to our understanding of social policy processes and practices; including through their theorization of the State. The State, and to a lesser extent social welfare, has been a recurrent topic of interest to sociologists, not least in the ways in which the State is viewed a vehicle for, and measure of, wider social transformations (Hay 1996). There have been functionalist analyses of the State and social welfare that have emphasized the ways in which the State has responded to changing welfare needs (Wilensky 1975), and more critical analyses that have linked the development of welfare states to class conflict (Esping-Anderson 1990; Pierson 1998). The development of modern welfare states has been conceptualized and understood through analyses of conflict and struggle, as well as industrialization and social differentiation. The actual extent to which social policy as a discipline has been informed by sociological theory is, of course, a matter for debate. However, it is certainly the case that conventional theoretical frameworks for undertaking analyses of social policy, such as social democracy, neoliberalism and conflict theories, can be set within broader discourses of social and sociological theory. Moreover, contemporary theoretical critiques of social policy, such as those that are offered by feminism, anti-racism and postmodernism, have, up to the present day, had a greater presence within sociological than within social policy discourses (Carlson 2004).

The aim of the remainder of this chapter is not concerned with tracing the theoretical origins of the discipline of social policy, nor with evaluating the contributions that particular theoretical approaches have made (for more detailed discussions of the relationships between social theory and social policy, see Pinker 1971; Townsend 1975; George and Wilding 1994; Lavalette and Pratt 2001; McBeth 2004). Rather the intention is to map, more broadly, the ways in which sociological approaches and ideas can inform how we think about, and make sense of, social policy worlds, processes and experiences. This means revisiting the commonalities of the sociological approach, and drawing upon the complementarity of different sociological and theoretical perspectives.

The individual and the social

As has already been noted, sociological theory places the individual within a social context, and helps us to explore relationships between people, structures, places and times. This is especially important if we are to understand the ways in which individual experiences, lives and biographies are shaped by, and in turn help to shape, social structures and social worlds. Hence socio-logical theory gives 'permission' to study and value the personal and private worlds of individual social actors; as well as the opportunity to understand how these relate to wider social, political, economic and legal contexts. For the understanding and analysis of social policy this is an extremely valuable position, not least because it provides a framework for identifying and rec-ognizing the ways in which individual welfare biographies are shaped by, and in turn shape, broader social policy processes. Social policy can be conceptualized in terms of broad social structures (through, for example, the State, the market, social institutions and organizations, and legislative and economic frameworks). Social policy can also be considered in terms of sets of individual, collective and auto/biographical experiences – with/in which social actors actively navigate social policy routes and pathways. Moreover, these pathways are navigated with/in specific temporal and spa-tial (as well as political and economic) contexts. Hence thinking sociologic-ally about social policy can mean an increased emphasis on understanding and making sense of the auto/biographical experiences of social policy, and exploring the ways in which these experiences are situated with/in social policy structures, processes and policies. A good example of this would be a consideration of the relationship between embodiment and social policy; rethinking the ways in which social policy 'shapes' the body, and how social policy is experienced with and through the body (see Chapter 6 of this volume).

Patterns and processes

Thinking sociologically is also to explore the general in the particular; to take specific actions, interactions and events and to identify more general patterns and processes. While different sociological theories and method-ologies place different emphases on the extent to which generalization is possible (or indeed desirable), they all share a commitment to systematically studying and documenting everyday social life in order to explore the ways in which complex social worlds are organized and patterned. It is these relationships between the specific and the broader view, or the particular and the general, that to some extent characterize the sociological enterprise. Sociological theory represents attempts to make sense of the complexity of these connections. For social policy, then, this invites systematic study of policy-making processes, settings and experiences, and developing the cap-acity to work at the interface between particular instances and broader cat-egories of understanding. Hence we can use detailed explorations of specific social policy 'events' – such as a primary school class, a health promotion intervention, the sale of public housing, life in a hostel for the homeless, a social work encounter, or a training scheme for young people – to begin to understand, not only the biographical realities of social policy, but also its broader social patterning (as gendered, racialized, generational, class defined, embodied, and so forth).

Making the strange familiar and the familiar strange

Sociological theorizing (and by inference sociological investigation) implicitly draws upon a notion of analytical strangeness. That is, the ordinary, mundane and 'everyday' social world – the familiar – is made 'strange' in order that it can be systematically analysed and explored. Hence taken-for-granted assumptions, experiences, processes and events are subjected to a sociological gaze and a critical scrutiny whereby 'normal' or 'expected' ways of doing things are problematized or questioned, and where familiar understandings of social life are challenged. Hence sociological explorations can enable us to 'see' the 'familiar' through a new and more critical lens. By contrast, those settings, experiences or events about which we have little tacit understanding or knowledge, which may appear alien, different or strange to us, can be made more familiar – subjected to the same kind of critical and systematic examination in order that we can begin to understand and make sense of them. Thinking sociologically invites us to take nothing for granted, nor to assume that there are whole areas or aspects that must remain beyond our understanding.

One of the defining characteristics of social policy (in its most general sense) is precisely the ways in which it is interwoven into all of our lives. Many institutions of, or settings for, social policy are very familiar to us – the family, the school, the hospital, and even the street. Equally many of our day-to-day experiences have social welfare implications or outcomes – relations of caring, for example. A sociological perspective can provide a framework for re-examining these institutions, settings and experiences. By the same token there are elements of social policy process and practice that are less familiar to some or all of us, or more difficult to understand precisely because they may appear 'strange'. Many of us will have had very little direct experience of homelessness, domestic violence or the higher echelons of policy-making. Sociological perspectives and systematic study can thus provide a forum for revealing and re-seeing both the familiar and the not so familiar aspects of social policy.

Continuity and change

Sociological theory provides frameworks for explaining social stability (for example, via processes of socialization, social differentiation and social reproduction) and for understanding the processes of social change. Hence, sociology is concerned with both continuity and transformation; with describing, mapping and explaining how cultures and societies stabilize, consolidate and change over time and through space. Social change is a common feature of all social worlds. Drawing upon the range of sociological perspectives enables us to explore the ways in which social transformation occurs, and to assess the significance and possible impacts of change (on individual social actors, social groups, social organization, social institutions, locales, specific societies and global contexts). Navigating across and between different theoretical perspectives also presents the opportunity to consider the role of conflicts and tensions; socialization and culture; ideas and social movements; and human action, interaction and agency in the development, transformations and re-visions of complex social worlds.

Social policy is concerned with social change in a whole variety of ways. Particular social welfare provisions are, in themselves, often responding to social transformations of various kinds – an ageing population, changes to the labour market or shifts in family formation, for example. Social policies can be used to recognize and consolidate wider social changes that are occurring (for example, it is possible to conceptualize the establishment of the post-war welfare state in the UK as a response to the aftermath of war, post-war consensus and a consolidation of changes to the relationships between the individual, the family and the State – see Alcock, Payne and Sullivan 2004). Social policy can also be used to provide catalysts for future social transformations, for example by providing legislative frameworks for the promotion of equality of opportunity or the mainstreaming of equality within organizations and institutions (Rees 1998; see Chapter 5 of this volume). The institutions of social policy are also situated within, and indeed can directly contribute to, wider processes of social stability and social change – schools, universities and teaching hospitals create as well as reproduce knowledge, for example. Moreover, welfare states regularly undergo revisions and transformations of their own, perhaps in response to shifting needs, demands and expectations, changing modes of provision, economic crises and reform, or new political agendas (Taylor-Gooby 1999; Alcock *et al.* 2004). Overlaying this is the academic discipline of social policy itself – concerned not only with documenting the State, social welfare provision and the processes of social policy over time, but also with contributing to the development of future social policy agendas – that is contributing in its own right to discourses of consolidation and transformation. Thus it is not difficult to see that there might be considerable analytical potential in thinking sociologically about the relationships between social policy, social stability and social transformations.

Conclusion

This chapter has begun to explore how the sociological imagination might be developed to encompass social policy. To an extent the chapter has had the task of setting the scene for the book as a whole, not least by providing an introduction to the discipline of sociology, to its historical development and to some of its overarching themes. The chapter has principally been concerned with providing an overview of what might be considered to be 'conventional' sociological perspectives and discourses. The emphasis on these should not be taken as a wholesale endorsement of grand sociological narratives. Indeed, in the next chapter this mini-tour of sociology is complicated by a consideration of some of the more contemporary developments and sociological critiques. Rather, the intention has been to introduce ideas from 'conventional' sociological positions in order to illustrate the potential of sociological discourses to make sense of social, and hence social policy, worlds.

Thinking sociologically about the social world means recognizing the complexity of social life, and thus the importance of systematic investigation and a critical perspective. At its simplest, sociological theorizing is concerned with asking questions about the social world, and seeking ways of systematically exploring these questions. Sociological theories and perspectives offer a range of analytical tools for critically thinking about (and in turn undertaking research on) complex, everyday social realities. As has been noted in this chapter, the kinds of questions that are asked, and the methods of social investigation that are promoted, will vary according to the particular perspective or position by which one is persuaded. However, all sociological perspectives offer the potential to 'unpack' social worlds in an attempt to make sense of them. For social policy, therefore, this provides an opportunity for adopting a critical stance and for promoting the systematic investigation of social policy worlds, processes, experiences, actors and settings. Thus it becomes possible to rethink the ways in which social policies are situated within wider social, economic, legal and political contexts, and in turn how social policy may help to reshape these contexts.

In the next chapter the focus is on the ways in which the discipline of sociology has developed in recent times, particularly in response to the theoretical and methodological challenges offered by feminism, postmodernism and other contemporary critiques. In particular, the chapter considers how these developments provide 'other' sociological perspectives from which to examine and understand the theory and practice of social policy.

Further reading

Craib, I. (1992) *Modern Social Theory*. London: Harvester Wheatsheaf; and Craib, I. (1997) *Classical Social Theory*. Oxford: Oxford University Press. Together these texts provide readable and systematic introductions to social and sociological theory, covering both classic theorists and contemporary developments.

Fulcher, J. and Scott, J. (2003) *Sociology*, 2nd edn. Oxford: Oxford University Press. A good introductory sociology text, which covers most of the mainstream sociological topics in an accessible way. This text also contains useful guides to further reading, and straightforward explanations of key sociological concepts.

Macionis, J.J. and Plummer, K. (2002) *Sociology: A Global Introduction*, 2nd edn. London: Prentice Hall. A lively and refreshing introductory text that engages with many of the contemporary debates within sociology. The book also includes interesting recommendations for popular films and videos that illustrate sociological themes, topics and ideas.

chapter

three

Social Policy, Feminism and Postmodern Times

Introduction

The theoretical underpinnings of sociology have been both consolidated and challenged in recent times. As contemporary societies have undergone cultural and economic transformations, the grand sociological narratives have become increasingly unsatisfactory as means of theorizing about, and making sense of, social life. The ideas, concepts and paradigms implicit within many 'conventional' sociological theories – such as social class, bureaucracy, manufacturing industry and rational science – have been challenged by theoretical developments and postmodern commentators. Some sociological theories have been seen as being too tied to modernist structures, institutions and assumptions, and too narrow to encompass the range of perspectives, experiences and 'voices' of contemporary (post-industrial, transforming) societies. Conceptualizations – of the family, sexuality, the State, leisure, the workplace, labour markets, education, welfare and leisure – have also been contested, challenged and recast in attempts to address contemporary social life and social change. Social, cultural and economic change – manifest in new ways of working, new family structures, new cultural arenas, new forms of governance, new information technologies and communications, as well as moves toward more globalized economies – has been accompanied by recast notions of the individual (Beck 1992) and the processes of self and identity work.

To make sense of, and understand these reformulations sociology has increasingly benefited from (and been challenged by) a range of new theoretical frameworks. Some of these theoretical frameworks have drawn upon and emerged out of dominant, 'conventional' sociological theories, while others have represented more radical critiques of, and departures from, 'conventional' sociology. We might include here the distinctive contributions of feminism and feminist sociology, postcolonialism and new racial theory, queer theory, gay and lesbian studies and postmodern social theory. These, among others, have contributed to the further theoretical development of sociology, offering complementary and/or alternative theories, perspectives and voices. These developments in sociological theorizing have highlighted an implicit feature of all sociological (and indeed social) theory. That is a recognition that any social theory can only ever be engaged in articulating partial perspectives. Hence the claims of particular social theorists or schools of thought to be able to throw light on, or to 'explain', society as a whole have come to be viewed as fundamentally flawed. This is not to say that 'conventional' sociological theory must be, or is, rejected out of hand. Rather it is to recognize the particular standpoints from which these theories are articulated, and the partiality of the contribution they are able to make. To put it another way, no theory can 'tell the whole story'; instead, all socio-logical theory comes from and with particular perspectives, views, stand-points and positions. Moreover, contemporary critiques have highlighted the particular perspectives and positions that have been dominant within 'conventional' sociology – primarily white, heterosexual, Western and male.

There is considerable debate as to whether these critiques and develop-ments constitute a crisis within the discipline or theoretical underpinnings of sociology. They certainly challenge modernist (and sociological) assump-tions that any one theory can provide a grand narrative or complete story of social, cultural and economic life. However, the new forms of theorizing consolidate as much as challenge the theoretical core of sociology, and certainly build upon what has gone before. The critical stance taken by 'new' sociological theories is underpinned by and draws upon earlier theoretical work, while at the same time recognizing the limitations of these existing theoretical models.

This chapter addresses some of these relatively recent critiques of, and trends in, sociological theory. In doing so it aims to provide an introduction to the contemporary developments that have been and are taking place, and to consider how these have and might contribute to the theorization of social policy. It is probably fair to say that as a discipline, social policy has been relatively slow to embrace some aspects of 'postmodern' theorizing (Taylor Gooby 1994; Carter 1998). It is certainly the case that the extent to which postmodern epistemologies and methodologies have influenced social policy research has been rather limited (see Chapters 8 and 9 of this volume). However, as Manning (1999: 67) suggests, the basic argument 'that different ideas or viewpoints, or "knowledges" ' coexist and that none can be seen in any 'essential sense as dominant or superior', does help us to 'understand the ideological and policy confusions' that characterize social policy. In contrast, while the extent to which postmodern theorizing has influenced the discipline of social policy might be considered to be rather limited, the impact of feminism on social policy has been somewhat more assured (although by no means mainstreamed within the discipline). Feminism, feminist sociology and the gendered analysis of social policy are discussed in the next two sections of this chapter. The chapter then returns to a more general discussion of the discipline of social policy in postmodern (social theoretical) times.

Feminisms and feminist sociology

It is helpful, and indeed essential, to talk about *feminisms* rather than feminism in the singular, as a way of highlighting the multiple meanings attached to contemporary feminist theory (and practice). Indeed, since the early nineteenth century there have been several different strands and brands of feminism. The feminist movements of the nineteenth century in themselves challenge any understanding that feminism is a relatively new intellectual and social movement. Banks (1981), for example, identified at least three feminist groups in Britain and North America in the nineteenth century – and traced their routes back to the eighteenth century. The most enduring of these early feminisms is perhaps one based on liberal, individualistic principles. As Weiner (1994) has argued, a version of liberal feminism – grounded in a social democratic, natural justice and equal opportunities tradition – is the most accepted of all the feminisms, underpinned by a belief that through democratic social reform all women (and indeed men) should be free to determine their political, social, educational and labour market roles and futures.

Contemporary feminism(s), most commonly dated from the late 1960s onwards, and like earlier feminist movements, incorporates a number of different theoretical orientations, epistemological positionings and practices. The 'three schools model' of feminism (liberal, Marxist/socialist and radical/separatist) that emerged in the early 1970s oversimplifies a more complex reality, and certainly pays little attention to the ways in which feminist ideas, theory, approaches and practice have developed over the last quarter of the twentieth century (Delamont 2003; Wise and Stanley 2003). Many contemporary feminist scholars would also wish to identify other feminisms alongside these three schools – for example, black and lesbian feminisms, which recognize the failure of some feminism work to adequately incorporate black and lesbian experiences, or to understand the processes and experiences of racism and heterosexism. Postmodern and poststructuralist feminisms should also be included, challenging the bases of (malestream) knowledge production and reproduction, and opening up new and novel discursive spaces (Nicholson 1990; Flax 1993; Weiner 1994; Haw 1998). Some leading feminist scholars also work the spaces across and between different articulations of feminism; and between social theory, epistemology and methodology (Wise and Stanley 2003).

Feminist sociologists have exposed sociological theory as 'malestream' and sociological research as drawing on data that are overwhelming male-referenced. Feminist sociologists in the 1960s and 1970s put forward the argument that the experiences and 'knowledges' upon which the discipline of sociology was based did not necessarily relate to the experiences or know-ledges of women. Women's voices were identified as absent from, or silent within, sociological theory and empirical practice. Hence the impartiality (or neutral) claim of sociology to represent or to understand 'society' as a whole was challenged and exposed; seen instead to represent at best only partial (that is male) perspectives. Abbott and Wallace (2000) provide a useful summary of the feminist critique of sociology, arguing that the discipline as conventionally conceived was at best sex- (or gender-) blind and at worst sexist. Feminist sociology has sought to reconceptualize sociological theory and practice in the light of this critique. There is, of course, consider-able variety in the ways in which feminists theorize about society (and the position of women within society) (see Humm 1992; Whelehan 1995 for good introductions to feminism thought), and how transformation might be achieved. This diversity is also evident within feminist sociology. In common is an approach that critiques the relative absence of women from socio-logical data and sociological work; recognizes and values the experiences and voices of women; and considers the ways in which the construction of (sociological) knowledge is gendered (Harding 1987).

Hence sociological theory has been exposed as gendered, and absences have been identified in the substantive work of sociology (for example, work on emotions, the body and the private sphere). Beyond these common con-cerns, different feminist perspectives propose alternative 'solutions' to recti-fying these gendered gaps. The most widely accepted approach has been to take active steps to include women as part of sociological research and sociological theorizing (Evans 2003). This has included, for example, a greater appreciation of gender as a factor in research samples, and the inclu-sion of research arenas in which women predominate (female-dominated work settings, for example), as well as repositioning women theorists within the discipline. This approach might usefully be conceptualized as seeking to integrate women into 'conventional' sociological theory and practice (Abbott and Wallace 2000), and certainly resonates with a liberal or equal opportunities model of equality (see Chapter 5 of this volume). It entails working with/in existing sociological theories and methodologies, while making them more relevant to women's lives and experiences. It is question-able whether this approach questions or challenges the discipline or theor-etical underpinnings of sociology *per se*; rather, it conceptualizes women (and gender) as an *addition* to existing research and theories. This approach recognizes that gender is a factor in social, cultural and economic life; that generalizations about 'society' can no longer be based on all-male samples; that women can and have made contributions to sociological theorizing and that more women are and should be encouraged to be engaged in sociological work.

Other feminist approaches have gone further in reformulating sociology in response to feminist critiques. Wise and Stanley (2003: 17) call for a wider view of social theorizing that is not simply content to rest on the laurels of expanding existing theoretical perspectives to take account of feminism: 'aren't there more interesting and more exciting ways to think of theory? And aren't there ways of configuring "feminist theory" and "feminist theorists" in ways that do not simply reconstitute the "male" hierarchies but peopling them with women.' This then recognizes the 'conventionality' of theorizing and the potential for new ways of seeing, knowing and thinking. It suggests alternative (parallel or different) theories, knowledges and practices. Women's studies courses, modules and degree schemes, and feminist texts and feminist publishing lists are some of the ways in which this approach might manifest itself at a very basic level. Indeed, women's studies itself is an interesting example, operating within and outside of the academy, and occupying a precarious border position (see Stanley 1997). A problem with this approach, however, is that it may not actually help to transform or reconceptualize sociological theory, and holds the risk of marginalizing or ghettoizing feminist sociology. Moreover, it may not necessarily challenge 'conventional' sociological theory at all (which by implication could go on marginalizing women, gender and feminism).

It remains questionable as to whether feminist critiques of sociology have led to a more wholesale shift within the discipline. Wise and Stanley (2003) are more optimistic than, for example, Delamont (2003) of the place of feminist sociology within the discipline as a whole. However, Stanley (1997) has also argued that, in general, feminists and feminism still occupy the 'borderlands' of academic life. Nonetheless within sociology, as elsewhere in the academy 'feminism is the analysis of old knowledge and the source of new knowledge: it makes you think' (Stanley 1997: 1).

It is perhaps difficult to argue that feminism has been 'mainstreamed' within sociology as a whole. Mainsteaming has increasingly been used within policy arenas to indicate a cultural transformation, whereby equality has become integral to the culture, policy and practices of an organization (Rees 1998). In terms of the discipline of sociology, this might mean recognizing that feminism(s) challenges many of the assumptions, generalizations and analyses of 'conventional' sociology, and that what is needed is revolution (or transformation) rather than the reform or 'patching' of existing theories and positions. It could begin from an understanding that 'conventional' sociological theory is at worst fundamentally flawed and at best partial, and that feminism changes the questions, methodologies and epistemologies that underpin sociological ideas, analyses and theories. Hence this is about creating new knowledge(s) and replacing old knowledge(s), to transform and recast the sociological enterprise. In the next section the impact of some of these feminist ideas on the discipline of social policy is briefly outlined.

Feminist approaches and the regendering of social policy

The concerns and preoccupations of nineteenth-century and early twentieth-century feminism were very much grounded in aspects of social policy and social welfare. Although, as Charles (2000: 1) has indicated, the feminist social movement from 1870 to 1930 was 'concerned chiefly with women's political and property rights', encapsulated within this movement were campaigns that focused (in various ways) on relations with the State and social policy. These included campaigns for economic independence (and participation in the labour market), citizenship (not least through the campaigns for universal suffrage), education (including women's entrance to higher education and the liberal, welfare professions), personal welfare and health care. More recent feminist social movements have both built upon and expanded these social policy agendas. Contemporary feminism(s) have formulated critiques of social policy, undertaken primary research in social policy arenas, and called for reforms that have specifically focused on social policy. Moreover, feminist perspectives on the State and social policy have highlighted the interconnections of private and public spheres.

> Indeed the slogan that the personal is political linked the so-called private domain of the home to the public domain of politics and the state. Feminists argued that domestic tasks are constructed as women's work through social and economic policies and that it is not simply a matter of personal choice that means women rather than men give up their jobs to look after children. Indeed, the state itself constructs the private sphere to which women are ideally confined.
>
> (Charles 2000: 1–2)

Contemporary feminisms and feminists have certainly raised the profile of and campaigned on a wide range of social policy issues – such as childcare, education and training, enhanced labour market opportunities, the domestic division of labour, equality of opportunity in public and political life, social care, women's health issues, poverty and housing. It is not difficult to see how social policy practice is of enormous importance to the everyday lives of women – for example, in their roles as mothers, carers, health workers, teachers and social workers. However, social policy as a discipline was relatively slow to draw upon feminist theoretical perspectives, and to recognize gender as an analytical and experiential variable. Indeed, until the 1970s the traditional world of social policy was peopled by ungendered subjects

(Lister 2000), and there was no systematic focus on the gendered clients, processes or outcomes of social policy.

During the 1970s and 1980s feminist critiques of social policy began to emerge. These critiques were articulated and consolidated in some key texts (see, for example, Wilson 1977; Ungerson 1985; Dale and Foster 1986; Pascall 1986). These authors variously highlighted the ways in which the discipline of social policy marginalized or ignored women's experiences and issues, and set about reconceptualizing the content (and analytic potential) of the discipline. At the heart of this work was an acknowledgement that social policy and social welfare issues were central to women's lives, and moreover that women were central to welfare (Maclean and Groves 1991; Hallett 1996; Williams 1997). With this recognition, however, came a contradiction:

> One the one hand, the welfare state has the potential to offer women greater freedoms (by providing childcare, for example, so that women may take up paid work and achieve a degree of financial independence). On the other hand, it has the capacity to constrain, control and restrict women's lives (by, for example, restricting abortion to certain groups of women).
>
> (Williams 1997: 258–9)

The insights offered by a feminist analysis of social policy have included a consideration of women as social policy actors (for example, as social policy clients, professionals, workers and providers), alongside a broader understanding of the gendering of social policy. There have also been explorations of the ways in which the State (through social policies) constructs and reproduces gendered identities.

Much of the substantive work on gender and social policy has primarily focused on women, and has been informed by feminist perspectives on the State, the labour market and the family. More recently this work has expanded to include wider considerations of gender and sexuality. Social policy and 'the problem of men' is a relatively recent concern within the discipline (Scourfield and Drakeford 2002). Scourfield (2003: 85–6) usefully identifies two different directions in which social policy's concern with men has developed – conceptualizing men as perpetrators and as victims: 'according to the first approach, men are a source of danger and disorder, an anti-social influence [. . .]. According to the second approach, men are facing greater disadvantage in society than women.' Both approaches can be located within contemporary discourses on the 'crisis of masculinity', and reflected in the ways in which masculinity is now being placed on social policy and political agendas (Popay, Hearn and Edwards 1998). For example, the relative underachievement of boys within the education system has preoccupied academics (including feminist scholars) and policy-makers over the last decade or so (see Epstein et al. 1998 for a good review).

Such work can be located within a broader and growing corpus of research and theorization on men and masculinities within contemporary society. The so-called 'new men's studies' (and the concurrent though not neccessarily comparable men's movement) actually encompass a number of different perspectives and agendas. These include men engaging with, responding to and drawing upon feminism in order to critique and change men's lives (sometimes referred to as pro-feminist men) (see Hearn 1987; Hearn and Morgan 1990; Lingard and Douglas 1999); as well as those reacting to the challenge of feminism through the reassertion of the rights of men and the dominance of masculinity (see Young 1993 for a review of this position). Some of the earlier critiques of feminism (for presenting women as homogeneous, for example) are equally applicable to men's studies. Moreover, feminism has had an uneasy relationship with this work on masculinities. Indeed, feminist scholars have increasingly turned their attention to the study of boys, men and masculinity (Raphael Reed 1999; Skelton 1999), while at the same time recognizing that (for some) men's studies represents a backlash to the success of feminism (see Canaan and Griffin 1990).

The gendered frameworks of social policy are usefully explored in a feminist analysis by Lister (2000). She considers how a 'gender lens' can provide a mechanism through 'which to describe and analyse the institutions, relations and discourses which constitute social policy' (Lister 2000: 22). Her framework reconceptualizes the discipline and practice of social policy through an exploration of the gendered contexts of social policy locales, people, resources and concepts. Lister's arguments are summarized and elaborated upon below.

Locales

The sites of, or localities for, social policy include the State and the labour market, and also the family (see Chapter 7 of this volume for a more detailed discussion of some of the spaces of and for social policy). By applying a 'gender lens' these locales can be complicated, contested and 'troubled'. Feminist analyses have explored the patriarchal nature of the State and the labour market, and the ways in which both reproduce and regulate gender inequalities (Walby 1986; Pateman 1988; Rees 1990; Charles 2000). Social policies that engage with education, training and the labour market often ignore gendered occupational segregation, and the differential rewards and power that such segregation usually implies (Rees 1998). As was discussed above, feminist analyses have also revealed the ways in which the State and its social policies can offer political, economic and social resources for women; and can be simultaneously oppressive and supportive to and of women (Charles 2000).

The family is where the practice and consequences of social policy are often most visible. Feminist analyses have highlighted the ways in which the family is a site of welfare production and consumption, as well as understanding familial ideology as gendered (and indeed racialized and heterosexist) (Gittens 1993; Jackson 1997). Moreover, feminists have identified the family as having contradictory implications for women, and have worked to expose the myth of separate and distinct public and private spheres (Somerville 2000). The relationships between the State, the labour market and the family have been revealed as multifaceted and complex. The family can be a site for oppression and the reproduction of gender inequalities. At the same time it can also be conceptualized (and experienced) as an arena for resistance by and identity construction for women. Feminist analyses of the family as a social, economic and political arena have also reconceptualized our understandings of the public and private spheres, and the relations between the two. The family is reconceptualized as a site for physical, emotional and mental labour (Finch and Groves 1983; Land 1991), as an economic system (Pahl 1990; Millar and Glendinning 1992) as well as a site for the provision and receipt of social welfare. By locating the (gendered) welfare work and consumption that takes place within family structures, the private sphere thus also becomes a legitimate concern for social policy.

Resources

Feminist analyses have systematically revealed the gendered distribution of material, temporal and practical resources, all of which are implicated within, and have implications for, the practice of social policy. For example, the distribution of income and wealth within families is far from equal, and is often differentiated according to gender. Pahl (1989) and others have argued that we cannot assume that material resources are distributed equally within families (Graham 1992; Jackson and Moores 1995). Rather, this distribution often reflects the gendered power relations within families, and has led to a distinction being made between 'his' poverty and 'her' poverty (Millar and Glendinning 1992). Even when women have (some level of) control over how income is distributed within families, they are more likely to 'go without' in order to support other family members (Graham 1992).

This material inequity within families has obvious consequences for the consideration of social policy processes and practices, particularly those concerned with income maintenance (between rather than *within* families!). Of course, this is part of wider analyses of the domestic sphere and resource distribution within it. The gendered division of domestic labour, for example (including physical and emotional caring), and the consequences of this for access to the public sphere, underpins the role of women as frontline providers of (private) social welfare, and as recipients of social welfare provision (due, for example, to their still-limited access to well-paid employment – see Equal Opportunities Commission 2001 for a report on gender and (un)equal pay).

People

Social policy is 'peopled' by a range of social actors in a variety of roles. Lister (2000) makes the distinction between social policy users (for example, consumers, clients or recipients), providers and shapers. All of these groupings can be analysed in terms of gendered (and indeed racialized and sexualized) social actors and social relations. Women are especially visible as the users and providers of social policy, but remain rather under-represented as social policy shapers or makers. In both private and public contexts, women deliver a majority of social welfare – as parents, daughters, wives, carers, nurses, home helps, social workers and teachers. They are most often the front-line providers of social policy. Similarly their (gendered) family and caring roles, restricted labour market opportunities (and indeed their longevity) means they are often over-represented as clients of social policy systems, either in their own right or as the mediators of the welfare for others (for example, male partners, elderly relatives and children). Women must navigate their way through welfare systems, often 'patching and quilting' as they go (Balbo 1987).

At the same time women's access to the processes of social policy-making are still limited by, for example, unequal labour market opportunities, limited political participation and gendered occupational structures. Feminist commentators still argue that the representation of women in political (and policy) life has not yet reached a 'critical mass' in many contexts, and hence the opportunities for women to influence policy and practice, and change the political culture have (up to now at least) been limited. This had particularly been discussed in relation to the increased number of women politicians and the impact they might have on setting (and shifting) the policy agenda (Lovenduski 1997; Puwar 1997). In Scandinavian countries, where there has been much higher representation of women in parliament for longer (over 40 per cent in some countries, compared with around 18 per cent in the UK Westminster parliament) there is evidence that women do have a greater impact on policy-making and political discourse, with more incorporation of women's issues and perspectives (Bystydzienski 1992). However, as Pilcher (1999) has argued, it is not inevitable that women in political power necessarily use their position to represent the interests of women.

Concepts

Feminist scholarship has challenged and reworked many of the concepts that are fundamental to social policy practice and analysis. For example, a sustained feminist analysis of the concept of care has been able to distinguish between the physical, material and emotion contexts of caring *for* someone, and the affective and emotional relations of caring *about* someone, as well as differentiating between paid and unpaid care-work (see Finch and Groves 1983; Baldwin and Twigg 1991; Baines, Evans and Neysmith 1998). Relatedly, the concept of work, so central to welfare policies of training and income maintenance, for example, has been complicated by a feminist analysis of labour market opportunities and realities, and by the reconceptualization of emotionality within work (Hochschild 1983 and 2003), as well as by an appreciation of the gender division of domestic labour and 'unpaid' work (Oakley 1974; Van Every 1995). As has been noted above, there has thus been a reworking of the relations between the public and the private spheres of social life, and the ways in which these are mediated by gender (as well as class, sexuality, race and ethnicity). Economic dependence or independence takes on new meanings through an appreciation of family economics and the distribution of resources within households. Likewise, the concept of citizenship, so central to the development of post-war welfare states has been 'troubled' by feminism (Lister 1997; also see Chapter 4 of this volume).

In summary, feminist analysis has thus helped to redefine the 'content' and concerns of the discipline of social policy, making gender more central to an understanding of it. Thus feminist perspectives on social policy have been important in reconceptualizing what counts as social policy – addressing how social policies reconstruct women's lives, and recognizing the contradictory relations between women, social welfare and the State. Williams (1997) also highlights the ways in which feminist work in social policy has now moved on to include an important comparative dimension, offering critiques and analyses of gendered welfare regimes in different countries (see, for example, Lewis 1992; Sainsbury 1994). These feminist analyses have considered the ways in which social policies are differentially experienced, and the processes by which social and welfare policies reproduce gender (and indeed other) inequalities. Thus there has perhaps been less concern with theorization about the State or modes of representation, and more empirical emphasis on the processes, outcomes and experiences of State intervention: 'thus feminists have tended to concentrate on social policies and their effects on gender relations rather than the way in which gender interests are constituted and represented at the political level' (Charles 2000: 17). Finch (1991), in an essay exploring the possibilities of feminist research in social policy, also considers the impact of feminist methodological developments within the discipline of social policy. She suggests that the general lack of engagement may have as much to do with the nature of the discipline of social policy as with feminists engaging with/ working within the discipline. Finch makes the case that as a subject area, or discipline, social policy has been less ready to engage in methodological debate and innovation than many other social science disciplines.

Although social policy has always had a strong empirical basis, methodological issues have never been high on the intellectual agenda. As such there
has not been an accessible methodological dialogue in social policy with
which feminists might readily engage (see Chapters 8 and 9 of this volume
for a more detailed discussion of these issues).

Social policy in postmodern times

Feminist analyses of, and influence on, social policy can be located within a
wider consideration of the influences of contemporary social theories and
social movements. In this section, therefore, the focus is broadened in order
to consider the discipline of social policy, and how it is situated within and
outwith contemporary sociological perspectives that might (generally) fall
under the auspices of postmodernism.

At a simple level, postmodernism can be described as a challenge to the
'modern' consensus seen to be held among the educated classes in Western
capitalist nations (usually traced to the Enlightenment movement at the end
of the eighteenth century). This consensus incorporated a belief that universal, objective, scientific 'truths' can be reached by the application of
objective, scientific methods. Postmodernist commentators have reflected
upon this with considerable scepticism, arguing that there are no universal
truths to be discovered about 'society', not least because all (social, scientific) investigations (and indeed social actors) are situated within particular
historical, cultural and economic contexts. Hence postmodern perspectives
emphasize the situatedness or partiality of empirical and theoretical insights;
the ways in which standpoints are dynamic and fluid, rather than fixed or
absolute (Lyotard 1992); and how accounts and experiences are located
within their particular contexts.

Postmodernism can thus be seen as a culmination of philosophical and
theoretical debate that has been going on at least since the 1970s (a debate to
which feminist scholars have contributed). These debates, within and
beyond the social sciences, have been concerned with the nature of knowledge and enquiry (Harding 1987; Nielsen 1990). And while postmodernism
has arguably had little fundamental impact on the natural sciences, the
impact on the humanities and social sciences has been more profound. In
particular, there has been a re-examination, by some at least, of the assumptions that underpin empirical research, methodology and theorization. For
example, some of the established dualisms associated with modernity – such
as rationality versus emotionality, objectivity versus subjectivity, or science
versus rhetoric – have been judged to be 'inadequate for understanding a
world of multiple causes and effects, interacting in complex and non linear
ways, all of which are rooted in a limitless array of historical and cultural
specificities' (Lather 1991: 21). Postmodern approaches to sociological

theory have thus embraced a postmodern condition that recognizes complex social realities, multiple voices and increasing diversity. Moreover, questions are asked about the extent to which conventional sociological theories attempt to, or indeed can, provide meta-narratives (or 'grand theories') of social and economic life. The form and content of ideas or theory are thus questioned, as part of a broader project that no longer assumes that there can be objective, all-encompassing or overarching explanations. Postmodernist perspectives have been engaged in the critique of the range of sociological theory, including those that emphasize structure or social action (see Chapter 2 of this volume), in their attempts to produce authoritative accounts of social life.

Poststructural theoretical perspectives have also illuminated the ways in which knowledge and ideas are produced, placing particular emphasis on human interpretation and social dialogue. Early articulations of (post)structuralism particularly illuminated the importance of discourse and discursive practices in the formulation of knowledge (Foucault 1974, 1982). In this context discourse refers to sets of arguments or 'languages' through which meaning is symbolically attached and derived. If social relations are viewed in terms of plurality and diversity (from a postmodern perspective), then there might also be a recognition that individuals are active in shaping discourses, through which they in turn are shaped (Weiner 1994). This re-emphasizes the importance of understanding the local situatedness of social discourse; as well as recognizing the ways in which the construction of knowledge and social identities are dynamic processes. Foucault, of course, linked knowledge and power, arguing that discourse constructs and legitimates knowledge, which in turn reinforces and embodies power relations. Thus discourses – as frameworks of meanings historically produced in a particular culture at a particular time – enable us to see knowledge and power as complex, constructed and negotiated, rather than fixed and static entities.

There have been other shifts in contemporary social theory that can be located within, or seen alongside, postmodern (and poststructural) frameworks, although the extent to which postmodern theorists have actually engaged with them is open to question. For example, Mac an Ghaill (1999) refers to the 'strange silence' surrounding issues of ethnic identity and racialized social relations within postmodernism, despite the fact that the discontinuities, fragmentations and uncertainties identified by postmodernism have clear resonance for ethnic minority communities. Mac an Ghaill argues that in most postmodern accounts, race and ethnicity are absent voices (which is a not dissimilar argument to that levelled at feminism by black feminists, see hooks 1982). The ways in which sociological theory on race and ethnicities could benefit from a postmodern, discursive framework are outlined by Mac an Ghaill (1999). For example, he argues that 'a more complex framework, with its suggestion that there are a range of subject positions that we may occupy within different contradictory discourses [. . .] helps us in understanding the contextual specificity in the cultural production and reproduction of ethnic formations' (Mac an Ghaill 1999: 45). New racialized discourses draw not only on the frameworks offered by a Foucaldian perspective. They can also be seen as emergent from more general (postcolonial) critiques that have emerged out of Said's (1978) sustained critical commentary on the orientalizing tendencies of Western colonialism. Said highlighted the ways in which 'other' cultures have been observed and represented through dominating discourses, thereby reducing them to subjugated and muted objects. New racialized discourses seek to replace conventional oppositional dualisms – such as black and white, them and us, east and west, and dominant and subordinate – with more complex, fluid and contradictory readings of ethnic identities and race relations (Madood and Bethoud 1997). Hence ethnic identification and reformation is framed within discourses of diversity and difference (Mason 2000).

The development of gay and lesbian studies, and the emergence of queer theory, have also challenged and reconceptualized social identities and social theory (Cranny-Francis et al. 2003). Contemporary gender studies, in various guises, and highlighting issues of power, identity and difference, have found intellectual space within postmodernist and poststructuralist discourses. Most sociological theory, however, still has a bias towards heterosexuality, and non-heterosexual voices are rarely 'heard'. In deconstructing and reconstructing gender and sexuality – and in making these silent voices heard – these perspectives have drawn on poststructuralist frameworks. Gay studies, lesbian studies, bisexual studies, transgender studies and queer theory have all adopted approaches to the understanding of social life that locate sexualities, identities and power within particular historical, local, cultural and situated spaces (Wilton 1995). The heterosexual bases of conventional knowledge and power have been deconstructed and new knowledges proposed and constructed (Garber 1994). Social theorizing has hence been further challenged, and reshaped to provide analytical and sense-making frameworks for complex, multiple and fractured social realities.

In the introduction to this chapter it was noted that social policy as a discipline has been relatively reluctant or slow to engage with postmodern and poststructural perspectives or discourses (see also Chapter 9). Yet our understandings of contemporary social policy can certainly be complicated or expanded by the range of social theoretical perspectives that might usefully be located under this broad umbrella. These approaches represent new ways of theorizing about society, and certainly move away from a notion that it is possible to construct grand theories or meta-narratives of social life. Instead, they offer views of societies that are more dynamic, fragmented, contradictory and shifting; where there are multiple and diverse voices to be heard; and where knowledges, power and identities are negotiated as well as reproduced. Of course, it is worth noting that such perspectives have not been universally accepted. There is ongoing sociological debate as to whether postmodern theorizing (and indeed the postmodern society it seeks to understand) represents revolution, or evolution of existing social theories (see Giddens 1990; Bauman 1993). Moreover, it is possible to argue that in rejecting 'grand' sociological theorizing, postmodern social theory does in fact attempt to provide a meta-narrative of its own – a 'single' view of the social world as fragmented, multiple and diverse. Feminist scholars have also reacted differentially to the challenge of postmodernism. For example, Fox-Genovese (1986) pointed to the ways in which some (for example, male, white and middle-class) scholars have used the excuse of postmodernism to render feminist research passé and outmoded (indeed Brodribb (1992: 8) goes further in describing postmodernism as 'the cultural capital of late patriarchy'); while others such as Flax (1993) and Weiner (1994) have identified considerable synergies between feminism and postmodernism. Despite (and indeed perhaps because of) these ongoing debates, postmodern perspectives have had a significant impact on recent work in and beyond sociology. The impact on social policy, however, has been less assured (as indicated in the introduction to this chapter), although a more critical engagement with such perspectives may well be conceptually and empirically fruitful. In the final section of this chapter some of these possibilities are briefly outlined.

Other voices in social policy

Social policy as an academic discipline has, to some extent, always been concerned with the varied and diverse 'lived realities' of social policy. There has been an ongoing recognition that individual and collective relationships to the State, and to social welfare, are marked by differential experiences and social inequalities. Indeed, the contemporary welfare state itself is in part a response to the recognition of difference. Academic commentary on social policy has mirrored this by revealing the diverse ways in which social policies can exacerbate, ameliorate or challenge social inequalities and dominant ideologies. Therefore the reluctance of social policy to work with/in postmodern discourses of diversity and difference may seem a little puzzling. In part, perhaps this reflects a reluctance to give up the 'empirical certainties' in which the discipline of social policy has its foundations. It can equally be seen as an uneasiness with the messiness or quirkiness with which postmodernism has often been associated (Twigg 2000, also Chapters 6 and 9 of this volume). It is possible, however, to speculate about the ways in which postmodern social theory (and associated perspectives) might offer potential for a reconceptualization of social policy agendas, topic areas, experiences and realities. For example, some commentators have indicated the ways in which the State can be reconsidered as a set of different, distinct and overlapping arenas, within which there are competing welfare discourses and a plurality of discursive forms (Pringle and Watson 1992; O'Brien and Penna 1998). This suggests a social policy analysis that is sensitive to the role of discursive practice, as well as to the temporal, spatial, local and specific contexts of social policy formation and practice. More generally, it may be useful to consider the shifting discourses within which contemporary social policy is located. Mac an Ghaill (1999: 134) highlights this shift in his discussion of the policy discourses of racisms and ethnicities, by arguing that 'it is suggested that we have shifted from the "simple" policy discourses of racial inequality (1950s/1960s) with their focus on selection, socialization and social mobility, through local authority anti-racist initiatives (1970s/1980s) to the "complex" policy discourses of social exclusion and the de-racialization of policy (1999s/2000s)'. These movements in themselves raise new challenges and areas for analysis. As Mac an Ghaill notes, these shifts also need to be seen within the contexts of other (political and social policy) discourses such as those of the New Right and New Labour. Moreover, within and across these discourses are differentiated and multiple lived realities and voices.

There is a long tradition of social policy scholars and practitioners 'giving voice' to under-represented groups. Indeed, advocacy in various guises has been an important part of the social policy agenda. In the past this has often meant 'speaking for' rather than 'speaking with' 'others', or enabling 'others' to speak for themselves. Shakespeare's discussion of the discourses of care highlights this tension:

> There is a tendency to ignore the voices of those people who are constructed as the problem: whether it is older people, disabled people, children or people with HIV/AIDS, it is not common for first-hand accounts to be available. We therefore rely for our information on the projections of policy-makers and academics, or professionals, or sometimes the testimonies of non-disabled relatives and carers'.
>
> (Shakespeare 2000: 56)

Alongside those 'voices' that have often only been (mis)heard by 'proxy' are other voices that have been relatively absent from the discourses of social policy. For example, Wilton (1995: 203) has argued that lesbians 'inhabit a precarious position within the nation state and are invisible as clients of welfare'. Within a more general discussion of lesbians and the State, Wilton considers the heterosexual contexts within which social welfare operates. She includes in her discussion considerations of health care, education, youth work and income maintenance systems, as well as highlighting the ways in which lesbianism and heterosexuality problematize social policy concepts such as citizenship (see also Chapter 4 of this volume).

Wilton concludes that 'social policy research, even that which derives from feminist principles, fails almost without exception to examine the effects of social policy on lesbians' (1993: 203).

These 'other voices' of social policy deserve to be heard, and in the recent past this has increasingly happened. There are now some good examples of research and scholarship that have listened to, worked with and given voice to previously invisible or silenced social policy actors – such as children and young people (Butler and Williamson 1994; Hallett and Prout 2003); lesbians and gay men (Sparkes 1994; Carabine 1996; Clarke 1996); and disabled people (Shakespeare 1998). More of this kind of work can ensure that the multiple perspectives and realities of social policy arenas are better recognized and understood. It can also enable a more careful consideration of the racialized, gendered, generational, disablist and sexualized discourses within which social policy is located.

Conclusion

This chapter has outlined some of the recent developments within, and influences upon, contemporary sociological theory. The extent to which sociological theory has undergone substantial change is, of course, open to considerable debate. It has certainly not been the intention within this chapter to suggest that there has been widespread or wholesale rejection of 'conventional' sociological analyses, or that we are all 'postmodern' now. Rather, the aim has been to consider how 'new' (and not so new) ways of thinking and seeing can create opportunities for social policy analyses. There has been a growing feminist analysis of social policy processes, arenas and practices, and there is some (though limited) evidence to suggest that social policy is increasingly recognizing the varied, different and diverse 'voices' that should be heard. However, there are many more possibilities for social policy to critically and constructively engage with contemporary theoretical and methodological agendas. Some of these possibilities are highlighted in later chapters within this volume.

Further reading

Abbott, P. and Wallace C. (1997) *An Introduction to Sociology: Feminist Perspectives*, 2nd edn. A systematic and accessible feminist introduction to sociology. The topics that are covered, such as stratification, the life course, family, work, health and caring, clearly demonstrate the overlaps between sociological and social policy arenas.

Carter, J. (ed.) (1998) *Postmodernity and the Fragmentation of Welfare*. London: Routledge. An edited collection providing a range of critical discussions on the relationships between social welfare, social policy and postmodernism. This text provides a range of interesting avenues for further discussion and debate.

Watson, S. and Doyal, L. (eds) (1999) *Engendering Social Policy*. Buckingham: Open
   University Press. Contributors to this volume analyse the gendered experiences
   and gender politics of social policy. The collection reflects upon both the historical contexts and contemporary discourses of social policy.

chapter

four

Social Policy, Citizenship and Identity

Introduction

The concept of citizenship is embedded within both historical and contemporary accounts of welfare states and social policy. The establishment of welfare states has certainly been associated with wider political and social struggles for citizenship, and with the recognition that all citizens should be able to enjoy similar life chances and opportunities. Access to social welfare is one way in which citizenship can be recognized and promoted. However, this conceptualization of citizenship in terms of the rights of citizens, and the responsibilities of the state to protect and promote those rights, forms one aspect of more complex understandings of citizenship. Citizenship can also be understood in relation to broader definitions of equality and social justice, as well as to rather elusive concepts such as nationhood, community and belonging. Moreover, who is recognized as a citizen – in legal, political, economic, social or moral terms – is open to interpretation and debate. Citizenship is a status that can be extended, given, restricted and withheld. Indeed, citizenship can be seen as a contested concept as well as a potentially contested status, and certainly one that is open to negotiation and renegotiation. Recent articulations of citizenship have increasingly included recognition of the obligations and responsibilities, as well as the rights, which come with being a member of civil society (Giddens 1998). The notion of the active citizen, and the increased role placed upon participation and community involvement are manifestations of revised political agendas and of approaches to social welfare that are uneasy with both wholly state or market provision of social welfare. Within the recent political project of the so-called third way, citizenship has been recast as an active status that carries with it the obligations of social inclusion, mutuality, participation and democracy (Hall, Williamson and Coffey 2000).

The discipline of social policy continues to grapple with, and the practice of social policy continues to work with/in, different conceptualizations and realities of citizenship. Notions of citizenship continue to underpin welfare strategies and wider social policy reform, while at the same time the ways in which citizenship is understood and experienced can be diverse and uneven. Sociological commentators, alongside other critical perspectives, have contributed in significant ways to these contemporary discourses of citizenship. In this chapter, the focus is on exploring these contributions with/in the social policy context. This includes a reconsideration of the definitions and meanings of citizenship, and a critical exploration of the ways in which particular articulations of citizenship are embedded within contemporary social policy realities. Thus citizenship can be recast as an analytical framework or lens (through which to view social policy), as well as being a legal or political status, or a set of social rights or moral obligations.

The chapter is thematically organized in four main sections. The first two sections consider the different and emergent ways in which citizenship is conceptualized and understood, and notes the contributions made by sociological commentators and other critical scholars. In the last two sections of the chapter attention is focused on particular realms of social policy, in order to explore the changing realities and discourses of citizenship. The first of these considers young people and the transitions to adult citizenship, while the second provides an overview of the changing relationships between education and citizenship.

The progression of citizenship

The post-war account of the development of British (or actually English) citizenship by the sociologist T.H. Marshall provides an important reference point for contemporary scholars. Marshall's formulation is an appealingly sequential one, in which civil, political, and then social citizenship rights are shown to have evolved serially in the course of the eighteenth, nineteenth and twentieth centuries respectively (Marshall 1950). Marshall tied the growth of the institutions of citizenship to the rise of industrial capitalism. He proposed that the development of citizenship (of social citizenship in particular) had brought about the substantial abatement of some of the inequalities of capitalism; that 'the preservation of economic inequalities has been made more difficult by the enrichment of the status of citizenship' (Marshall 1950: 77). Marshall's account gave intellectual expression to the optimism of the post-war consensus, and coincided with the creation of the modern welfare state. Marshall provided what was to become a 'dominant paradigm of social citizenship' (Roche 1992: 21), specifically focusing on the substantive rights of citizenship as guaranteed by the welfare state (Rees 1996).

Various commentators have since challenged aspects of Marshall's account – including his rather neat and sequential chronology of citizenship, his tripartite division of citizenship rights (civil, political and social), his exclusive focus on Britain, his lack of attention to the gendered contexts of citizenship, and his neglect of the role of conflict in the attainment and extension of citizenship. One of the most consistent criticisms has been that Marshall adopted an evolutionary perspective in which the historical development of citizenship appeared as a more or less inevitable process, which looked set to continue indefinitely. In fact, as Turner (1990) points out, Marshall did acknowledge something of the specificity of the socio-historical conditions under which he was writing, and the possible compromise between the logic of the market economy and the egalitarian principles of citizenship which he outlined (and aspired to). Nonetheless there is a general sense in which Marshall's account did lend itself to a rather sanguine view of the ongoing development of citizenship as an inevitable and more or less irreversible process. However, recent decades have seen the unravelling of some of the post-war certainties within which Marshall based his thesis – what Hobsbawm (1995) termed the 'golden age' of the twentieth century; a period characterized, in the developed capitalist world at least, by high employment, technological revolution, rising incomes, and expansionist welfare policies. The economic and social traumas of the last quarter of the twentieth century – for example, significant industrial decline, economic recession, high levels of unemployment, increased disparity of incomes, and crises in state welfare provision – marked a decisive break with the post-war era on which Marshall based his thesis of social citizenship. This prompted a resurgence of interest in citizenship precisely because the possibilities for social inclusion were no longer as widely guaranteed as they once were (or at least appeared to be). In recent years, the paths to citizenship, and the meanings that are invoked by citizenship, have thus become the subjects of renewed political interest.

The citizenship with which Marshall was concerned was, by definition, an evocation of 'national' citizenship. One characteristic of the late twentieth century was the seeming decline in the autonomy of the nation state, and the growth in significance of the European, transnational and global – in political, economic and cultural terms. These are developments that potentially problematize and challenge understandings of citizenship, and by implication notions of membership and social inclusion (Dahrendorf 1996). For example, some commentators have argued that the nation state has been forced to give ground to international and global processes, while simultaneously facing a resurgence of sub-national, regional and ethnic challenges to its authority (Turner 1994). The global and the local have thus both mounted challenges to the conceptualization of 'nationhood', and have raised difficult and challenging questions about identity, affiliation and citizenship for the twenty-first century.

The structural and contextual transformations of contemporary industrial societies have been accompanied by social and cultural changes in the life experiences, affiliations and interests of *citizens* themselves. New, non-class forms of collective action (feminism, the peace movement, and green politics, for example) have contested more established citizenship discourses and political formulations. Indeed, as Hall and Held (1989: 176) suggested, a modern politics of citizenship must come to terms not only with the questions of membership and entitlement posed by such new social movements but also 'with the problems posed by "difference" in a deeper sense: for example, the diverse communities to which we belong, the complex interplay of identity and identification in modern society, and the differentiated ways in which people now participate in social life'. These comments were made with particular reference to arguments that there have been shifts in the social structures of capitalist societies, such that established identities and understandings (such as those based on social class) have lost much of their significance and explanatory validity. This development can be seen as a part of, and as a consequence of, a wider range of changes in the character of contemporary societies, variously referred to as a move to a post-industrial, post-Fordist, postmodern world. The first two of these terms signal changes in the organization and character of economic production, while the third denotes the subjective and cultural quality of these changes, which have variously been seen to include the celebration and increased recognition of 'difference' in identity, politics and philosophy, as well as a pluralization and diversification of cultural identities, and an 'emphasis on a flexibility and self-consciousness in personality and life-style' (Turner 1994: 154).

While there is some general agreement that such developments are taking place, there is also considerable debate about their extent and consequences (not least for citizenship and social policy). As part of a more general sociological commentary, Giddens (1996: 73) argues that the contemporary social environment is one of heightened social reflexivity, in which 'most people have to take a variety of life decisions that cannot be settled by appeal to past tradition . . . in the context of diverse information sources and malleable knowledge claims'. Similarly, Beck (1994: 14) has written of *individualization* as a social form derived from 'the disintegration of the certainties of industrial society as well as the compulsion to find and invent new certainties for oneself'. These developments have prompted new conceptualizations and discourses of and for citizenship.

Contemporary discourses of citizenship

There has been a considerable amount of academic debate about the conceptualizations of citizenship, and the ways in which these are undergoing contestation and change (see, for example, Turner 1986; Barbalet 1988;

Andrews 1991; van Steenbergen 1994; Bulmer and Rees 1996; Clarke 1996; Lister 1997; Faulks 1998). Citizenship has gained a new prominence in political debates and policy agendas, as well as in academic discourses. On the whole there has been a shift away from a 'passive' rights-based (and primarily 'national') language of citizenship towards a new emphasis on citizenship responsibilities, obligations and active participation. The notion of the 'active citizen' has been central to this reconceptualization, emerging in the late 1980s among those on the Right of the political spectrum alarmed by the finality of Margaret Thatcher's assertion that there was no such thing as society. Active citizenship stresses the importance of personal responsibility, and also a wider duty of care for neighbours, locality and community, thereby mitigating, to an extent at least, the New Right ethic of individual self-interest. This emphasis on responsibility – for oneself and towards others – has not been confined to any one political party. Under the UK Labour governments since 1997, notions of good citizenship have shown some considerable continuity with, and support for, the idea of the 'active citizen'. For example, speaking in January 1998 the then Lord Chancellor, Lord Irvine, argued for a concerted effort to engage with a more active conception of citizenship, participation and mutuality within society (as reported in *The Guardian* newspaper, 28 January 1998). In line with many recent pronouncements on the importance of citizenship, Lord Irvine's comments were directed specifically at young people, and disadvantaged young people in particular (see France 1996).

Inevitably, recent and current debates have at their root the question of what is actually meant by citizenship. There is no fixed and final answer to this question, and certainly no single definition that has stood the test of time (Bynner, Chisholm and Furlong 1997). In societies undergoing social change and transformation it is perhaps inevitable that there will be contestation over the meanings attached to citizenship. Citizenship can be rather narrowly defined as referring simply to legal membership of a political, economic or geographical community; a status that is afforded to an individual, whose relationship with the community will entail reciprocal rights and duties. This definition does not readily admit to differing degrees of citizenship or allow an appreciation of qualitative differences in the lived experience of citizenship. Instead, a person's citizenship – their status as a citizen – appears fixed as a matter of fact and law (see Lister 1997). A narrow definition such as this has the advantage of clarity – if citizenship is simply a legal definition or status, then that potentially makes for a straightforward analysis. Working *within* such a narrow definition might make for a rather limited discussion, but this does not make it impossible to work *with* such a definition. We might, for example, accept the legal definition but aim nonetheless to look beyond this in order to contextualize citizenship in a broader sense, exploring other factors which interact with this status, hence aiming at a kind of differentiated universalism (Lister 1997). This is an approach that Jones and

Wallace (1992) adopted as they investigated the extent to which external factors (principally economic inequality) structured access to citizenship for young people in their transitions to adulthood.

It is also possible to define citizenship in much more generous and general terms than those of legal status and entitlement. This moves towards an understanding of citizenship as a normative ideal, incorporating a notion of membership while evoking a range of other factors – for example, a sense of belonging, independence, equality, responsibility, participation, collectivity and identity. In present-day political exhortations about the importance of good citizenship, and of being a good citizen, it is invariably this normative sense of citizenship that is being shaped and redefined rather than the actual legal framework of citizenship status, rights and duties (Hall, Williamson and Coffey 1998). However, process and agency can still be missing from these articulations, as can a meaningful recognition that there may be *multiple citizenships* – in terms of status, experiences, understandings and the construction of social identities. Citizenship is thus not just about a political relationship to the State, or even the rights and responsibilities that are afforded by such status. Rather, it can also be viewed as a means through which we can explore and articulate differentiated social identities and experiences, and the ways in which these are mediated by factors such as age, gender, race or social class.

Questions of gender certainly 'trouble' definitions and conceptualizations of citizenship. In the debates that have ensued over citizenship, little attention has been afforded to gender, although arguably citizenship *should* be located within broad analytic frameworks such as gender equity and social justice. Moreover, it is impossible to separate social identity and citizenship from its gendered (and indeed racialized, localized and generational) contexts. As Billington, Hockey and Strawbridge (1998: 191) have noted 'citizenship is often conceptualised as part of the public world of politics but [. . .] the public and the private overlap and what happens in one area affects the other'. Feminist theoretical perspectives have revealed the ways in which women have been systematically excluded from both the theory and practice of citizenship, as part of a wider feminist project of critiquing the ideals of equality and universality that are traditionally articulated within citizenship discourses. As Lister (1997: 66) argues 'the universalist cloak of the abstract, disembodied individual has been cast aside to reveal a definitely male citizen and a white, heterosexual, non-disabled one at that'. Hence Lister poses the challenges of diversity and difference for citizenship alongside an analysis of the ways in which women have played key roles in various citizenship struggles (not least the campaigns for suffrage and emancipation). In re-engendering understandings and realities of citizenship, the task is more than the summative one of 'adding women' into existing definitions of citizenship. Rather this entails, firstly, rethinking the ways in which women are *included*, as well as excluded from theories and practices of citizenship, and secondly recognizing the gendered *process(es)* of citizenship. That is, the ways in which citizenship(s) are negotiated, (re)produced and articulated. This model

> encourages an approach to theory and practice that gives due accord to women's agency rather than simply seeing us as victims of discriminatory and oppressive male-dominated political, economic and social institutions . . .[] recognising women's agency and achievements as citizens, both individually and collectively, without losing sight of the deep-seated inequalities that still undermine many of their citizenship rights.
>
> [Lister 1997: 5–6].

There is a distinction to be made between citizenship rights and responsibilities. Much of the current focus has been on the *responsibilities* of active citizenship. The notion of social and civic responsibility has been foreshadowed in various discussions of what it means to be a citizen. However, if responsibility is excessively foregrounded such that it overshadows other components of citizenship, it can come to imply an unthinking subordination. Where such a formulation informs areas of social policy (such as citizenship education, civic duty, respect for the law, and so forth) active citizenship becomes a quality to be instilled (in young people) without question, not part of a wider status to be understood and *negotiated* in a more open and reflective fashion. Here the individual becomes more a 'subject' than an 'active' citizen. Similar observations can be made about the notion of 'rights' attached to citizenship status. Again these can be rather formally noted in terms of legal rights (and indeed there are differentially afforded legal rights to different categories of citizen – for example, the 'right' to marry or undergo fertility treatment is not afforded to all citizens), or broadened to encompass the right to participate, to have a 'voice' and to actively negotiate the theory and practice of what it means to be a citizen.

Contemporary discourses of citizenship draw upon a range of frameworks and analyses. Rethinking citizenship as gendered, multiple, contested, shifting and active implicates sociological understandings of the self and the social construction of identities; of relationships between the individual and society; and of the distinction between the public and private spheres of social life. By working with/in these new discourses it is certainly possible to rethink the implicit and explicit relationships between social policy arenas and (the concept and practice of) citizenship. In the sections that follow two such arenas are considered. The transition to adulthood (and adult citizenship) has been conventionally seen as a phase for considerable social policy intervention. In contrast citizenship education is a recurrent and explicit social policy that attempts to instil the values of citizenship.

Young people, citizenship and transitions to adulthood

It has been widely acknowledged that youth transitions to adult citizenship are different for young people today than for previous generations (Furlong and Cartmel 1997). Explanations for this lie with a combination of factors that include long-term socio-structural, economic, and demographic changes, and also policy responses to these changes. These shifts have affected different young people in different ways and to different degrees. Nonetheless there is a general agreement that a process which was once more-or-less straightforward has become increasingly protracted and complex (Morrow and Richards 1996). In part, this complexity reflects a freeing up of established patterns of transition to adulthood. There is a sense in which youth transitions are now more open-ended and fluid than perhaps they once were. Beck (1992, 1994) has suggested that an enhanced 'individualisation' may have signified a decline in the coherence and certainty of once-established patterns of social reproduction, and a corresponding increase in individuals' capacity for self-determination. Beck maintains that new ways of life now require people to 'produce, stage and cobble together their biographies themselves' (1994: 13). To the extent that this is the case, youth transitions are not only more complex but are perhaps increasingly young people's to decide upon. This has implications for the identity-work that young people undertake, and the social policy mileaux within which this takes place. Protracted transitions can leave young people ambiguously placed in respect of an adult status – 'waiting in the wings' for a longer period of time than they might have expected. Some may be able to take advantage of this extension of youth, while others may find it a frustrating time during which their sense of themselves and of their place in society seems indeterminate and unresolved.

Citizenship as the end product of youth

This notion of a possible postponement of adulthood (see Willis 1984) has resonated through much writing about youth transitions over the last two decades. The negative consequences of the economic restructuring which began in the 1970s have been experienced perhaps 'more acutely by young people than by any other group in the labour force' (Doogan 1988: 90), exposing many school leavers – already vulnerable in the labour market and poorly organized to protect their interests – to considerable economic hardship. In addition to which, throughout the 1980s and 1990s, young people were on the receiving end of a number of social policy measures, including the withdrawal/realignment of a range of benefit entitlements and various youth training programmes, intended to ease the burden on the social security budget, advance the New Right's ideological opposition to the 'nanny state', and cope with new labour market realities. However, any notion of an indefinite suspension of adult status has been substantially qualified and revised as sociological attention has shifted from an early focus on youth unemployment to consider a wider range of public and private thresholds, and citizenship contexts. There is a general agreement that a combination of factors, including long-term demographic change, shifts in economic and educational structures, and recent social policy decisions, have left young people to negotiate transitions which are more diverse and complex than those undergone by previous generations (Jones and Wallace 1992). In this context, there has been an increased recognition of the role played by families in supporting young people through an extended indeterminate status towards adulthood. While many families manage, some albeit with difficulty, to 'take the strain' of supporting young people through periods of extended dependency and into eventual adulthood (Hutson and Jenkins 1989), not all are able to do so. Where the burden proves to be too much, this can lead to unsustainable levels of family conflict. Large numbers of young people forced to leave home under such circumstances in recent years have found themselves exposed to the risk of homelessness, a status that severely curtails their citizenship entitlements (and indeed responsibilities). Youth homelessness, as visible social problem, was a particularly pervasive media image of the late 1980s and early 1990s (Hall 2003). However, as Jones (1995) has argued, the struggle over the interpretation and control of young people's position in society during the last two decades has been marked by a whole series of moral panics, which, in addition to fears about the young homeless, have included panics over teenage mothers, 'dole scroungers', street crime and drug use. These debates are explicitly tied to social policy agendas, and have contributed to the notion that Britain may be witnessing the emergence of an underclass. This possibility has generated a substantial amount of sociological and popularist debate (Murray 1990 and 1994). Although it has not been construed as exclusively a youth phenomenon, much of the popular concern about the possible existence of a British underclass has focused on young people (see Rees et al. 1996; MacDonald 1997; Williamson 1997).

In the 1990s citizenship was increasingly used as a way of talking about young people's membership of adult society – what this should and does mean, and how it is attained. The legal and administrative components of citizenship – for example, criminal responsibility, the right to forge consensual sexual relationships, the right to vote and to sign a tenancy agreement, the entitlement to state welfare benefits, and to leave school – are acquired automatically with age, demarcate an individual's economic or social status, and appear to make the eventual attainment of formal adult citizenship more or less inevitable (Jenkins 1990). However, there is a distinction to be drawn between the legal and administrative aspects of adulthood and the capacity to exercise these with/in more complex understandings of citizenship. To focus on citizenship is to recognize the extent to which this status has been substantially withheld from many young people. As they enter upon full legal citizenship status, many young people today find themselves to be among those least able to exercise some of the entitlements, and indeed the responsibilities, that this status brings.

Citizenship and the construction of youth identities

In contemporary political and policy arenas, much of the rhetoric of citizenship is about citizenship as an identity – encouraging young people in particular to think of themselves *as* citizens. This may seem something of an inversion of what is more usually supposed to be the case – that citizenship is a status that is demanded, as it were, from the bottom up. As a status attributable to an individual by virtue of a relationship with the State, citizenship has a rather formal and asocial character. This does not really capture the everyday and personal complexities of social engagement and interaction. And it is through social engagement and interaction – for example, at home, in education or training, or peer groups – that young people are most actively involved in negotiating their emergent social identities. This negotiatedness of social identity stands in contrast to formal articulations of citizenship which are, more often than not, a matter of no negotiation at all, even between the individual and State. This is not to suggest that the issues which citizenship encompasses are not of common importance and the subject of everyday discussion for young people. Nonetheless, the fact that our citizenship is not a status that we call upon ordinarily in our interactions with others should alert us to a certain disjunction in considering citizenship as an everyday source of (young people's) identity.

Young people's capacity to construct a sense of who they are also extends beyond national and even European boundaries. This is particularly so in respect of youth cultures – some of them global – in which many young people are enthusiastic participants. As was noted earlier in this chapter, expanded global reach is only one aspect of developments which have been described, variously, as post-industrial, post-Fordist and postmodern. To the extent that it can be agreed that these developments are taking place, young people – facing a fragmented and fluid opportunity structure in which risks are increasingly individualized, and lifestyle choices, collectivities, and politics are encountered outside the bounds of traditional social formations – may find citizenship an increasingly outdated and inflexible discourse. It is important, however, to interject a note of caution here and to recognize the possibility that many young people's lived experiences and identity-work in postmodern times may in fact not be all that different from that of previous generations. Certainly the developments referred to are uneven, and it would be naïve to deny the persistence of traditional collective social identities and structures which may resonate much more obviously with established citizenship discourses. Furlong and Cartmel (1997), for example, have argued that young people growing up in late modernity face a paradoxical situation in which powerful determinants such as class and gender continue to constrain life chances but obscurely so, giving the impression of greater equality and individualization without any real substance.

Discussions of young people's transitions often use the terms 'adulthood' and 'citizenship' interchangeably. While there are dimensions to adulthood that are essentially those of 'formal' citizenship (a range of rights and responsibilities acquired more or less universally as one grows older), adulthood also entails other, more diffuse, components not central to some definitions of citizenship: for example, socially recognized themes of competence, maturity and independence, which are in turn tied to practical accomplishments such as starting work, leaving home, marriage or cohabitation, and parenthood. Thus adulthood is not only a broader, but also a more *social* category than citizenship is often perceived to be; its achievement is not simply matter of fact and law, but rather something an individual must demonstrate and have validated by others. As such, it is likely that adulthood is an identity that is altogether more meaningful and tangible to young people than citizenship. Yet, where adverse conditions such as economic hardship interrupt or delay transitions to adult roles, the formal entitlements of citizenship can be vitally important to young people precisely because these are attained independently of circumstance. Hence, the 'core' status of citizenship can enable young people to continue to assert their social majority when they may otherwise be unable to demonstrate this (see Hutson and Jenkins 1989 for a discussion of this with regard to youth unemployment).

Young people's routes into adulthood are of course plural and lead into correspondingly plural adult identities. Citizenship is, more often than not, conceptualized as a singular, undifferentiated, and universal status (Lister 1997). The transitions to adulthood (or citizenship) are mediated by other social identities – woman, white, Muslim, Jewish, Welsh or gay, for example. Thus it may be equally as useful to consider the ways in which transitions to different adult identities can skew young people's experience of and even access to citizenship. There are both normative and material dimensions of citizenship and a need to recognize and stress the 'differential nature of citizenship experiences'. (Harrison 1991: 210). These kinds of distinction become particularly sharply focused when social policies and initiatives are put in place to foster citizenship in young people. In the next section this is addressed directly, by considering the trajectory of citizenship education within the discourses of social policy.

Citizenship and education

Legislating for active citizenship seems something of a contradiction. An arena in which this contradiction is perhaps less glaring (but by no means absent) is that of education. It is here, with children and young people (those whom Marshall called 'citizens in the making' (1950: 25)), that governments can more easily make the case for intervention in order to set the agenda, and prepare the way, for citizenship. As Fogelman has indicated, 'the debate about citizenship education, and its place in British schools is far from new' (1997: 214). However, there has nonetheless been a discernible intensification of interest in citizenship education in recent years, matching the emergence and diffusion of the notion of active citizenship. The 1990s began with the identification of citizenship as one of the five cross-curricular 'themes' of the UK National Curriculum (see National Curriculum Council 1990) and with the publication of the report of the Commission on Citizenship (1990), which recommended that citizenship should be a part of every young person's education from the very earliest years. There was an emphasis here, shared by other public pronouncements at the time, on the teaching of citizenship as more than the teaching of 'civics', combining the inculcation of moral values, the learning of practical competencies, and the fostering of a willingness to contribute at a community level – all characteristics of active citizenship.

Some commentators (for example, Wringe 1992; Beck 1996), however, have been keen to point to the ambiguities inherent in a notion of (active) citizenship as something young people should be educated *for* and not only *about* – a set of dispositions to be somehow instilled in and elicited from young people. The final report of the Advisory Group on Education for Citizenship and the Teaching of Democracy in Schools (1998: 5) cited 'worrying levels of apathy, ignorance and cynicism about political and public life and also involvement in neighbourhood and community affairs', and paved the way for renewed calls for compulsory education for citizenship in schools. The report was explicit in its support of active citizenship, with education for citizenship defined as combining social and moral responsibility, community involvement and political literacy. While its principal focus was on compulsory education, the report also stressed that adequate preparation for citizenship should extend beyond school and the school-leaving age into post-16 education, training and youth work. In 1999, the then UK Secretary of State for Education outlined plans for an increased emphasis on citizenship as an explicit part of the school curriculum in England and Wales. These proposals were met with a mixed reaction, not least from teachers already overburdened with a National Curriculum in a finite school day, and from commentators stressing the difficulties of defining and operationalizing (for the purposes of teaching and learning) the concept of citizenship (see Hall et al. 1998). Citizenship is, however now an integral part of the English National Curriculum, and is similarly foreshadowed in the education agendas of the devolved administrations within the UK (see for example National Assembly for Wales 2001).

The notion of active citizenship has informed recent developments in the provision of citizenship education for young people. Beck (1996) certainly found that it informed the general curriculum guidance pertaining to education for citizenship in schools, and Evans (1995) identified similar influences in the post-curricular and training field. Likewise it is an understanding of active citizenship that has informed social policy projects in the youth work field – such as the Prince's Trust Young Volunteer Scheme, the Community Service Volunteers Action Programmes, The Millennium Volunteers and the European Voluntary Service Schemes (European Commission 1996). This notion of active citizenship (and the active citizen) combines communal values and social responsibilities with an ideological commitment to self-interest. Often targeted at disadvantaged young people, active citizenship impresses on young people the responsibilities and obligations that come with the status of citizen (France 1996). In this formulation 'active citizens are charitable, public spirited individuals who make a voluntary contribution to society at a local level' (Hall *et al.* 1998: 308). While the notion of active citizenship has substantially informed debates about education for citizenship, commentators have also been quick to question the conceptualization of citizenship that is supported and proposed as a measurable outcome of citizenship education (Hall et al. 1998).

Attention has increasingly focused on what education for citizenship actually means in practice. Certainly there are concerns that an education for citizenship, as it is currently articulated, reflects an agenda that focuses on skills and competencies for an active contribution to a fluid economy, as well as realigned understandings of nationalism and social and community responsibility. This is in marked contrast to more expansive, innovative and democratic understandings of citizenship espoused by, for example, the democratic schools movement (Gordon 1986; Harber and Meighan 1989; Smith *et al.* 1989). Moreover, some forms of citizenship education have always gone on in schools, but these have rarely been acknowledged or discussed in renewed calls for an increased role of education for citizenship in schools. Education has long been involved in teaching about the everyday experiences or realities of citizenship, and one outcome of educational experiences has long been the social reproduction of citizens/hip. For example, commentators have systematically revealed the ways in which citizenship issues concerned with social class, 'race', and gender identities are routinely 'taught' or 'learnt' in schools (Gillborn 1992; Gordon 1992). Gillborn, for example, has argued that schools were already teaching about (the limits of) citizenship for black people in the UK in the early 1990s. Responding to an early curriculum guidance document (National Curriculum Council 1990), Gillborn suggested that citizenship education discourse was in danger of ignoring 'the important day-to-day messages that schools transmit concerning the citizenship of their students, that is the degree to which students truly belong and may expect full participation and equal access within society' (Gillborn 1992: 59).

While citizenship education may be a worthy *outcome* aim of schooling, there remain degrees of contestation over its meaning and how it should be delivered through education policy and practice. Like the concept of citizenship itself, there are different interpretations that can be levelled at education for citizenship, which reflect different agendas and different outcomes. Citizenship education, with its current emphasis on social responsibility, community participation and politic literacy, does little to recognize the ways in which citizenship and social identities may be differentially experienced and understood. It also, to an extent, masks a contradiction in the discourses of citizenship – whereby citizenship can be perceived as part of a system of social control, or as a recognition of rights and social inclusion (Connell 1992: 133). The contrast between the social control and social justice aspects of citizenship is a longstanding dichotomy within education and training, and indeed within social policy discourses more generally.

Citizenship and youth work

Alongside education and training arenas, youth work in general, and the youth service in particular, has also been identified as a particular social policy arena that has 'great potential value' as a possible contributor to citizenship learning (Advisory Group on Education for Citizenship 1998: 27). It is certainly the case that a significant amount of contemporary youth work practice, with its emphasis on participative activity, community involvement, and support for the development of self-confidence and inter-personal skills, is cognate to particular articulations of citizenship education (Williamson 1997b). Furthermore, the language of citizenship is by no means new to some youth work settings. Indeed, citizenship is an established element of the youth work 'curriculum' (Jeffs and Smith 1996). Youth work has always had an educative agenda, and implicit in that has been the promotion of citizenship.

Youth work itself is a somewhat amorphous concept, encapsulating a range of ways of engaging (with) young people in a variety of organizational and institutional contexts. A key aspect of defining youth work in this context of diversity has been to focus on the principles that inform its work – which might include empowerment, participation, and the provision of space for young people to negotiate, experiment with and challenge their identities and sense of self. This implicates particular aspects of citizenship, – and indeed the *practice* of youth work – incorporating participative activity, community involvement, the acquisition of core skills and competencies.

This in turn draws heavily on some of the contemporary formulations of citizenship (and resonates with the proposals for increased citizenship education in schools). This coincides closely with the concept of the 'active citizen', promoted from a variety of standpoints, both left and right of the socio-political spectrum.

Sociological research has been cautious about youth work's potential as a vehicle for enabling young people's citizenship, for a number of reasons (France 1996; Hall et al. 2000). The numbers of young people actually involved in youth work provision remain a matter of contention (OPCS 1995). Youth work also remains on a precarious footing within social policy, attracting declining resources and (certainly in the UK) without a firm statutory base, despite some arguments that sufficient youth work provision is an essential component of young people's overall educational experience (see Bell *et al*. 1994). The assessments of the efficacy of youth work, as with other arenas for informal or tacit learning, are problematic, with measurable 'outcomes' (beyond the most superficial) difficult to establish and even more difficult to attribute with confidence to the interventions of youth work. Moreover, the promotion of active citizenship, while capturing one aspect of youth work participation or provision, does not necessarily recognize the social and economic inequalities that structure many young people's opportunities and everyday realities (and indeed some arenas for youth work practice are particularly concerned to connect with and provide space for young people excluded from education, training or labour markets). Nonetheless, under conditions in which young people are struggling to negotiate complex and extended transitions to adult citizenship, and in which the notion of active citizenship substantially informs much of the debate over education for citizenship, there is a clear relevance in looking at youth work settings as social policy sites that may or could have increasing importance to young people in the negotiation of their entry to citizenship.

Conclusion

This chapter has considered the ways in which citizenship can be reconceptualized and challenged by broader sociological perspectives. It has done this in a number of ways:

- Through a revisiting of the work of T. H. Marshall as one sociological starting point for making sense of the progression of citizenship;
- Through an engagement with contemporary theoretical and policy discourses;
- By considering the extended trajectories into and multiple meanings extended to adult citizenship;

- By considering the role of schools and other educative settings in the teaching and learning of citizenship.

The aim of the chapter has not been to exhaust the analytical possibilities, but rather to begin to explore the sociological mileage in rethinking relationships between citizenship and social policy. There are, of course, a wide variety of other arenas and agendas of social policy through which conceptualizations and experiences of citizenship are manifest – including, for example, access to and participation in housing markets, the provision and receipt of income maintenance measures, the experiences of and services for 'looked after' children, and the realms of employment policies and training provision. Hence there is considerable further work that could be done in exploring the social policy spaces, places and experiences of and for contemporary articulations of (and indeed inequalities of) citizenship.

The concept and realization of citizenship also provides a means of exploring the relationship between the individual and the State. It provides a framework for considering social policies, their aims and their outcomes. Moreover, we can also use the idea of citizenship in a more qualitative way, recognizing it as part of the context within which individual and collective identity work is undertaken and accomplished. Some of the elements of a more expansive understanding of citizenship, and its linkages to social policy, can be explored through a broader appreciation of the processes of identity work. For example, citizenship is also embodied, spatially situated and biographically constructed (see Chapters 6, 7 and 9 of this volume). To an extent the same set of issues can also be addressed through a critical and sociological consideration of other key social policy 'concepts' – such as equality, diversity and equality of opportunity. Attention is turned to these themes in the next chapter.

Further reading

Faulks, K. (2000) *Citizenship*. London: Routledge. A comprehensive sociological overview of citizenship, which considers the implications of globalization, postmodernity and changes to the nation state. This book explores the rights and responsibilities of citizenship, and the extent to which it is a status that has relevance across public and private spheres of social life.

Lister, R. (1997) *Citizenship: Feminist Perspectives*. London: Macmillan. In this volume, Ruth Lister provides a critical feminist analysis of the concept of citizenship, and considers some of the ways in which feminism complicates how citizenship is experienced and understood.

Van Sternbergen, B. (ed.) (1994) *The Condition of Citizenship*. London: Sage. A thought-provoking edited collection that attempts to make sense of the conditions for, and condition of, citizenship. Leading scholars debate what citizenship is, and what it might become in the future.

chapter

five

Social Policy, Equality and Difference

Introduction

The concepts of equality and social justice have been central to the development and analyses of contemporary social policy. Equality of opportunity was a principle that guided the post-war development of the British welfare state; and was a foundation stone of many social policy institutions (such as the National Health Service) and structures (such as the post-war tripartite system of education). Despite these rhetorics of (and commitments to) equality, commentators of the British welfare state during the 1970s and early 1980s remained sceptical of the extent to which social policies, and more particularly the modern welfare state, had been successful in achieving equality. Critics pointed to the ways in which systematic and structural inequalities remained – for example, with regard to access to health care, mortality and morbidity rates, educational achievement, access to housing and dependency on the State.

The New Right social policy agenda, actively pursued during the last quarter of the twentieth century, also questioned the legitimation of the State to redistribute, or to artificially manipulate equality, preferring instead to relocate the State as the promoter of freedom and liberty, best achieved through the free play of the economic market. This too implied a version of equality, but one based on an understanding of, and re-emphasis upon, the meritocracy and fairness of the marketplace. Hence rhetorics of equality were replaced with discourses of choice and the freedom of individuals to determine their own educational, health, social care and labour market futures. The New Labour social policies of the late 1990s and early twenty-first century have continued to grapple with the concepts and realities of equality. The labour governments since the late 1990s have not retreated completely from the delivery and organization of social welfare within a market framework. Hence equality has become seen as an implicit aim of social policy that can be delivered through a diversification of welfare choices. Moreover, equality has been repositioned within a broader or social democratic framework, and set alongside other discourses such as social inclusion and exclusion, difference and diversity. Hence while equality could still be said to underpin social policy, the meaning that is attributed to this, and the ways in which this is translated into policy and practice, have undergone considerable repositioning in recent years.

Concepts of equality, and their multiple meanings, have formed part of more general historical and contemporary theorization and commentaries of social policy. Equality was certainly a factor within 'classical' philosophies of social provision. For example, Rawls (1972), in his development of principles of social justice, aspired to the idea of equality of opportunity (although he was less than clear as to what he perceived this to be in practice). Similarly, R. H. Tawney (1964) articulated a desired movement toward some notion of equality (which he equated with the establishment of minimum acceptable standards). At the other end of the (socio-political) spectrum, writers such as Hayek (1960) foreshadowed New Right criticisms of equality as a barrier to economic efficiency and personal freedoms. And, as has already been noted (see Chapter 3), academic commentary and critique of contemporary social policy has continued to use equality as an analytical framework. Feminists and others have also scrutinized the theory and practice of social policy, and the extent to which they promote equality, lead to inequality or indeed exacerbate existing inequalities.

There is little doubt, therefore, that equality, and equality of opportunity continue to feature in the ways in which social policies are conceptualized, practised, experienced or evaluated. Nevertheless, the extent to which these are not straightforward or undisputed concepts should be acknowledged in any analysis. Equality and equality of opportunity can mean different things to different people, and hence the pursuit of equality through social policy will always be open to interpretation and debate. Sociological and feminist perspectives can contribute to these debates, not least by providing frameworks through which the different meanings, understandings and experiences of social policy can be explored. Thus this chapter takes equality, and more specifically the concept of equal opportunity, as its focus, drawing out some of the contrastive and complementary conceptualizations. In the next section of the chapter the relationships between equality of opportunity and contemporary social policy are briefly explored. This is then followed by sections that consider different conceptualizations of equality, and the consequences of these for the theory and practice of social policy.

Equality of opportunity and social policy

Equality and equal opportunity are essentially contested concepts (Drake 2001). However, the general principle of equality of opportunity is now widely accepted as both fair and legitimate, within and outwith social policy. The concept can be seen as compatible with liberalism and notions of meritocracy, as well as with more general and radical egalitarian agendas. However, there is still considerable debate as to how equality of opportunity should and indeed can be implemented (Walby 1999). Policies and practices aimed at fostering equal opportunities vary considerably, both in their scope and effectiveness. Some of these differences are rooted in different ideological commitments, such as contrastive feminist perspectives (Whelehan 1995). Others represent alternative responses to equality and diversity agendas. Some of the contemporary discourses of diversity, for example, have repositioned diversity as a potentially 'lost' opportunity for industry and the workplace that should be recognized and harnessed (Kandola and Fullerton 1994). Thus it is possible to reconceptualize equality of opportunity, not only in terms of social justice, but also as a means of improving business efficiency through the removal of barriers to the effective utilization of the skills and labour of all (Walby 1999). This is certainly in contrast to more sceptical views that equality of opportunity policies may favour some groups to the detriment of others, or that equality concerns serve as a distraction from the 'real work' of the economy. However, the positive harnessing of diversity is not unproblematic, not least because it could be seen to represent a rather weak version of equality, grounded in improved economic efficiency rather than more expansive notions of equity and social justice.

Why might it be useful to consider equality of opportunity in an analysis of social policy? Aside from the historical and philosophical underpinnings of contemporary social policy, considerations of equality can also serve as frameworks for addressing the policy-making process, the outcomes of policy, and the lived realities of welfare provision. For example, policy formation can be considered in terms of underpinning models of equality (of opportunity) and the extent to which these are followed through in the implementation of policy. A consideration of equality provides a mechanism for tracking the transitions from the theoretical dimensions of social policy (such as values and principles) to the empirical articulation of social policy; from policy writing through to implementation and outcomes. The concepts of equality and equality of opportunity can be, have been and are used to formulate research questions about the outcomes of social policies. For example, questions such as 'who benefits?' or 'who loses?' are central to the assessment of social policy, as are broader questions as to whether inequalities are being reproduced, exacerbated or challenged. Just as important to contemporary understandings of social policy are the notions of work and experience (both of which are core to sociological understandings of the social world). These too can be explored through a framework of equality. Social policy or 'welfare' is often (and formally) an 'employer' as well as a provider of services. Hence social welfare and social policy can be viewed as parts of the labour market and the economy. Thus equality of opportunity issues within social policy can straddle work as well as welfare issues. The legal and moral obligations of employers with regard to equality of opportunity are just as salient to social policy 'work' settings as to any other form of employment. Moreover, the 'providers', 'recipients' or 'clients' of social policy are not passive consumers. They experience policy and practice in a variety of ways, both as individuals and as social groups. To understand and make sense of these experiences is, by definition, to engage with discourses of difference, diversity and (in)equality.

Equality of opportunity (and equality more generally) can be defined in terms of both theory and practice. As analytical concepts and frameworks they are open to different understandings and interpretations. Moreover, these different theorizations lend themselves to different solutions in terms of policy and practice. While widely used, and indeed widely accepted as desirable, equality of opportunity is a very flexible term. As Weiner (1986: 266) noted 'for some, achieving equality means enabling certain under-represented groups to attain their rightful place in the existing social, economic and political order; for others it means offering radical alternatives to an essentially biased social and political system'. This flexibility can be considered a strength (enabling groups with differing ideological persuasions to 'sign up' to a 'version' of equality), or a weakness (whereby it is difficult to achieve a consensus of meaning and action). In the sections that follow some of these different conceptualizations of equality of opportunity are described, drawing on both sociological and feminist contributions. The implications for the formation, implementation and practice of social policy are then considered in this context. While it may be argued that these conceptualizations or models offer (potentially radically) different visions of equality, in terms of policy they can be seen to represent a continuum. These approaches are not in themselves necessarily mutually exclusive, and can perhaps more helpfully be seen as cumulative, or, as Blakemore and Drake (1996) suggest, a spectrum of approaches.

Liberalism and equality of opportunity

A most readily accepted and adopted conceptualization of equal opportunities has its roots in the notion of the liberal state and the individual's right for self-advancement. This can be seen as a legacy of nineteenth-century liberalism, drawing on the work of liberal thinkers such as John Stuart Mill (1869) and Mary Wollstonecraft (1792). This conceptualization of equality of opportunity does not seek to change fundamental social structures, but rather aims to seek formal (legal) equality for all within those accepted structures. The issue, then, is not to challenge the theoretical underpinnings of the State or the organizational structures of institutions, but rather the individual's opportunity to access those structures in an equitable fashion. Hence this conceptualization can be used to consider a framework of civic, political and legal rights to promote equality of access (to welfare, employment, education, services, wealth and opportunities for self-advancement, for example) and equality of treatment within social organizations, institutions and structures. This implies a rather tightly defined concept of social justice, concerned with the removal of formal barriers to equity; and grounded in social democracy, natural justice and meritocratic understandings of social reform. This encapsulates a basic belief that all individuals (regardless of gender, ethnicity, sexual orientation and age) should be free to determine their political, social, educational and labour market roles and futures (Coffey and Delamont 2000).

This is not a model that aims to necessarily equalize experiences, or wealth, and indeed would recognize that social differentiation is a necessary aspect of society. Rather, it is a model that strives to ensure that such social differentiation is based on choice and merit, and not on formal barriers to progress. This model can perhaps be viewed as a resolution between equality of opportunity and a *laissez-faire* or free market. In Blakemore and Drake's (1996) terms this represents a minimalist approach to equality, concerned with 'securing fairness in the *procedures* used to fill offices and positions, to forbid direct discrimination and to disallow the use of irrelevant criteria in processes of selection' (Drake 2001: 41). It is hard to argue against such a basic definition. Indeed this version of equality of opportunity has been adopted within and beyond social policy institutions and procedures, as well as being enshrined in what might now be considered landmark equality legislation – such as the 1975 Sex Discrimination and 1976 Race Relations Acts in the UK.

This approach to equal opportunities has, however, been open to criticism, and can be conceived as a relatively weak approach to equality (Riddell and Salisbury 2000). Few commentators would argue with the basic premise that enshrining equal access and treatment in legislative and policy frameworks is a desirable and necessary part of advancing equality. However, there are limits as to how far such an approach can advance broader social change, or successfully tackle inequalities. Policies to encourage equal access (to education, training, employment, social services, income maintenance and the professions, for example) do not benefit all individuals equally. Some individuals and social groups will not be in a position to access particular educational opportunities, or welfare provisions or labour market positions, even if formal (legal) barriers to entry have been removed. For example, the removal of the formal barriers to women entering the liberal professions in the nineteenth and early twentieth centuries did not initially lead to large numbers of women accountants, medics, lawyers or dentists (Witz 1992). The fact that women have been legislatively permitted to become Members of Parliament in the UK for three-quarters of a century has not resulted in equal numbers of men and women entering that Parliament. Thus formal equal access does not necessarily tackle in equality – and alone cannot compensate for differences in experiences, family commitments, domestic responsibilities or cultural capital. Moreover, legislating for equality in the 'public' spheres of, for example, policy and employment, does little to address inequalities in the 'private' and domestic spheres (the home, for example), which in turn mitigate against some individuals (for example, some women) taking up the opportunities that may be afforded by equal access. The significant increases in female labour market participation, for instance, have not been matched by anything like similar shifts in the domestic divisions of labour (Pilcher 1999).

Despite statutory frameworks designed to ensure equality of access and treatment, there are also many examples where this has not resulted in equality of outcome. Within the labour market, for example, there is still substantial evidence of both vertical and horizontal segregation – in terms of gender, ethnicity and age (Hakim 1979; Crompton and Sanderson 1990; Equal Opportunities Commission 2001). The 'labour market' realm of social policy is not immune from these segregations. For example, in education, nursing, social work, the civil service and political life, the workforce can still be characterized in gendered and racialized ways (Finlayson and Nazroo 1997; Halford, Savage and Witz 1997; Lovenduski 1997; Coffey and Delamont 2000). While legal commitment to equal access or equal treatment removes formal exclusion from certain spheres of public life, it does not necessarily tackle segregation within public life (Walby 1990). Certain occupations remain highly gendered, as do occupational hierarchies (Halford et al. 1997). Moreover, there remains a significant gender pay gap in the UK despite the Equal Pay Act that legislated against pay discrimination 30 years ago (EOC 2001).

Policies that recognize the rights of individuals to equal access and equal treatment are, of course, significant milestones in the pursuit of equality. However, this rights-based view can be seen to be a rather passive approach to the complex realities of equality. By focusing on the individual there is a danger of ignoring organizational or structural dimensions of inequality (such as, for example, institutional racism, the gender pay gap, systematic age discrimination or non-transparent promotion procedures). Within such formal and narrow definitions of equality there is also a danger of not paying sufficient attention to the many dimensions of difference and diversity. This in turn might make it difficult to make a case for special treatment in order to counter discrimination (Gregory 1999). Thus ensuring equal access to welfare services or public positions or areas of (social policy) work may not necessarily result in equality of opportunity becoming a reality.

For example, commentators have drawn attention to the ways in which social care and health services, while enshrined within policies of equal access and treatment, are actually insensitive to ethnic and cultural diversity, for example in matters of diet, gender sensitivity, religious observance and dress (Ahmed 1992; Blakemore and Boneham 1994; Gazdar 1997). Moreover, having a 'policy' in place without actively promoting or monitoring that policy – for example, through a robust monitoring system, or equality awareness training – may actually prove ineffective in the actual observance of (even) formal equality. Thus it is possible to consider moving beyond basic liberal articulations and the removal of formal barriers, towards a more pro-active approach to equality. This begins to recognize the organization and structural constraints on realizing equality of opportunity.

Positive approaches and additional support

Formal approaches to equal opportunities, enshrined within liberal models of individualism, natural justice and equal access, often assume that all individuals start from the same vantage point (Rees 1998). However, assuming such a 'neutral' stance can be problematic if equality is an explicit goal, as Gregory (1999: 107) argues (in this case with respect to gender, but equally applicable to other aspects of inequality):

> There is an assumption of symmetry in this approach which suggests that men and women both suffer equally from discrimination, thus deflecting attention from the specific disadvantages experienced by women. Spurious gender neutrality in reality endorses a male norm and restricts the possibilities of remedial action designed to compensate for historical and structural disadvantages, on the grounds that such action discriminates against men.

Thus it is possible to develop the argument that additional measures may need to be taken to ensure that equality (of access and treatment, for example) is actually realizable; recognizing that some individuals and social groups may require additional support in order to compete effectively in the public sphere, or to secure 'equal' access to services. This approach, sometimes referred to as affirmative action (Bacchi 1996), maintains a belief in a system of merit ('the best person for the job') but recognizes that not everyone begins from the same starting position. In this conceptualization of equality, formal (legal) equality is not enough on its own. Rather, potential barriers to access and progression are identified, and measures put in place in an attempt to remove or ameliorate them. There might, therefore, be cases when there are exceptions to strictly equal treatment in order to facilitate equality of outcomes.

Affirmative action can take a variety of forms. For example, positive action measures can include specific service provision for particularly 'vulnerable' or disadvantaged groups; career breaks and family-friendly hours for working parents; dedicated training courses for particular groups; equal opportunities awareness training; mentoring systems; or the appointment of an equal opportunities officer. Measures such as these can be designed to raise the profile of equal opportunities in general and/or be used to accommodate real or perceived 'disadvantages' that certain individuals or social groups might face which may be preventing them from taking advantage of opportunities that are available to them (such as those of education, training or the labour market), or engaging with service provision. These kinds of measures can be used to further promote and encourage equal opportunities. Bacchi (1996) contrasts these sorts of measures with more direct action, which might be better defined as positive discrimination. Rather than simply offering additional support to some individuals and social groups, Bacchi argues that there might sometimes be a need to sanction explicitly unequal treatment in order to redress discrimination. Thus this recognizes, not only that some may need 'special' provision to compete effectively, but also that there is discrimination (implicit or explicit) that needs to be counterbalanced. Examples of this kind might be the imposition of quotas in recruitment or selection (for example, in favour of women or ethnic minorities), or all-women shortlists for public or private positions. One danger of such actions is that they could be perceived as discriminatory in their own right, and of actively creating inequities, although this is a line of argument that is difficult to sustain once there is an appreciation of existing inequalities (Rees 1998). More significantly, as Gregory (1999) argues, these forms of action are very often short-term, temporary measures, and do not necessarily require organizations or policy-makers to reflect upon their policies and practices, or make longer-term, structural changes.

This conceptualization of equality, and equality of opportunity, still operates within a broad liberal framework, while at the same time recognizing some of the barriers that individuals and social groups may face in attempting to realize their potential. Affirmative measures such as positive action and positive discrimination certainly provide mechanisms for under-represented groups to have a fairer (more equal) chance of taking advantage of the policies of equal access and equal treatment. As such, they are often used in conjunction with more formal legislative frameworks. However, these measures can still be limited in their capacity to challenge organizational structures or to ensure parity of experiences and outcome. Such approaches still make the assumption that once individuals have been 'helped' on to a particular trajectory, the 'neutral' systems of merit and ability will reign supreme. For example, this assumes that once lone parents have been 'helped' back to the labour market (through income maintenance policies and retraining opportunities), they will not require any further support, as they will then be in a position to compete on equal terms.

This takes little notice of ongoing domestic commitments, discrimination in the workplace, unfair recruitment and promotion procedures, and so forth. More generally, positive measures are less satisfactory in tackling the less tangible aspects of inequality, such as sexual harassment. Positive measures also assume some kind of deficit or disadvantage that needs to be accommodated or addressed. While positive discrimination recognizes some aspects of inequality and puts in place mechanisms to create a better balance, there is an overarching concern with 'perfecting or skewing the rules of the contest' (Rees 1998: 40), rather than abandoning the contest completely. Thus this conceptualization does not necessarily tackle organizational cultures, the 'neutral' system of merit (clearly not neutral given the inequalities in terms of outcomes that persist) or the differential valuing of skills, knowledges and experiences. This calls for more radical understandings of equality, ones that 'trouble' what is meant by equality and how it can be assured.

The politics of difference

The conceptualizations of equality described thus far begin from a recognition (and position) of disadvantage, and seek to put in place measures (formal or otherwise) to counterbalance this disadvantage. They do not necessarily challenge organizational structures, processes or knowledges, but rather recognize that some individuals or social groups have been and continue to be better able to take advantage of opportunities that are presented to them (whether these be access to health care, education, housing, income maintenance, training or the labour market). Hence formal equality legislation, and the range of positive measures that can be put in place to facilitate this, can be viewed as a desire to ensure 'sameness' or neutrality. Following this through to a natural conclusion, there is an implication that services, opportunities, organizations, outcomes or treatments can be and should be gender-neutral, race-neutral, age-neutral, and so forth. Some sociological and feminist commentators have argued that this still represents a rather limited approach to the complex realities of equality and difference. Moreover, some commentators have challenged the possibilities and desirability of neutrality. There has been scepticism expressed at the potential of these various equality of opportunity measures to achieve equality, precisely because they attempt to mask (or compensate for) difference. This critique can be located within a cultural politics or 'politics of difference' approach (Giddens 1994). Such an approach does not deny that there may be disadvantages that may need to be overcome, but takes issue with the notion of neutrality and the pursuit of sameness. Thus there is recognition of different lives, experiences and voices that need to be heard, and built into employment practices, service provision and policy-making.

Postmodern agendas have recognized the diversity of social life and the multiple (and shifting) identities and voices that make up the social world. This recognition (and celebration even) of diversity invites a rethinking of the meanings and realities of equality. In doing so, the notions of the 'norm' and the 'other' are disrupted. As Maynard (1998) argues, postmodernism and calls to diversity problematize the 'accepted' version of 'normality' – as overwhelmingly white, male, heterosexual and able-bodied. The politics of difference approach rethinks equality – by engaging with the ways in which sameness (such as equal access) and specialness (such as positive measures) both deny the importance of power in the persistence of inequality (Snitow 1990). This is a far more challenging approach to issues of equality, not least because of the potential to reveal organizations, processes and services as (for example) androcentric, racist, homophobic and disablist. It brings to account the ways in which organizations and institutions are structured and run, and the sets of values and knowledges on which they are built. This approach, thus, draws upon more radical theoretical perspectives (such as, but not exclusively, those associated with radical feminism, new racial theory, queer theory and lesbian studies – see Whelehan 1995; Wilton 1995; Mac an Ghaill 1999). Equality is thus positioned alongside difference and diversity, as a factor to be recognized, 'accommodated' and 'mainstreamed' (Rees 1998). Or to put it another way, the pursuit of equality should not assume or imply some kind of deficit or disadvantage to be 'compensated'.

Of course there are many different ways of responding to a diverse society (in terms of, for example, gender, race and ethnicity, age, religion, culture, sexuality and disability). Drake (2001) identifies at least three – ignoring differences and imposing *uniformity*; accommodation through some *reconfigurement* of the social and political environment; and *compromise*, whereby all parties undertake some change. Mainstreaming equality (Rees 1998) implies reconfigurement and compromise, but supports a more radical transformation of the culture and structures of organizations. Mainstreaming equality in part reflects a belief that if equality of opportunity is a significant part of the ethos of an organization then this should be reflected in its power structures and should permeate all its activities (Farish, McPake, Powney and Weiner 1995). This approach positively recognizes difference and questions the pursuit of sameness without adequate recourse to questions of diversity. This does not, however, imply nothing should be done to actively counter inequalities. Rather, there is an implication that differences need to be positively acknowledged and accommodated in definitions and practices of equality. A further implication of this is a more significant shift – through which equality is made central rather than peripheral to *all* aspects of organizational structures, processes and practices. Rees (1998: 46) describes this transformative process as 'designing programmes and projects informed by knowledge of the diversity of the needs of potential participants', as opposed to 'fitting [women] into existing structures and systems, or seeking to adjust structures to ensure a better fit'.

This conceptualization can be seen as building on basic good practice, such as that of formal equality of opportunity policies, the setting of equality targets, undertaking equality monitoring, and equality awareness training. However, from this perspective these practices are seen as a small (though important) part of more substantial change that may be needed. What is at stake here is not so much the capacity of individuals or social groups to take advantage of opportunities that may be (made) available to them, but the capacity of the organization to ensure that equality and the positive appreciation of difference is the accepted and desired norm. Hence this is concerned with challenging structures, values, processes and practices of the organization, and how these are embedded within systems of (for example, male, white, heterosexual) power and privilege. This is, to say the least, a challenging agenda. As Gregory (1999: 111) has argued, mainstreaming may be an excellent idea, 'but if it is regarded by those responsible for its implementation as little more than a paper exercise, providing the appearance but not the reality of equality, it becomes a sham'.

Labour market commentators have increasingly come to recognize the advantages of a diverse workforce, and in working with (rather than trying to reduce) difference (Kandola and Fullerton 1994; Rubery and Humphries 1995). However, equality mainstreaming is not the same as some of the more superficial management articulations of 'managing diversity' (which may actually assume a halting of equality measures, or of monitoring equal opportunities). Mainstreaming is a much broader concept, wider in its remit and more far-reaching than simply a management tool. Mainstreaming is certainly not an excuse for abandoning existing examples of good practice, or the development of new ones. Rather, these are the foundations and building blocks of wider transformation. Mainstreaming equality, and responding to positive discourses of difference, does not necessarily deny the importance of measures such as positive action or equal access (better these than nothing at all), but would be critical of such measures as a long-term strategy for ensuring full public participation for all on equal terms. Mainstreaming argues for the integration of equality issues and the recognition of diversity within policy planning, decision-making, service provision and practice (McCrudden 1996). It also assumes participation and anticipation – whereby meaningful consultations take place as part of the routine policy-making process, and equality of opportunity is built into policy planning and evaluation as a matter of course.

All of the conceptualizations of equality that have been discussed thus far in this chapter present analytical frameworks and challenges for the theory and practice of social policy. While versions of equality of opportunity may be enshrined within historical and contemporary articulations of the welfare state, in itself this tells us very little about the conceptualization of equality with/in social policy formation, process, practice or experience. In the next section of this chapter the analytical potential for social policy of working with this broader theoretical spectrum is explored.

Policy, practice and experience

The formalization of equality of opportunity through law and policy ensures a minimum, basic commitment. Ensuring equal access and equal treatment in legal terms can also be seen as a first step toward more radical and far-reaching approaches to equality. A more proactive stance, perhaps through the adoption of positive measures or affirmative action, recognizes some of the difficulties of realizing equality of opportunity and makes provision to remedy or neutralize difference. Taken further, the recognition of the politics of difference, and the pursuit of equality mainstreaming seeks to disrupt values, structures and hierarchies; promoting a more challenging version of equality realized not least through a positive appreciation of diversity. These different conceptualizations or approaches can be seen as cumulative, rather than mutually exclusive, or as points along a fluid continuum of policy and practice, each representing a step along the way to a fully integrated ethos of equality (Farish et al. 1995). In an exploration of the practice and policy implications of these different approaches, Rees (1998) adopts the terms 'tinkering', 'tailoring' and 'transforming'. Tinkering refers to establishment of legal, policy frameworks while leaving structures and processes relatively untouched. Tailoring refers to particular measures that may be put in place to 'tailor' equal opportunities policies to individuals and social groups. Transforming recognizes the structural, organizational and cultural changes that may be necessary to mainstream equality. These terms, and the approaches they represent, can be utilized in an analysis of the theory and practice of social policy.

Ensuring legal equality with/in social policy

Social policy arenas, alongside public policy more generally, have increasingly adopted formal definitions of equality, usually enshrined within equality of opportunity legislation. Such policy frameworks are designed to legally ensure a basic, minimum compliance to equality through policy, and often represent a formal or organizational commitment to equality of opportunity (see European Commission 1995). They can also be viewed as a necessary precursor to any wider pursuit of equality, although they may not, in isolation, be sufficient to bring about long-term organizational change. A policy does not in and of itself ensure compliance or effective delivery. Formal policy commitments to equality can also be accompanied by institutional mechanisms for monitoring particular dimensions of (in)equality –

such as gender and ethnic balances in the workforce, or in levels of achievement or pay differentials – and programmes of equality awareness training. An equal opportunities employer might, for example, be expected to have a clear (and empirically grounded) understanding of how their organization operates or 'measures up' in terms of the allocation of opportunities, positions and rewards (Rees 1998). Equal opportunity policies also provide employees with a legislative framework for redress. In terms of social welfare services this can be extended to providers and clients – ensuring formal obligations to attempt to give equal access to services, and citizens the right to certain levels of care, consideration and provision.

There is little doubt that this formal articulation of equality of opportunity was part of the development of the post-war welfare state in the UK. It was a key element in its formulation. Moreover, equality of opportunity, in formal terms, remains part of the discourses of contemporary social policy. Hence equality of opportunity, often expressed in terms of citizenship rights (see Chapter 4 of this volume), was enshrined in the establishment of many of the core social policy services such as health and education, as well as being reaffirmed through various legislative measures (such as the Disability Discrimination Act and Regulations of 1995 and 2003 respectively). Indeed, it is now (almost) unthinkable that any public or social policy organization – for example, social service department, school, university, health trust, youth work setting – would not have a policy of and formal commitment to equality of opportunity. However, despite these formal and legal commitments to equality, there is considerable evidence to suggest that inequalities within social policy arenas and experiences have not been eliminated. For example, sociological research on health continues to highlight the persistence of inequalities of health experience and health care. Class, race, gender and age have all been highlighted as significant factors in the ways in which we gain access to and benefit from health care (Smaje 1995; Annandale and Hunt 2000; Iganski and Mason 2002; Popay *et al.* 2003). Furthermore it has been argued that the health service has been and continues to be heavily reliant upon the (low-paid) labour of women and ethnic minorities (as carers, nurses and auxiliary health-care workers) (Williams 1989; Nettleton 1995; Halford, Savage and Witz 1997). Moreover, while there are no longer formal barriers to women entering the welfare and health professions (and indeed while the welfare state continues to be one of the largest employers of women), the increased numbers of women entering medical school has not translated into a feminization of the higher echelons of medicine, or the most 'respected' specialities such as surgery (Riska and Wegar 1993). The NHS has also been accused of institutional racism in its procedures and practices (see Esmail and Etherington 1997; Esmail *et al.* 1998).

Other spheres of social policy can also be considered in terms of the ways in which formal redress to equality has not necessarily resulted in the elimination of inequalities. Education and training, for example, are arenas that have not been immune from accusations that they have failed to achieve equality of opportunity and equal access, in spite of legislation. Social class still remains the biggest determinant of educational performance (Brown *et al.* 1997). Despite the introduction of a National Curriculum in 1988, which removed some of the gendered subject choices up to the age of 16, it is still the case that when there is subject choice, for example at post-16, young men and young women continue to 'choose' different routes (Arnot, David and Weiner 1999), and hence have different training and labour market trajectories. There has been recurrent concerns over the underachievement of some groups within the education system – for example, there have been recent debates over the poor performance of some boys (see Epstein et al. 1998; Francis 1999 for critical commentaries of these debates), and exclusions from school continue to be framed by gender, class and race (Wright, Weekes and McGlaughlin 2000; Osler and Vincent 2003). As an employer the education system also continues to show substantial inequalities. A gendered division of labour exists within the teaching profession. Despite the fact that in principle 'teaching is a career in which men and women enjoy equal opportunities' (Measor and Sikes 1992: 111), the numbers of women securing senior teaching posts remain disproportionately low (Boulton and Coldron 1998; Coffey and Delamont 2000; DFES 2002). Within higher education the picture is even less encouraging, with few women present within the senior decision-making or professorial levels (Bown 1999). There also continue to be significant gender pay differentials within higher education (see Bett 1999), although this is not surprising given the persistence of a gender pay gap within the UK labour market in general (EOC 2001).

Measures and actions to address inequities with/in social policy

Tailoring is a useful metaphor to describe the various measures that can be put in place to encourage a more active pursuit of equality of opportunity for some individuals or social groups. As has already been noted in this chapter, these measures can vary enormously and can take many different forms, but might include the scheduling of training opportunities to 'fit in' with other life commitments; offering particular services or opportunities to specific groups; the appointment of equality officers; the development of mentoring or role model programmes; and equality 'proofing' of organizational literature and committee structures. Such measures might imply an operational equality audit of the organization as well as proactive strategies to address inequalities of access and treatment. Operating within a distributive framework of justice, this model thus attempts to ensure more effective equality of access and treatment without disrupting organizational cultures and structures. What can occur through this approach are examples or pockets of good equality practice that can be used as a catalyst for greater change.

Many of the arenas of social policy are examples *par excellence* of the 'tailoring' of equality of opportunity. Social security and income maintenance are obvious areas where *de facto* positive measures are used. Indeed, one could argue that the State provision of income maintenance is predicated on this notion of a 'helping hand' in order to ensure a level playing field. Hence there are a series of benefits targeted at particular groups – such as lone parents, the elderly, the unemployed, low income families, parents, the disabled and long-term carers. It would clearly be unwise to argue that such measures should not be in place, although it is difficult to argue that these have been successful on their own in achieving longer-term equality. We know, for example, that women are still more likely to experience poverty than men, even if they live within the same household, that lone parents continue to make up a substantial proportion of the poor, that State pensions leave many elderly people in a vulnerable position, and that the disability benefit system does not encourage (or make possible for many) financial independence and autonomy (Glendinning and Millar 1992; Drake 1998; Oliver and Barnes 1998; Bradshaw and Sainsbury 2000). On their own State benefit provisions do not necessarily address the structural causes of disadvantage – for example, differential educational outcomes or training opportunities or discriminatory labour market practices.

More generally, so-called positive measures have been extensively used as a social policy mechanism of recognizing and responding to inequality. Hence there have been a range of programmes and provisions designed to provide extra support and resources to 'disadvantaged' groups, areas and individuals. A good example of this would be the identification of and support given to Education Action Zones by the UK government – designated geographical areas deemed to be in need of additional resources in order to improve educational experiences and outcomes (DfEE 1998; Skidelsky and Raymond 1998). The extent to which these measures are effective in the removal of inequalities in the long term is a moot point. Certainly they do not necessarily tackle wider structural inequalities, although we should not be dismissive of the short- (and indeed longer-) term benefits to some individuals and groups. Similar arguments can be made about much smaller initiatives that have been set up to redress specific equalities in social policy provision. For example, the various projects that have been developed to encourage girls to take up a wider variety of school subjects and career opportunities have had a limited impact on changing educational trajectories (Whyte 1986; Whyte et al. 1988).

Mainstreaming quality with/in social policy

It is more difficult to identify specific examples of equality mainstreaming or transformation within the spheres of social policy. A move away from a notion of a monolithic welfare state of the post-war years to a more eclectic, mixed economy of welfare could be seen as part of a recognition of diversity in terms of need and provision. Policy documents and statements now pay more attention to gendered and racially sensitive language. The increased emphasis given to user consultation and participation in some welfare services could also be said to denote a shift in the power relations of welfare (Pithouse and Williamson 1997). There is clearly more recognition of diversity within social policy than there once was, and more commitment to finding ways through which all citizens can actively engage in the policy process (from citizenship education, to public consultation exercises and formal user panels). More fundamentally, UK governments (in Wales, Northern Ireland and Scotland, as well as the Westminster Parliament) have embraced the concept of equality mainstreaming, particularly with regard to gender. While this is at a relatively early stage, it may have a significant impact on the future making and monitoring of social policy (Women and Equality Unit 2003).

However, there are a number of ways in which equality (and diversity) has not (as yet) been 'mainstreamed'; that is made an integral and vital part of the processes *and* practices of social policy. Social policy-makers are still, by and large, white, male, heterosexual and middle class – and are rarely by contrast disabled, black, elderly or female. Of course, we can always point to exceptions – an increasing number of women in government (indeed the Welsh Assembly Government is the first gender balanced parliament in Europe, and has the only cabinet to contain more women than men!), the first openly gay cabinet minister, a disabled chair of a select committee and so forth – but these should not be used to assume equality with/in social policy-making. Similarly there are still many social policies that support certain kinds of family structures, or personal relationships, or gender roles, and in part contribute to continuing inequalities in status, service provision and welfare experience. Mobility audits of public buildings or public transport or social welfare institutions are still not done as a matter of course (although this is set to change under the new disabilities legislation). Gender pay audits (whereby organizations subject their pay structures to a rigorous gender analysis), argued for by the Equal Opportunities Commission (EOC 2001), can still be highly resisted, and are certainly not the norm within the realms of social policy and welfare provision. User groups and welfare clients still yield little real power in policy-making or in the delivery of services. And here lies the problem with advocating mainstreaming and the politics of difference. Not only has this transformation not happened within social policy; it may not happen at all if recognizing difference and celebrating diversity becomes used as an excuse (even a well-meaning one) for 'ignoring' differences and inequalities, or removing positive measures, equality monitoring, equal opportunity officers and other mechanisms that work toward formal and practical equality of opportunity, within and ultimately beyond social policy.

Conclusion

This chapter has explored some of the ways in which equality, and more specifically equality of opportunity, can be used to reconceptualize and reanalyse the theory and practice of social policy. In particular, the chapter has explored a range of different ways in which the concepts of equality, equality of opportunity and diversity can be defined and put into practice. Equality was central to the formation of the post-war welfare state and remains an important element of the philosophy and practice of contemporary social policy. As a concept it is, and looks set to remain, an integral part of the discourses and aims of social policy. However, the meanings that are attached to terms such as equality or diversity are far from fixed or incontestable. On the contrary the critiques that have been levelled at various social policies, institutions and welfare practices have drawn on a range of definitions and understandings. These in turn have benefited from broader sociological and feminist perspectives. The pursuit and realization of equality with/in and through social policy must be understood in terms of these different understandings. Moreover, in making sense of social policy, what is meant by equality, or diversity, or equality of opportunity is paramount – as the conceptualization and strategies that this implies can make a significant difference to the ways in which social policy is formulated, practised, experienced and analysed.

The theoretical understandings and practical realities of 'equality' enable a consideration of competing definitions and evaluations of, and consequences for, social policy. Moreover, this broader and sociologically informed approach also enables us to take a wider perspective on social policy. A consideration of equality provides one mechanism for relating social policy (formation, practice, experience and analysis) to 'mainstream' sociological concepts – such as class, race, gender and generation. Moreover, while it is increasingly usual to consider social policy as a process, discipline or set of welfare services, by reconceptualizing equality with/in social policy it is also possible to view social policy as a place (or places) of work and as an arena for personal, biographical experiences. Thus a focus on equality is a way of rethinking social policy – as a labour market (or indeed as multiple labour markets), as social organization(s), and as space(s) for the development of social, cultural and indeed professional identities.

Further reading

Bagilhole, B. (1997) *Equal Opportunities and Social Policy: Issues of Gender, Race and Disability*. London: Longman. This text outlines some of the legislative frameworks for equal opportunities in the UK, before going on to consider the extent to which equality of opportunity has been achieved in each of the core social policy areas. The book particularly focuses on issues of gender, race and disability.

Drake, R.F. (2001) *The Principles of Social Policy*. London: Palgrave. An excellent introduction to key concepts and principles of social policy, and the ways in which these have shaped modern welfare states. Includes a systematic and critical treatment of equality and social justice.

Rees, T. (1998) *Mainstreaming Equality in the European Union*. London: Routledge. This text provides a systematic and detailed description of the different approaches to equality, and considers these in relation to social and public policy within the European Union. The book primarily draws upon research from education, training and labour market arenas.

chapter

six

Social Policy and the Body

Introduction

The body and the processes of embodiment have become an increasingly important topic within sociology. However, relatively little attention has thus far been paid to the body by scholars of social policy. This chapter draws on the sociology of the body and embodiment, and explores the ways in which the body is sited within social policy practice, experience and discourse. There are a number of reasons why the discipline of social policy may have been rather reluctant to draw upon a sociology of the body. Much of the contemporary work on the body has been located within 'the post-modern turn', and social policy has not embraced this with ease (see Chapter 3). Moreover, sociological work on the body has (albeit implicitly) contributed to a critique of some aspects of social policy – for example in identifying its practitioners and institutions as agents and sites concerned with exerting control over bodies. These and other explanations for the absence of a significant corpus of literature on social policy and the body are discussed in more detail over the course of this chapter. This is done alongside an exploration of how considerations of the body and embodiment could be more explicitly utilized to make sense of the processes and experiences of social policy.

The chapter is organized in three main parts. Firstly contemporary work on the sociology of the body is outlined and key aspects identified. This provides a context for the second section, in which the potential for considering 'a social policy' of the body is explored. In this section the reluctance of the discipline of social policy to engage with the body and processes of embodiment is discussed, alongside an exploration of the ways in which the body might be considered central to what social policy is and does. In the final substantive section of the chapter these relationships are further developed with the aid of empirical examples. The work of social policy is considered and reconceptualized as processes of embodiment – the ways in which the body is managed, organized and reproduced within everyday (social policy) work, institutions and discursive practices.

Towards a sociology of the body

The body is now firmly established as a topic of sociological investigation and theorization. In recent years, there has been an outpouring of empirical and theoretical work on the centrality of the body and embodiment to social and cultural life. This work has spanned a number of disciplines, including social anthropology, psychology, linguistics, social philosophy and education as well as sociology (Featherstone and Turner 1995). Sociology had conventionally shied away from analyses of the body, and its importance has only really been highlighted in sociological work since the 1980s (Shilling 1993). Other disciplines, such as social anthropology, have had a much longer concern with the body and matters bodily. For example, the symbolic and physical presence of the body has been the subject of sustained anthropological work, as too have issues of body privacy and pollution (see for example, Douglas 1966).

The reframing of the body as a legitimate area for social inquiry and social theorizing has thus largely taken place over the last two decades or so. Turner's text *The Body and Society* (1984) repositioned the body within mainstream sociological theory. By the early 1990s the body had a new significance within the discipline (Frank 1991), becoming 'a physical and conceptual space in which the recurring issues and tensions of sociology are revisited and reworked' (Howson and Inglis 2001: 300). The body has hence moved from the sociological margins into the mainstream; no longer an absent presence (Shilling 1993) but increasingly an area for empirical and theoretical investigation.

Howson and Inglis (2001) usefully map the conceptual development of a sociology of the body. They identify three 'moves' within sociological work on the body. These are not necessarily chronological, but rather represent three (complementary) approaches. The first locates the body as a legitimate area for sociological study, adding the body onto and into existing sociological analyses. The second is concerned with 'rediscovering the body' in classical social theory, and identifying the corporeal concerns of the classical theorists. The third establishes 'the body as a conceptual centre-piece of sociology in an attempt to achieve integration between "troublesome" dualisms' (Howson and Inglis 2000). This repositions the body as lived experience; a space for knowing and for discursive practice; and as a conceptual frame for rethinking conventional distinctions (such as between mind and body). The development of a sociology of the body can also be contextualized within broader theoretical and social movements, from the Enlightenment of the eighteenth century to contemporary postmodern discourses. The dualities that formed the post-Enlightenment modernity sidelined the body and all things bodily. Science, rationality, logic, reason, abstraction and evidence were prioritized in the Modern society. The body was discredited alongside persuasion, opinion, emotionality and rhetoric. The historical development of social science adopted the language of modernity – neutral, scientific, logical and objective – and a view of social actors as rational, unemotional and fundamentally 'disembodied'. The body was thus excluded from grand social theory and distanced from sociological analyses. Bodies were to be managed, transcended or more likely ignored (see Shilling 1993 and Turner 1984 for accounts of the failure of classical sociology to generate a sociology of the body). Historically, then, the social sciences tended to neglect the fact that social actors have bodies and that social action and institutions are embodied.

In calling for a more embodied sociology, Scott and Morgan (1993) argued that attention *should* be paid to the physical, social, emotional and sexual body in theorizing about and understanding the social world. This concords with Frank's view that modern sociology had failed to accord due attention to the body (Frank 1991). In critical reviews Frank (1990, 1991) illustrated the centrality of the body in social life; the body 'talks' and interacts; it is disciplined through social processes and in institutions; the body is both sexualized and medicalized with/in society. The emergent sociological (and other social scientific discourses) of the body have expanded upon these kind of analyses, and have contributed to the argument that everyday social life and experiences are necessarily embodied. These ideas build upon the work of key social theorists, particularly Goffman (1963, 1968) and Foucault (1977). These were exceptional in their positioning of the body as central to social action and social agency. For example, Goffman's work on the presentation of self, and the distinction he made between 'backstage', 'frontstage' and 'off-stage', located the body within the theatrical (dramaturgical) performance of everyday life.

Foucault's work on discourse has also been a powerful and recurrent influence on contemporary analyses of the body. Foucault highlighted the false assumption of the body as a neutral or natural entity; instead rendering the body visible through the creation of discourses. Hence Foucault presented bodies as reproduced, regulated, disciplined and ordered – and hence a mechanism for the exercise or denial of power. Foucault intertwined power and knowledge, understanding knowledge as constituted within power relations (Watson 2000). Within this understanding the body took centre stage. The two articulations of power that Foucault identified – disciplinary power and bio-power – both invoke the body as the site for the power-knowledge nexus. Interestingly in the context of this chapter, Foucault developed his arguments through an analysis of many of the institutions of social policy, such as the prison, the asylum, the hospital and the school (Foucault 1979). These institutions invoked versions of disciplinary power, not least through the surveillance, manipulation and social production of the body. The body is physically controlled, and hence disciplinary power is exerted over patients, criminals, school children and the mentally ill. Bio-power relates to other kinds of body-control, for example the nineteenth-century 'professional' interest in the body, including the collection of data on morbidity, mortality and levels of health. Twigg (2000a) particularly points to Foucault's work on sexuality and bio-power as being influential to the social science literature on the body, arguing that much of the current work starts from his analyses of discourse, and the ways in which bodies are historically, spatially and temporally mediated. That is the ways in which the body is not a fixed or neutral entity, but rather is shaped, controlled, negotiated and reproduced through and with/in everyday social life.

Contemporary theoretical and empirical interest in the body also owes much to feminism, particularly contemporary feminisms. Feminist researchers and theorists have challenged contrastive representations of the male and female body, and the ways these have been mapped onto conventional dichotomies of, for example, hard/soft, defined/fluid, strong/weak, and contained/leaky (Twigg 2000a). Feminist theoretical, political and research agendas have resituated the body as central to the enactment of social, cultural, economic and political life. Hence there has been a critiquing of the positioning of the body within conceptualizations and articulations of patriarchy, alongside a reclaiming of the female body. Hence feminists have sought to locate the female reproductive and sexualized body within discussions and theorizations of patriarchy and oppression (Firestone 1971; Corea 1985; Walby 1990), and alongside critiques of the commodification, medicalization and abuse of women's (and children's) bodies.

Feminist empirical work has also shown the ways in which women are responsible for the servicing and well-being of other bodies – through, for example, the provision of physical care, taking responsibility for the family's health, family food preparation and so forth (Finch and Groves 1983; Murcott 1983; Land 1991). The feminist reclaiming of the body has also encompassed an appreciation of the ways in which the body can and has been used as a channel for political action and protest, from furthering women's knowledge of their own bodies (Boston Women's Health Collective 1973) and control over pregnancy, childbirth and reproduction (Stanworth 1987; Raymond 1993; Brain 1998), through to 'embodied' feminist protests such the feminist campaigns of the late nineteenth and early twentieth centuries (Liddington and Norris 2000) and the Greenham Common campaign against nuclear armament in the 1980s and early 1990s (Young 1990; Junor 1995). Feminist analyses of the body have also included work on the ontological status of feminist agendas, experiences and challenges, bringing the body back into understandings of the social. For example, Stanley and Wise (1993) reject abstract and essentialist conceptualizations of the body in feminist ontology, and argue that

> 'The body' is seen rather in terms of *embodiment*, a cultural process by which the physical body becomes a site of culturally ascribed and disputed meanings, experiences, and feelings. Here 'the body' is positioned within culturally specific – and sometimes competing – discourses of meaning, authority and control. For us 'the body' is rather to be conceptualized as a *becoming*, its meaning is never fixed to a particular type of person, but rather these different meanings have to be achieved and re-achieved in order to be seen as constituting a particular type of person [. . .] 'the body' is actually different *bodies* around which different readings, significations and judgements are made.
>
> (Stanley and Wise 1993: 196–7, their emphasis)

Postmodernity and attendant calls to diversity have given new significance to the theoretical and empirical conceptualizations of the body. Attention has particularly been paid to the ways in which reconstructions and reproductions of identity and selves are embodied, and the meanings that individuals attach to and through their bodies. Hence physical, sexual and emotional bodies are located as central to our experiences – of self, health, work, play, family, consumption, the environment, and so on. Selves are created and reproduced – and the body is centrally located in this process. The body moves from a vessel of sin to an object of display (Featherstone 1982) and the self is performed 'finely tuned, cared for, reconstructed and carefully presented' (Shilling 1993: 35). One outcome of this is the resituating of the body and emotions within multiple subjectivities and realities, hence recognizing multiple embodied narratives. Weiner's work on feminist poststructuralism links these notions to discourse and discursive practices, recognizing that individuals (with and through their bodies) are active in engaging in discourses through which they in turn are shaped (Weiner 1994). Thus concepts of identity formation and power are multiple, shifting, contradictory, emotional and embodied. This relates to what Shilling (1993) refers to as a crisis in our knowledge of what the body is. What constitutes a body is no longer (if it ever was) a certainty. Alongside Frank's identification of talking, disciplined, medicalized and sexualized bodies, we can also add bodies that are consumed, commodified, redesigned and performed. Bodies can be discursive, material and indeed virtual.

The foregrounding of the body as a legitimate area of sociological analysis and theorizing has not resulted in a singular 'sociology of the body' but rather a plurality of theories and empirical investigations. These have responded (and continue to respond) to developments in and beyond sociology, drawing on a range of approaches and perspectives. Integral is a concern with relationships between the body, social action and agency. The body has become a project to be worked upon, but also a site for the playing out of discursive practices. It is a vehicle for consumption, self-expression and self-identity, as well as a vehicle for and a form of representation. In the next section the implications of these embodied perspectives for the discipline of social policy are explored.

Social policy and the body

Social policy as a discipline has been relatively untouched by theoretical and empirical work on the body. There has certainly not been any sustained social policy engagement with contemporary understandings and articulations of the body that have arisen out of sociological and other social science analyses. This is interesting given the centrality of the body to the everyday work of social policy and social welfare, as Lewis, Hughes and Saraga (2000: 7) have argued.

> The irony of the relative failure of Social Policy to engage with the theorization of the body – as either socially constructed; constituted at the intersection of biology and culture; or as 'performance' – is that the body in diverse forms is central to the practices of social policy. Disabled bodies, 'ethnic bodies', children's bodies, sexualized bodies, old bodies, bodies in need, bodies in danger, bodies at risk, are all at the heart of social policy.

The body as an 'absent presence' (Shilling 1993) is a useful concept to invoke here. The body is 'there' but 'not there' in social policy. In social policy discourses there is an almost unquestioning acceptance of the body – as a pre-social, basic or fixed entity. Yet, the body is at the heart of the most fundamental welfare needs, and there are obvious ways in which social welfare practices and processes have always focused on bodies – 'on bodily potential, bodily functions and bodily needs' (Dean 2000: xi). Moreover, welfare professionals and administrators 'gaze' upon client, patient and student bodies; are often 'concerned with the capacity of such bodies to produce, consume and be orderly'; and direct their skills 'to ensuring the fitness of such bodies for labour, leisure and social interaction' (Dean 2000: xi). Yet within the academic discipline, there is little evidence of critical engagement with corporeal discourses. And as a substantive field, bodies have remained as objects to be worked on or managed, rather than cast as subjects to be worked with or as vehicles of agency in and of themselves. Hence the invisibility or absent presence of the body is in stark contrast to a lived reality of social policy – its work, processes, clients and knowledges – where the body and processes of embodiment might be seen as central.

Social policy, in its broadest sense, denotes a variety of ways of conceptualizing, assessing and responding to embodied needs – be they physical, emotional, material or psychological. Social policy practitioners are charged with working with a diverse range of issues related to:

- the challenged body (for example, bodies that are ageing, or are in need of physical or emotional repair, or bodies that hinder mobility);
- the abused body (for example, bodies that are addicted, harmed, hurt or violated);
- experiences encompassed within, or lived through, bodies (bodies are housed, contained, restrained and manipulated).

Moreover, the legitimacy of social policy practitioner knowledge claims often rely upon these diverse, though ontologically stable, embodied subjects – practitioners are 'body experts' of various kinds (Lewis *et al.* 2000). Hence the body cannot help but be present in the practices and processes of social policy. The body is an implicit empirical subject for social policy; a site through which it operates and functions. It is even possible to go as far as to say that bodies are at the heart of social policy. Bodies are both what social policy 'does' and what it leaves behind as 'cultural artefacts', as Lewis *et al.* (2000: 11) argue.

> Representations of subordinated bodies are central to the ways in which social policy has historically marked out its areas of expertise and practice and constituted the very persons on whom these practices will be deployed [. . .]Embodied subjects are there to be photographed, tested, hospitalized, institutionalized, categorized, analyzed and 'removed' by the relevant policy and practice experts.

Given the centrality of the body to the 'business end' of social policy, the lack of embrace within the discipline remains stark. Twigg (2000) in an insightful analysis offers some explanations as to why this might be so. Twigg makes a useful distinction between explanations that are offered in defence of social policy and explanations that critique the contemporary sociology of the body. In defensive mode, one can argue that many of the practices and processes that form the basis of a critical sociology of the body implicate (and indeed criticize) social policy processes and social welfare practice. As indicated above, Foucault's influential theorizing of the body drew on critical analyses of the embodied contexts of social policy institutions – such as the prison, the hospital and the school. In this embodied critique, social policy institutions, practices and practitioners play a central role in regulating, disciplining, categorizing, observing, ordering, medicalizing and (de)sexualizing the body. Moreover, this appropriation of the body, in a variety of guises, is essential to the knowledge-power nexus of social policy professionals. It is not necessary to agree with the proposition that the desired outcomes of these practices imply control and power, to see control and regulation as a potential, or indeed in some instances an unintended outcome. Social policy as a discipline, and as a set of social practices, has a long tradition of confronting and attempting to ameliorate inequality and power differentials. We might want to re-emphasize the aim of social policy to bring about change and make a difference – to individuals, social groups and society. Nevertheless, the embodied critique of social policy questions the means of achieving this through the disruption, manipulation and appropriation of the body. Hence it is not hard to see how theoretical and empirical work on the body can be perceived as an attack on the work of social policy, and why in turn there may be a reluctance on the part of the discipline to embrace an embodied critique of welfare practices, processes and professionals.

Set alongside this rather defensive position is a recurrent unease within social policy with the empirical emphasis and theoretical leanings of contemporary sociological engagement with the body. One could argue that a preoccupation with the body is at odds with the remit of social policy to try to move away from oppressive accounts of social actors. Indeed, social policy (and sociological) studies of gender, ethnicity, disability and ageing have attempted to move away from biological or bodily reductionist models of social experience; preferring instead to focus on notions of structure and agency, and on the social processes by which inequality and difference are reproduced and maintained. Thus the female body as deficit and non-male, the disabled body as abnormal and dysfunctional, the black body as non-white, and the ageing body as declining and failing have increasingly been rejected in favour of more social and structural explanations and understandings. Thus, in one sense, a return to the body, however reformulated, could be perceived as a backward step. However, this is perhaps a difficult position to sustain given the substantial contribution that sociological work on the body can make to understandings of the embodied experiences of identities and selves. In this sociological reformulation, the body is not reduced to an object but rather becomes a subject of, and vehicle for, the enactment of structure, agency and identity work.

Some commentators have also alluded to the relatively 'data free' nature of much sociological work on the body (see Bury 1995). It is certainly the case that early work took a theoretical rather than empirical focus (Turner 1984; Shilling 1993). This could well be perceived as at odds with a discipline like social policy, which has a strong empiricist tradition. However, as the sociology of the body has grown as a subdiscipline, so too has the empirical data-set on which that sociological work is based. This does not necessarily address the unease of social policy in engaging with this material. Twigg (2000a: 134), for example, has argued that empirical data on the body has, thus far, been skewed towards the more 'fashionable' and voguish – to 'cyborgs, female body-builders, transsexuality, internet sex'. This is somewhat of an exaggeration, as the body has become more firmly embraced within the sociologies of, for example, health, education and work. However, this perception of the fashionable, sexy or 'wacky' empirical bases could be used to explain the reluctance for social policy engagement. These topics may seem somewhat removed from mainstream (and moral) social policy, which 'has always been a meat-and-potatoes sort of subject' (Twigg 2000a: 134) (though this categorization is not a 'high echelon' to which social policy should necessarily aspire or indeed defend!). It is certainly true that work on the body has enabled and encouraged a widening, shifting and redefining of research boundaries. And to some extent this has come at the expense of using the body and ideas about embodiment to study the more everyday and the mundane (perhaps of most relevance to social policy). Thus there are examples of research that has focused on topics such as body-building and body adornment (Butler 1998; Monaghan 2001). However, there are also plenty of examples of where 'body-theorizing' has and can be used to increase our understanding of social policy arenas – such as schools (Shilling 1993; Gordon, Holland and Lahelma 2000b), care settings (Ungerson 1987; Lawler 1997; Twigg 2000b) or social work (Scourfield and Coffey 2002). Thus the paucity of social-policy-relevant empirical engagement with the body is neither wholesale nor irretrievable.

What is less clear is whether the more general theoretical positions that have underpinned the contemporary sociology of the body are compatible with the discipline of social policy. The body has, to some extent at least, been 'captured' by postmodern discourses, and theorized within shifting frameworks of free-floating selves and multiple realities. For some within the social sciences, postmodern approaches to knowledge have opened up opportunities for complicating the social world and recognizing the need to capture the polyvocality of social life. For others postmodernism denies a 'reality' that can be recognized and documented, and hence problematizes the relevance of empirical work to an understanding of the social world (for there isn't in that sense a social world to know, nor a set of empirical data that can represent a 'true' picture). Twigg (2000a) suggests that this is not something that the discipline of social policy can incorporate with ease. More generally, the discipline of social policy has been slow to engage with postmodern discourses, research agendas and representations. As Carter (1998) has noted, the 1970s and 1980s postmodern makeover of other social science and humanities disciplines has been slow to reach the shores of social policy. Taylor-Gooby (1994) has argued that, as an intellectual trend, postmodernism serves as a smoke screen that masks social developments, inequalities and power differentials. Gibbins (1998) is less circumspect, and has argued that the postmodern theoretical project, as an academic project, poses real questions for the discipline and practice of social policy. Gibbins (1998: 34) defines this project as 'an attempt to understand and respond to a world being transformed, without the supports found in modernism, namely a confidence in absolutes and foundational structures, truths, knowledge,

meaning and methods'. He rejects claims that postmodernism has no prag-
matic or political value, in favour of a more fruitful relationship between
postmodernism and social policy. Hence a social policy of the body does not
necessarily need to reject postmodernity and attendant calls to diversity.
Rather, there is the potential to work with/in postmodern discourses to reveal
the ways in which the body receives and generates social meaning within the
substantive practice and discipline of social policy. While Twigg (2000a:
138) cautions a wholesale adoption of embodied perspectives, she nevertheless argues that empirical and theoretical work on the body has much to offer
social policy, creating analytical and substantive spaces that are 'currently
locked away'. In the next section some of these spaces are explored.

The embodiment of social policy

A consideration of the relationships between the body and social policy, and
the adoption of a more embodied perspective, can offer new analytical
purchase on the processes, practices and discourses of social policy. Social
policy implicates, works with and constructs individual and collective bodies. A disembodied social policy is actually untenable, once the 'work' of
social policy is scrutinized. There are a number of different approaches that
can be taken in working towards a consideration of a more embodied social
policy. Twigg (2002) argues that the territory of social policy can be re-
examined through a consideration of the literature on the body. She argues
that there are areas of social policy where the body is taken for granted (for
example, health care), central but overlooked (for example, community
care), and central but consciously ignored for reasons of good practice (for
example, with regard to disability or old age). As well as rethinking existing
social policy topics and themes, Twigg also suggests that a focus on the body
can open up new domains for social policy analysis – for example, bio-
power and the disciplining of the body, consumption and pleasure – as well
as contributing to understanding the gendered, racialized, sexualized and
generational contexts of social policy. This section develops some of these
themes through three categories of analysis:

- 'body work' – the presence of the body in the everyday 'tasks' of social
  policy;
- 'body organization' – the ways in which the institutions and spaces of
  social policy manage the body;
- 'body discourse' – the construction of bodies through social policy discursive practices and talk.

These are not mutually exclusive categories, but rather might serve as overlapping analytical frameworks from which to begin a refocusing of social
policy through a 'body lens'.

Body work

The practice and everyday work of social policy is fundamentally concerned with the moving, tending, cleaning, caring and sheltering of the
physical (and indeed emotional) body. Health services, residential care
settings, services for the elderly, voluntary and statutory facilities for the
homeless; all of these and more represent spaces where 'body work' takes
place. Personal care represents a particularly apposite example of the
juxtaposition between social policy activities and body work. The everyday activities of personal care include bathing and tending the body.
Based on a series of qualitative interviews with older and disabled people,
care workers and managers, Twigg (2000b) sought to reconceptualize care
work, and in particular personal care, within embodied perspectives. By
concentrating on washing and bathing she considers how personal care
transgresses boundaries of adult life and the taboos associated with naked-
ness and touch. Twigg argues that care work involves a kind of 'body
work' – which she defines as working directly on the bodies of others; 'Typically it involves touching, manipulating and assessing the bodies of others,
which thus become the objects of the workers labour' (Twigg 2000b: 137).
Twigg suggests that this body work is also ambivalent work – potentially
demeaning, highly gendered, caught up in aspects of subordination and
domination, as well as dealing with 'taboos' such as sexuality and human
waste.

These factors were foreshadowed by earlier studies of community and
personal care (Finch and Groves 1983; Ungerson 1987), which revealed the
physical, bodily aspects of caring *for* someone. Not only that care work is
physically (and bodily) demanding; caring also involves close and intimate
interactions with other bodies (Ungerson 1987). A vivid example of this was
revealed in Bates' ethnographic study of a group of young women undertaking a youth training scheme (YTS) on social care (Bates 1990, 1993). The
'care girls' undertook work placements in homes for the elderly, alongside
college-based training. There is no doubt that their on-the-job training
involved significant amounts of body work. One aspect of the personal care
that these girls engaged in focused on the same kinds of hygiene and bathing
issues highlighted by Twigg, Ungerson and others. This is what the care girls
referred to as 'shit shovelling' (Bates 1993: 17) – dealing with incontinence,
bathing, washing and toiletting. This quickly became accepted by these
young women as part of their job, and something they must just get used to.
Another kind of body work for these trainee carers involved the caring for
the dying and dead, including bathing the body after death. Most of the girls
gained first-hand experience in this aspect of the job. While this was a source
of considerable distress during their first year of training, the girls still
'expressed a pride in what they did' (Bates 1993: 19). Indeed, the various
ways in which these girls engaged in body work as part of their training

became an important source of their emergent labour market and personal identities.

There are then obvious ways in which the body work of caring can be revealed. There is no doubt that caring involves 'dirty work' in a literal sense. That is, the practical management of corporeal dirt and leaky bodies. Gurney (2000: 65) has argued that bodies are 'essentially unfinished social products which are inherently prone to disorder and in careful need of management, training and presentation'. Care work is partially concerned with these unfinished social products and their various discharges and leaks – such as blood, urine, mucus, vomit, phlegm and faeces. Twigg highlighted some aspects of this dirty work, giving examples of things carers find the hardest to cope with – the smell and 'muck' of incontinence, flaky skin, the coughing up of phlegm, hearing someone being sick. 'It is other people's bodies and especially the by-products of bodies, or the parts of bodies that are anomalously connected, that are the main focus of revulsion' (Twigg 2000b: 144). This focus on body work as 'dirty work' does, however, have broader dimensions, as commentators such as Ungerson (1987) and Lee-Treweek (1998) have revealed; the gender dimensions of this body work, for example, and the association of the realm of bodily waste with women's work. Hence a focus of the bodily aspects of social care can also be used as a way of exploring gender segregation within the social policy labour market, and can lead to a reconsideration of the gendered, bodily contexts of 'informal' social policy contexts of the home and family. Caring, alongside other social policy work, straddles a gap between the public (policy and work) realm and the private (home and family) sphere. The ways in which the body is implicated within these different contexts, and the gendered mediation of body work can provide a fruitful frame for analysis. Similarly, the ways in which care settings are spatially managed to create front- and back-stage regions, with the 'dirty work' hidden from view, can also be useful in understanding the embodied contexts of caring practices (and the 'absent presence' of the body). As Bates (1993: 20) argued in her description of care work in residential homes for the elderly,

> To the outsider, the 'caring' world may have appeared as one of pink overalls, cleanliness, jangling keys, 'Come along Annie', wheelchairs, walks around the grounds, trolleys, laundry, the ubiquitous institutional smell, dozing residents in television lounges. This was the re-presented, more acceptable face of an occupation, which in effect, in terms of contemporary cultural constructs, was a 'heavy', 'dirty' job, steeped in taboo subject matter such as the body, age, 'shit-shovelling' and death. These social responsibilities were transported from the wider society to a sub-society, staffed largely by women.

Concentrating on personal, social or 'bodily' care might be seen as an all too easy example of the body work inherent in social policy spheres. Health and social care are obvious sites for body work. Yet there is still relatively little attention paid to the body in community care literature and policy (or indeed in the wider literature on nursing, medicine, and health care, for that matter). Despite the seeming centrality of the body to the work and experiences of care, it would be an overstatement to maintain that embodied perspectives are widespread or embedded. If we venture beyond the obvious body realms of health and personal care, the foregrounding of body work is even more tenuous. And yet comparable observations and analyses could be made – for example, the ways in which facilities for the homeless shelter the body and are routinely concerned with its re/production, through washing, clothing, feeding and grooming, and indeed how homelessness itself is experienced and managed in bodily ways (Wardhaugh 1999); or the role of educational policy and the school in the development and articulation of adolescent bodies, through sex education and physical education (Epstein and Johnson 1998); or the use and regulation of the body through custodial and community sentencing – the use of physical 'body' labour and the incarceration of the body. These all imply that bodies are worked on, worked with, reproduced, managed and organized with/in everyday social policy.

Body organization

The institutions, organizations and processes of social policy can also be reconceptualized in terms of bodily presence and embodied practice. Social policies are enacted through physical places and spaces (see Chapter 7 for a more detailed discussion of social policy and space). These spaces of social policy – for example, schools, hospitals, prisons, residential homes, short stay facilities, training centres, job centres, social security offices – all participate in the organization and management of bodies. The school provides a good illustration of the embodiment of the places of social policy. As Shilling (1993b: 57) argues, the body is central to the 'very business of schooling'. Education is important to the formation of particular orientations by children to their bodies. Moreover, schools serve as sites for the regulation and control of these bodies. In their account of ethnographic research in secondary schools in London and Helsinki, Gordon, Holland and Lahelma (2000a and b) consider the ways in which school organization and experience are embodied, and in particular the ways in which the school is engaged in the restriction and surveillance of student bodies. They note that prevalent modes of teaching rely overwhelming on relatively still and/or quiet bodies 'moving from station to station, or sitting at their desks, upright, facing the teacher' (Gordon *et al.* 2000b: 82). And even where movement is encouraged or required at school – for example, in sport, drama, dance, science, design and technology – there are usually body-rules to be followed: when and how to move, what to wear and how to interact with other bodies. Rules about the presentation and adornment of the body are also evident in schools – rules about school uniforms, the wearing of jewellery, hair length – or restrictions on physical behaviour – walking (not running) in corridors, one-way systems around the dining room to manage the flow of bodies, not eating or shouting or running in class. The everyday routines of the school are thus dependent upon the restricted and regulated movement and representation of bodies through the physical school over the course of the day.

> Students learn what is acceptable and appropriate in relation to their bodies, voice and movement in school contexts, 'sit up straight', 'don't use that tiny voice, like a mouse', 'you do not talk when I am talking', 'I will wait for you to be quiet', 'walk, don't run', 'wipe that smile off your face'. Their bodies are constrained in time and space, they must learn the time-space paths that dictate their trajectory through the school day.
>
> (Gordon *et al.* 2000b: 93)

This focus on bodily comportment as a mode of regulation and control is not the only way in which the body can offer analytical insights into school and educational life. Students can also deploy their bodies in order to exercise agency – conforming to, resisting or challenging school rules and regulations – in order to assert their identity, cope with peer group pressure, express sexuality, reclaim autonomy, set themselves apart or disappear into the crowd (Gordon *et al.* 2000b). As staff and schools can discipline young people through controlling their bodies, so too can young people use their bodies to resist and rebel, to disrupt lessons and trouble boundaries.

The embodiment of school practices can thus be used as a mechanism for making sense of gendered educational experiences, the reproduction of feminine, masculine and sexualized identities, and indeed young people's identity construction more generally. Hence a focus on the body can reveal the informal and social, as well as formal, regulatory and pedagogical aspects of schooling. Transfering from primary to secondary school is also an embodied process, whereby the body is enmeshed in the reconstruction of adolescent, secondary school identities. The body is also an important aspect of school 'folklore' and story telling, for example in the stories that are told about school transfer (Measor and Wood 1984; Pugsley *et al.* 1996). These transfer stories include the fears and anticipations of cross-country running (punishing and challenging the body), the dress requirements for PE and the sanctions that will be given out for failure to comply (regulating the body), and worries over communal school showers and teachers 'watching' exposed bodies (the surveillance of the body). These school transfer stories have been explained in terms of the anxieties, fears and coping strategies of young people moving from the familiar environment of the primary school to a secondary school that is usually larger, often further way from home, where lessons are more differentiated and there are more (male) teachers. The prevalence of stories about physical education and the body again suggests that there are important embodied aspects to these school experiences and that school is a social organization in which bodies are exercised, exposed, controlled, sexualized and socially produced.

The school is, of course, the site for the enactment and implementation of one particular aspect of social policy – namely educational policy. It represents a social policy 'space' where the regulation, control and indeed potential agency of the body is distinctive. An embodied perspective thus provides a lens through which to consider and seek to understand the organization and lived reality of social policy in practice. Similar analyses can be introduced into considerations of other sites for the enactment of social policy. A cursory glance into a primary care surgery or social security office will reveal the ways in which bodies are managed and controlled. Desks, chairs, counters and screens mark out boundaries for the containment of bodies. Gatekeepers restrict movement, and there are often rules governing appropriate bodily behaviour – for example, about eating, drinking and levels of noise. The body here can also be used as a source of agency – bodies being placed where they are not meant to be, the use of the raised voice or the transgression of physical boundaries. Likewise institutional settings such as residential care homes, young offender centres and prisons are concerned on a day-to-day basis with the movement and restriction of movement of the body in much the same way as the school – bodies here are also located in time and space (see Chapter 7).

The organization, control and potential agency of the body are not restricted to the clients of social policy. Practitioners also experience the organization of their 'work' in embodied ways – the bodily presence of a social worker in a client's home; the physicality of teaching and the (formal and informal) body boundaries between students and teachers; the 'volunteering' body, cold from a soup kitchen session or sitting still and listening at a telephone helpline. Bennett's work on the embodied 'lived' experience of (women) equal opportunities officers working within state bureaucracies presents an even broader picture of embodied social policy (Bennett 2000). By considering the ways in which these officers (as makers and implementers of policy) work to sustain an embodied female identity within (male) bureaucracies, Bennett explores both the regulation and the potential agency of the body in enacting change, and the ways in which embodiment is a matter for legitimation and negotiation. These women equal opportunities officers found ways of 'legitimating their different embodied positions in the organization through spatial, behavioural and verbal strategies' (2000: 201). This provides a useful link to a third consideration of an embodied social policy, which focuses on the ways in which the body is also constructed and reproduced through social policy discourses.

Body discourses

The construction and reproduction of the body through professional and organization discourse represents a further way in which we might explore the embodiment of social policy. Through various discursive practices – such as talk, visual images, documents, institutional regulations, concepts, and professional codes – particular kinds of bodies are constructed and reproduced. Social policy practitioners and professionals also draw on these various discourses in their own 'body knowledge' and identity work (Brewis 2000). Moreover, professional and organizational discourses are navigated in the reconstruction of 'client' bodies. Child and family social workers, for example, construct and position the body of the child in child protection work. For example, Scourfield (2000: 368) argues that 'creative constructions of embodied children have particular power in the organizational culture of the social work office'. Scourfield's ethnography of a social work team demonstrated the ways in which case workers drew on professional discourses of child neglect, and in doing so concentrated on children's bodies and on the 'parental body maintenance work for children' (2000: 370). Hence the hungry, dirty, smelly, poorly clothed bodies of children featured heavily in the identification of cases of child neglect. These exterior 'bodily' signs were used as signifiers of child welfare, and parents' (mainly mothers') inadequate servicing of the child's body became a focus for concern. Hence children's bodies are reconstructed as 'evidence' within the professional discourse on neglect, and are subjected to, and reconstructed through, the professional gaze. An ethnographic study of critically ill children in an intensive care unit provides an interesting comparison here. Place (2000) considers the ways in which the sick child's body is reconstructed through discourses of technology. The critically ill child becomes 'technomorphic', externalized by machines, and represented at the nexus of technology and corporeality. Nursing staff draw upon technical and occupational discourses to re-present the child and the child's body to parents and others.

This analysis of the reconstruction and representation of client bodies could, of course, usefully be extended to include other 'social policy' bodies – for example, the ways in which elderly bodies are constructed and subject to the 'gaze' of care workers and health practitioners, and the implications this has for service provision – the elderly body as, for example, 'public property', frail or failing; as (in)capable or (dis)abled. Similarly professional and organization discourses are navigated in the construction of the sick body, or homeless body, or disabled body. The dominant discourses in these contexts and the ways in which they are enacted and enforced can be revealing of social policy culture and practice.

There has been little attention paid to the ways in which social policy professions or practitioners develop their own body knowledge and negotiate embodied discourses. Joanna Brewis (1999, 2000), for example, interviewed women working in a range of social policy occupations (including housing and social service management, probation, nursing and higher education) about their experiences of their own bodies at work. While few explicitly felt that their jobs were physically (or bodily) demanding, there was evidence to suggest that they drew on prevailing discourses of the female body in their everyday working lives – for example, cultural discourses of bodily beauty, the gendered, sexualized or ageing body. The female body was often a marker of difference in the workplace, and had to be carefully 'managed'. This categorization of the body as *other* was reacted to in different ways – for example, 'power dressing' the body, and adopting a more masculine appearance; emphasizing the femininity of the body; spending various amounts of time on morning beauty regimes; rearranging work to accommodate difficult menstrual cycles; emphasizing a smaller body size as non-threatening; being a bit 'girly'. As Brewis (2000: 181) concludes 'these women see their bodies as materially real (possessing sex, weight, age and so on), but that this materiality is accessible only through the operations of discourse. These women's bodies, then, are sites which discourses (re)inscribe in various complicated ways'. Hence like the bodies of social policy clients, practitioner and policy-maker 'bodies' can also be mediated by and constructed through various discourses. Understanding these discursive practices can further promote an appreciation of social policy as embodied social practice and bodily experience.

Conclusion

A focus on the body and processes of embodiment has the potential to give new analytical purchase to social policy. It is clear that the body and bodily matters are highly relevant to the processes and practices of social policy. This in itself is not a remarkable statement. As Twigg (2002: 436) notes 'the body is indeed everywhere by virtue of the fact that we all have and are bodies'. However, it is possible to argue that a more explicit 'social policy of the body' can open up new, as yet hidden, aspects of the subject matter of the discipline, as well as providing new ways of making sense of familiar welfare experiences. There are elements of social policy of the body that already exist, and the discussion in this chapter has demonstrated that the capacity to develop these into a more systematic approach is considerable. Social policy clients, practitioners and policy-makers can be reconstituted as (differentiated) embodied subjects, and their experiences recast by and mediated through processes and discourses of embodiment. Moreover, an analytic focus on the body is also a potentially useful tool for rethinking the spaces and places of social policy, and how these are organized, experienced and represented. Perhaps less obvious is the way in which a consideration of the body and embodiment could be utilized to explore and give new meaning to the more 'conventional' subject matter of contemporary social policy. Issues such as social inequalities, diverse welfare experiences, gender, power, practitioner knowledge, work organization and the everyday work of social policy could all be approached through a social policy of the body. Thus far the contribution of an embodied perspective has perhaps mainly been at the level of understanding the lived experiences of welfare practices and social policy, as they are experienced by and through the body. It can also provide a platform for understanding the consequences of embodiment for social policy, and for exploring further social policy discourses, institutions, work, practitioners, clients and policy-making processes.

Further reading

Ellis, K. and Dean, H. (eds) (1999) *Social Policy and the Body*. Basingstoke: Macmillan. A text that explicitly addresses the corporeal discourses and practices of social policy. The contributors look at shifts in corporeal discourses of social welfare over the twentieth century, and draw on a range of topic areas, including care management, organ donation and health promotion.

Scott, S. and Morgan, D. (eds) (1993) *Body Matters: Essays on the Sociology of the Body*. London: Falmer. This accessible collection of essays provides a range of sociological insights into the everyday work of and on the body. It is a good introduction to the sociology of the body, drawing on a range of empirical examples.

Shilling, C. (1993) *The Body and Social Theory*. London: Sage. This book reviews sociological literature and analysis on the body and embodiment, and establishes a strong theoretical case for a sociology of the body. The book includes discussions of classic and contemporary social theorists, and covers a wide range of 'body' topics such as gender, age and health.

Twigg, J. (2000) *Bathing: The Body and Community Care*. London: Routledge. A book that provides an excellent empirical illustration of the embodiment of social policy, located within a broader discussion about the body, care and social welfare.

chapter

seven

Time, Space and Social Policy

Introduction

In recent years sociologists have begun to pay more attention to the ways in which time and space are central to social, cultural, economic and organization life. For example, the spatial and temporal changes that accompanied the move to modernity, during the eighteenth and nineteenth centuries, have been increasingly acknowledged and documented within sociology. This sociological analysis has explored, among other things, the process of urbanism and the 'creation' and restructuring of the city (Harvey 1973); the routinization of workplace time, and the adoption/surveillance of clock time that accompanied the advance of industrial capitalism (Adam 1990); the differentiation or separation of public and private spheres of time and space – work and home or labour and leisure (Gamarnikow *et al.* 1983); and the impact of globalizing communications in redefining time and space (Lull 1995). This sociological analysis of time and space has also been extended to embrace more postmodern concerns – for example, explorations of biographies, life times and the construction of the self (Evans 1993; Plummer 2001), or of cyberspace and communication in the digital age (Markham 1998; Crang *et al.* 1999). There has been an increasing recognition that social structures, processes, organizations and lives have temporal and spatial dimensions. By utilizing the concepts of time and space as analytic tools it is possible to re-examine a variety of everyday social settings, processes and activities, such as the workplace, bureaucratic organizations, leisure experiences and family life.

This chapter explores the potential of drawing upon temporal and spatial perspectives for understanding the institutions, processes and experiences of social policy. In doing so the chapter seeks to illuminate some of the ways in which social policy inhabits specific spaces and places, and to draw attention to the timings, temporalities and rhythms of social policy.

The chapter is organized into four main sections. In the first section, a brief overview of the sociology of time and space is given, and some emergent themes highlighted. Secondly, some of the interconnections between time and social policy are described, including the interweaving of life times and social policy times. The third section concentrates on social exclusion as a case study, to illustrate the lived temporal realities of social policy. This case study also makes connections between time and space. Finally, the fourth section explores some of the ways in which the concepts of space and place can be employed to make sense of social policy processes and welfare experiences.

A sociology of time and space

Sociological interest in the concepts of space, place and time is a relatively recent phenomenon. Indeed, these concepts have been rather neglected within mainstream sociology, both theoretically and empirically. Many introductory sociology texts still pay little, if any, attention to time and space; major texts in the sociologies of time and space remain few (although these have made significant contributions to the discipline – see Adam 1990; Lash and Urry 1994; Adam 1995; Urry 1995). However, it would be wrong to assume that the contemporary work that is now being undertaken lacks an historical context. As Urry (1995) has noted, many early twentieth-century sociologists and writings did take account of space and place, although they may not have explicitly recognized that they were doing so. Hence contributions to sociological thinking by social theorists such as Durkheim, Weber and Marx (see Chapter 2 of this volume) did have time–space dimensions. Collectively these and other early social theorists contributed to social understandings of time and space, within the specific contexts of advancing societies and the advent of industrial capitalism. They highlighted, for example, the increasing reliance on clock time in industrial work organizations, and more generally 'the tyranny of the clock' (Bilton *et al.* 1996: 28) in economic and social life. They also made distinctions between urban and rural spaces, and observed the temporal and spatial movements between these two different spaces (Wirth 1938). Such 'modern' concerns foreshadowed subsequent sociological work on time and space, which has continued to explore themes such as 'clock time' (in social and domestic as well as economic organizations), the nature of urban 'city' space and the growth of the metropolis, among other things. From these beginnings has grown a critical appraisal of the spatial and temporal contexts of social life, and the development of distinctive sociologies of time and space. It is possible to identify a number of emergent themes within this sociological exploration of time and space.

Consuming space(s)

Places and spaces have been reconstituted as arenas for various kinds of consumption (Urry 1995). It is relatively straightforward to recognize that all goods and services are provided, viewed, evaluated, purchased and used in specific places of consumption – *supermarket* groceries, *restaurant* meals, *hospital* surgery, *school* education, and so forth. Goods and services are spatially located and consumed. Thus places provide sites of and for consumption. As well as this, places and spaces can themselves be consumed. For example, physical places or spaces feature in the pursuit of leisure activities – theme parks, white-water rivers, golden beaches, formal gardens, stately homes, mountain passes and forest walks. These are places that provide locations for leisure activities. They are also spaces to be consumed – through our senses and experiences. Equally particular places are interwoven with working lives. Paid employment often means travelling to and then occupying a variety of spaces. For example, the steel mill, the textile factory, the call centre and the office are all sites that are experienced and, to some extent, used and consumed. Our homes are also used and consumed (and indeed manipulated and neglected) as particular spaces and places. In all of these instances the sense of consumption can be sensual, emotional and indeed literal. Mountain footpaths can wear away; stately homes and gardens are subjected to wear and tear; theme rides are broken; offices become 'tired'; factories can become defunct; our homes are often in need of decoration and repair. Places are subjected to physical and emotional investment, and can consume time, resources and emotions.

Processing spaces

Spaces and places can also be used to mark social, cultural and economic processes. Massey (1984), for example, has argued that social processes take place over and in space – and that spatiality is an integral and active feature of the processes of capitalist production. Hence a sociology of space can enable a consideration of fluidity and movement between spaces; the significance, for example, of nearness and distance; the conditions for and importance of locality and belonging; and more generally the symbolism that can be attached to spaces. Thus, it is possible to reconceptualize industrial production in terms of spatially organized processes, whereby materials and social actors move within and between spaces. The significance of space can similarly be explored in understanding and making sense of 'community', or in the context of life transitions such as the rituals of leaving home, marriage, parenthood or death. Relationships between work and home can also be considered in terms of the processing of different activities within differentially defined (physical and social) spaces. Within all of these examples the demarcation of space, and the 'troubling', blurring or maintenance of boundaries between different places can be used as analytic concepts. Other processes can similarly be analysed in terms of space and place – the consumption of the arts, for example. Opera, theatre or film occupies and is experienced through specific settings of the opera house, the theatre and the cinema. The experience of these cultural events is different if the locations are altered – opera in the park, community theatre in the leisure centre, a film on television at home. Social welfare processes such as health and social care or education are also spatially organized – the surgical procedure, primary care appointment, social work interview or physical education class are all concerned with the occupation and processing of space; equipment and social actors move between, are located within and are contained by particular places.

Living spaces

Lives are also 'lived' in and through space, and identities constructed with/in certain places. For example, spaces are appropriated by and differentiated through social identities such as gender, social class, sexuality, age, 'race' and ethnicity (Massey 1994). These dimensions can mark out spaces and places as (for example) working class, female, young, gay or black. Hence places become associated with different social groups and social identities. And at the same time, spaces can provide identity markers. Thus the bus shelter or street corner becomes a place for young people to 'hang out'; the back-street hairdresser's becomes a place for women of a certain age to socialize and share stories; or the football terrace can be seen as a space, perhaps, for the articulation of working-class masculine identities. Similarly, the home can be reconceptualized as a series of overlapping spaces – the physical demarcation of rooms are embedded with/in notions of public and privates spaces (the family sitting room versus the teenage bedroom), gendered spaces (the kitchen, garage or den), generational spaces (the study versus the nursery or playroom). Home can also be experienced as a quiet or noisy space, as confinement and sanctuary, as a haven or hell. It is a place to retreat to and feel safe in, but can also be a place for abuse or trouble (Hague and Malos 1993; Mama 1996). Thus individuals and social groups can gain a sense of belonging and derive identity from the sharing of spaces. Equally, exclusion from certain places can also be used to mark different identities, and might contribute to alternative life experiences. Spaces and places in these contexts are not static. Rather they are dynamic and subject to shift and change. Within them social actors can exercise agency to include or exclude, to alter, consolidate, appropriate, and source identity.

'Living' spaces and places can hence be transformed, as well as maintained; can be sites of struggle and sites for sharing.

Biographical space

Biographies and lives also have a spatial dimension. Not only do we live with/in and through space(s), our memories and lives are also spatially situated. Lives are remembered, retold and contextualized with regard to a sense of place. Particular spaces and places mark the accounts of our lives. Take, for example, the favourite hiding place as a child; the tree 'down the lane' under which a first kiss was experienced; the empty study-bedroom that greets a new arrival at university; the first house bought 'together'; the place of a proposal of marriage; or the place where a first child is conceived or born. Equally a question such as 'where were you?' is a way in which individual and collective memories are organized and reconstructed. Lives are also marked out by the places 'where we were' at key moments in history. For different generations this might be the place where you were when the American President J. F. Kennedy was assassinated in 1963, when British Prime Minister Margaret Thatcher was elected in 1979, or when news came through of the air attacks on the World Trade Center in New York in 2001.

The omnipresence of time(s)

Time, like space, is implicit to social, cultural and economic life. Contemporary sociological understandings reveal the omnipresence of time. Time is everywhere and ever present (Adam 1995), and moreover can be measured, defined and experienced in a variety of different ways. Time is not just related to formal understandings of the clock and 'clock time' – although of course there is much to be said about the ways in which these formalizations of time inhabit everyday lives, activities and experiences. Think, for example, of the timings of lessons and classes (signified by a bell or buzzer, or undertaken within the gaze of the clock); the appointments diary and the work of scheduling; the setting of the morning alarm clock (and the occasional luxury of not setting it, or being able to ignore it); the timings of film showings at the cinema and the consequences of arriving late; or the booking at a restaurant, when a designated clock time is part of the contract that is made. There are other understandings and experiences of time. Time is situated and contextualized with/in our everyday experiences.

Time for life

Biographies are embedded with/in notions of time; lives have pasts, presents and futures. Hence lives and biographies are also temporally situated and experienced. They happen, and are reproduced, in and through time.

Memories, as well as being spatially located, can also be conceived as the remembering and retelling of events and lives through time. As Adam (1995: 14) observes, memories – 'sudden, sharp ones and generalized amorphous ones – are integral to every moment of our being'. Memories are situated in the time they are remembered and are part of the ways in which lives are (re)created. With a resurgence in sociological interest in (auto)biographies has come an appreciation of the ways in which lives are captured through socially shared temporal resources. Hence the individual and collective passing and recapturing of time has increasingly been seen as a legitimate way of making sense of the social world (Stanley 1993). Lives, then, have a time as well as a place. Time can be marked, regained, halted, truncated, elongated through the associations with lives being remembered, lived or anticipated.

Social life itself also has its own temporal rhythms. The chronology of an individual life, traditionally framed in terms of life cycle, has more recently been reconceptualized as the life course. The life cycle suggests a biological, developmental model – consisting of a series of chronological stages that individuals and families move through in relatively unproblematic ways. More recent commentators (see Pilcher 1995) have highlighted the ways in which this model is suffused with medicalist and modernist assumptions about what is the 'normal' development or sequencing of a life. The concept of the life course is more fluid in nature. It rejects life cycle assumptions of the normal or developmental, and offers instead a more dynamic way of conceptualizing lives. A life course approach suggests a more interpretive approach to the construction of biographies, recognizing that these are differently constructed through time. Hence the life course embraces contemporary notions of diversity and difference, and acknowledges that lives are offered a range of possibilities, less rigidly patterned than some (more life cycle) models would suggest. The concept of the life course thus enables us to rethink the transitions and temporal rhythms of individual and family lives. For example, this approach is better placed to recognize and allow for an 'extension' of adolescence and youth through elongated transitions from home to the labour market (Morrow and Richards 1996; Furlong and Cartmel 1997); a contraction of childhoods as a possible consequence of media (and other forms of) consumption; a postponement of parenthood and the advent of pregnancy in later life (Craig 1997); the absence of parenthood as a part of the life course, through being childless or choosing to be child free; and the extension of the 'third age' through early retirements, flexible working lives and extended life spans.

The body of/in time

Time is also an embodied experience. Time is experienced through and with the body. The body is a marker of time. This body-time is encompassed in both physical and emotional ways. The tired body, ageing body, menstruating body, fit body, aching body, pregnant body, the failing body – these all mark time and are located in time. The 'body clock' can be interpreted in a number of ways. Often the term is used in relation to the natural cycles of (female) fertility. It can, however, also be used to denote the daily, monthly, yearly or generational rhythms of our bodies – the ways our bodies interact with biological cycles – but also with other concepts of time such as night and day, the seasons of the year, the weather and other 'time-markers' such as working days and holidays. Some body-time rhythms transcend familiar or taken-for-granted understandings of time. For example, Adam (1995: 48) argues that women's experiences of labour and childbirth can be 'simultaneously temporal, timeful, timeless and extended in time'.

The resource of time

A particular concept of time as resource was sharpened by the advent of industrial capitalism. The differentiation of work and non-work time, and the surveillance of the clock, are still relevant to contemporary understandings of time. These though can be extended into more general observations of the resourcing of time and the temporal. Hence it can be productive to think of time as a resource. Certainly in everyday language time is conceptualized in tangible ways. Time is used, preserved and spent. We make time, take time out, save time, do things just in time and run out of time. Time is also a commodity that can be sold, used to negotiate or bargain with, and indeed be 'stolen'. Contemporary discourses of work are also redefining the organization of time. There is a growing momentum for the introduction of family-friendly time, and the creation of a better balance between work time and home time (the work/life balance). In addition *some* working times have become more flexible, diverse and fragmented.

Time–space

It is, of course, difficult to separate the concepts and dimensions of time and space. Sociological work on both draws on many of the same understandings, as the preceding discussion has outlined. Social, cultural and economic life transcends spatial and temporal boundaries. Space and time are both biographically situated, and in turn help to situate biographies. Both are consumed, used, abused, preserved and reproduced. Both can be overlaid by an embodied perspective. Both can be used in an analysis of transitions and turning points. New conceptualizations of time and space also prompt new interweavings and interconnections to be made. For example, the growth of global communications, the World Wide Web and the advent of 'cyberspace' give new meanings to space (that can be virtual and no longer tied to place) and to time (that is simultaneously instant, present and absent).

In the sections that follow sociological understandings of time and space are brought to bear on the field of social policy. These discussions are by no means exhaustive, but serve to illustrate the analytic potential of rethinking social policy with/in these temporal and spatial contexts.

Time for social policy

A temporal perspective provides an opportunity to reconsider the processes, practices and experiences of social policy. Indeed, there are a number of ways in which the times, timing and temporalities of social policy can be explored as part of broader analyses. For example, time is a factor in the processes of social policy-making. Policy-making has, almost by definition, frameworks and structures that are guided by schedules, timetables and sequencing; dates of committee meetings (often published well in advance); timings of consultation meetings with clients, practitioners, residents and other significant groups; scheduling of publication and the release of documents (often embedded within governmental timetables); and the reading and debating of policy as part of established parliamentary cycles. All of these give a temporal quality to the formal mechanisms of social policy-making. The implementation and practice of social policy perhaps has a more fluid set of temporal rhythms than these formal timings of policy-making. However, arenas and sites of social policy still have their own timetables and temporal structures. There is, for instance, an established sociological literature on the temporal qualities of hospital life and the ways in which timetables of various kinds structure health care and work (see, for example, Roth 1963; Zerubavel 1979). Time has also been explored as a feature of school life (Adam 1992). For example, Gordon *et al.* (2000a: 148) argue that time in schools 'appears as a variable to be managed and controlled', as well as providing a potential point of teacher–student negotiation (for example, asking for more time to complete a task, staying after hours or being permitted to leave early).

Other areas of social policy can similarly be reconceptualized in terms of time. For example, one factor in the implementation of community care legislation has been the increasing emphasis placed on individual social care plans and packages. While these are constituted in terms of access to various care services, institutions and practitioners, they can also be considered in terms of timings and temporality. Care packages address *present* caring needs, and anticipate *future* caring needs. Home and residential care is *scheduled*. Carers visit at certain *times* of the *day* and *week*. There will be a schedule of visits to day care, hospital and other facilities. Respite care may be arranged for evenings or weekends or longer periods to give carers time to themselves. Thus the practical accomplishment of caring are suffused with timetables and temporal cycles. Similarly, the experiences of being cared for are embedded in and through time. Although the caring literature has paid relatively little attention to the experiences of the cared for (see Shakespeare 2000), it has given some consideration to the experiences of being a carer. It has been well documented that 'informal' care (usually unpaid care provided by partners or other family members) is physically arduous, emotionally demanding and time-greedy work (Finch and Groves 1983; Dalley 1988). Caring can place significant time constraints on carers, who may find that time – for paid work, for leisure or for themselves – is severely curtailed. As much of this informal care is carried out by the elderly (caring for their spouse) and by women, the time consequences and constraints of informal care can also be conceptualized as generational and gendered (Baldwin and Twigg 1991; Parker and Lawton 1994; Arber and Ginn 1995; Baines *et al.* 1998). Thus a focus on time in the context of social care can generate a variety of analytical starting points – thinking about the organization, rationing and rhythms of social care, as well as the experiences and consequences of caring. Similar analytical frameworks could usefully be applied to other social welfare settings. Consider, for example, the 'timings' of income maintenance payments such as state pensions and child benefit. Time is made visible by the queues of young mothers and older people at post office counters on certain days and times of the week or month. Waiting is a particular use of and understanding of time. These arbitrary timings and schedules in turn structure routines, everyday experiences and patterns of (welfare) consumption.

The times of and for social policy are, of course, interwoven with other times, and embedded within individual and collective experiences of time; the professional, training and work time of social welfare practitioners; family building time; the body-time of illness; stressful or emotional times; unemployed times; time to care for and care about; biographical and life times. Social policy is overwhelmingly situated within life course times. The client groups of social welfare are embedded within, and correspond to, generational and life course moments – childhood, young adulthood, parenthood and old age. Moreover, social policy works at, and with, lifetime transitions – the loss of employment; the advent of parenthood; the moves into and out of education; the transitions to adulthood; the loss of mobility; the onset of illness; the break-up of relationships; the move to retirement. These are all movements and moments through and in time, and represent potential 'settings' for social policy interventions.

The experiences of social policy are also biographically located, and form part of the construction of social identities. For example, the reconstruction of children's identities through education, child care and social work teams, or the reconstruction of disabled identities through policies for the disabled, or the reconstruction of carer identities through community care legislation and social care practice. These identities are changed, challenged or consolidated over and by time. Social policy encounters themselves also serve as markers of pasts, presents and projected futures; our memories and autobiographies are reconstructed through engagements and interactions with the 'business end' of social policy – for example, the first day at school, sitting school examinations, the first time in hospital, leaving home, giving birth, becoming unemployed, lean financial times, seeking refuge from a violent relationship, and the ageing of a parent. Hence social policy is intimately interwoven with everyday times and the reconstructions of autobiographies.

Social policy 'times' are complex and multiple. Through a consideration of institutions, practices and experiences, it is possible to see how time is central to social policy. It is also possible to explore the ways in which time is embedded within social policy concepts such as need or equality or social justice. An example of how this might be achieved is given below, drawing on the concept and experience of social exclusion.

The temporal rhythms of social exclusion

Social exclusion is a term and a status now embedded within sociological and social policy discourses (Byrne 1999). Social exclusion has been increasingly used as a means of describing social actors and social groups who are not able to fully participate in social, cultural and economic life (because of, for example, low incomes or poor skills, housing or health). Social exclusion has been the subject of considerable sociological and policy debate. It has also become part of official political discourse in the UK, not least through the establishment of the Social Exclusion Unit in 1997, set up to improve government action to reduce social exclusion, and now located within the office of the deputy prime minister. Social exclusion (and by contrast social inclusion) can be conceptualized and understood in a number of ways, including:

- Access to resources: Social exclusion is most readily associated with exclusion from the labour market (or parts thereof) and from economic resources that are associated with (well) paid employment. Of course, poor access to resources is not limited to money. Social exclusion can also mean exclusion from other (social or cultural) services, for example poor or no access to education, training, child care, transportation or decent housing.
- Space and place: The explanations and experiences of social exclusion can have geographical and spatial dimensions. The city has long been associated with poverty and social decay. Equally, rural life can exacerbate the experiences of exclusion, with welfare services spread out over larger areas, and reduced access to resources such as public transportation. Specific places can also serve as the locations of and for the socially excluded – for example, the street, shop doorway, drop-in centre, the hostel, job centre, or indeed the home.

- Political and participative exclusion: One of the explanations for, or consequences of, social exclusion is the inaccessibility of democratic processes. At one level this might be about the lack of opportunities for the 'voices' of the socially excluded to be heard – through, for example, community organizations and pressure groups. At other levels this can mean informal and formal exclusion from participating in elections, and contributing to political debate at local, national and international levels.
- Diversity and difference: The experiences of, and meanings that are attached to, social exclusion are not uniform. These are mediated by social identities and complex social realities. For example, age and generation have been noted as crucial factors in the determination and experience of poverty more generally. The prevalence of poverty among the elderly (and very elderly) is significant (Vincent 1995; Jamieson, Harper and Victor 1997). Similarly, socially excluded *young* people have been the subject of sociological investigation and policy intervention. The increasingly prolonged transitions into adulthood and an extended youth are especially profound for those young people not in education, training or employment (so-called status zero young people – see Rees *et al.* 1996). There is a range of other factors that can contribute to differential experiences of social inclusion – for example, family building, 'race' and ethnicity, gender, sexuality, and of course social class.

These factors, outlined above, all contribute to a more complex sociological understanding of social exclusion. Moreover, they can be subjected to a temporal or time perspective. Most obviously, factors such as age, generation and the life course encapsulate a (biographical) time dimension. The body is a marker of age but also of time. Generations are indicative of differences over and through time. The life course is time-marked and measured by different events and experiences. Hence, as has already been noted elsewhere in this chapter, there is a temporal dimension to life course phases, transitions and movements. This, in turn, can be used to explore the experiences of, and policy responses to, social exclusion – focusing, for example, on the ways in which social exclusion is linked to markers of time, such as youth transitions and old age, or to individual or collective biographies.

It is possible to look beyond this most obvious temporal dimension of social exclusion towards a more general 'time' analysis. Biographies experienced and constructed through and in time have their own temporal rhythms and ruptures. But other aspects of social exclusion can also be reconstructed with/in time frameworks. Economic activity, for instance, is grounded in notions of work time and industrial time (and thus social exclusion could be conceptualized in terms of what happens when these temporal frameworks are removed or disrupted or fail to materialize?). Similarly, education and training are also concerned with times and timings. Education acts as a time-marker for children and young adults, and training can be perceived as part of time and status transitions – from young person to adult, or from learner to worker, or from one kind of worker to another kind of worker. An understanding of education and training as 'life-long learning' also extends and reworks these time dimensions (Coffield 1999). Indeed, 'life-long' in and of itself is indicative of a certain appreciation of time. How social exclusion fits with a concept of life-long learning is a fascinating analytic question to be posed, both in terms of explanation and solution. Indeed, social *inclusion* as a goal fits well with the aspirations of life-long learning.

Transport and travel also have temporal rhythms, and by their very nature imply movement in time and through time. Poor access to transportation is one factor associated with social exclusion. At a simple level, relying upon public transportation in itself imposes particular kinds of timetables on social life. More broadly, physical and geographical movement through time (travelling and transportation) can take on particular significance for the socially excluded. Journeys (to job centres, advice offices, leisure facilities, colleges, shops) are temporal and timed. Transport and travel can be used to progress time or mark time. For the socially excluded, transport can be 'time to somewhere' or can be 'time to nowhere'. Travel can make time, save time, kill time and take time. Exclusion from transport resources and networks (through financial, geographical or other factors) can also make travel problematic and thus demand a rethinking of daily, weekly and life rhythms.

The spatial dimensions of social exclusion are also embedded with/in notions of time – daily and weekly 'timetables' are spent 'somewhere'. Organizational, institutional and formal settings (hostels, care homes, job centres, training settings) may provide new markers of time and ways to spend time. Similarly, informal settings, such as drop-in centres, street corners and the home, are also places to spend time, waste time, make time or plan time (Hall *et al.* 1999). The conceptualization of young people not in education, employment or work as 'status zero' (Williamson 1997) itself provides a particularly powerful articulation of social exclusion. 'Zero' (like nought or nil) embeds within it powerful understandings of time (and indeed space). Zero implies nothing. This can denote a slowing or stopping of time, no time, timelessness, empty time or wasted time. Similarly, it can evoke empty space, an absence or destruction of place or spatial displacement.

Participatory and democratic exclusion (or inclusion) can also be considered in terms of time. For example, there are distinctive 'times' for participation, and manifest calendars of democracy (such as dates of elections, campaign scheduling or the timetable for devolution). There are recognized cycles of democracy and prescribed times to exercise particular kinds of democratic rights (for example, through the ballot box). These can be contrasted with other participatory or democratic 'times' – time to take part in debate, to be heard, to be informed or to protest. These are different from the formal political process, but nevertheless can be construed as important aspects of social inclusion, with their own cycles, rhythms and moments. These participatory times are also spatially organized – for example, the electoral station at the local school or village hall, the connections between electoral registers and place of residency, the debating chamber or place for public meetings. Thus to be excluded from participation is embedded with differential experiences of these democratic times and spaces.

The example of social exclusion can be used as a case study to explore the analytic potential of a time perspective for the understanding of social policy. As a feature of contemporary social policy discourse, social exclusion provides a particularly apt illustration of the ways in which time and temporality can be used to explore experiences and policy processes. A consideration of time allows individual, collective and institutional perspectives to be considered afresh, and provides a new lens for viewing social policy. It allows for the exploration of the ways in which concepts, experiences, statuses, policy-making and implementation are embedded with/in different times, temporalities and temporal rhythms. Social policy and social welfare can thus be reconstructed in terms of pasts, presents and futures, transitions and movements, cycles and rhythms, time to and time for, making time and taking time. In this section the interconnections between time and space have also been noted. The spatial dimensions of social policy are explored in the following section.

Spaces for social policy

Social policy is situated within particular spaces and places, and hence it is possible to explore its spatiality as well as its temporality. Social policy is made, implemented, practised and experienced in and through space and place. The location, organization and meanings that are attached to these places contribute to the ways in which we understand and make sense of social policy processes and practices. Of course, social policy inhabits a diverse array of places and spaces. There are, for example, obvious physical places that might usefully be designated as institutions of social policy. The hospital, school, further education college, residential home and prison are institutionalized spaces for social policy and social welfare activities and provision. These are (usually) purpose-built, rebuilt or designed in order to provide dedicated, and (by definition) appropriate, space for the implementation and practice of health care, education, social care, rehabilitation, incarceration, and so forth. These spaces are physically and socially organized in order to promote or support particular approaches to social policy and social welfare. Schools are constructed in order to put into practice particular approaches to learning and teaching. Similarly, the hospital is organized in order to facilitate particular enactments of medicine and health care relationships. Places such as these are sites for the supply and consumption of social policy 'services'. The ways in which these places are organized, and the spaces that are fashioned within them, can be considered as part of an understanding of how social policy work, practice and experience are accomplished.

These physical settings themselves represent one way in which social policy has a spatial dimension. The organization and differentiation of these settings can take the analysis further. Consider again the school. Classrooms, science laboratories, sports halls, dining rooms and staffrooms organize and define the school in terms of differentiated spaces, and particular approaches to learning and teaching. Children in the primary school setting, for example, usually have a base classroom within which they undertake the majority of their lessons. The classroom 'belongs' to a teacher and her class. The classroom will, within it, have tables often organized in clusters, separate play areas, painting areas, places for 'water' activities, and a corner with a rug for end-of-day stories. Primary classrooms are often brightly coloured, decorated with the children's own work and other pictures and posters. This approach to the organization of the classroom space can be contrasted with other kinds of learning environment. For example, desks that are arranged in straight rows, all facing the teacher's desk positioned at the front of the room, suggest a rather different approach to the learning event, compared to clusters of desks and a 'mobile' teacher. Similarly, classrooms that are designated and arranged for particular school subjects (science, mathematics, art or geography) prompt particular understandings of knowledge – arranged into discrete, subject-specific packages. The point here is not necessarily to evaluate some kinds of spatial organization of learning and teaching as better or worse than others. Rather, it is simply to appreciate that the physical and spatial environment in which learning and teaching takes place might make a difference.

Moreover, learners and teachers are not fixed in space in these settings. Education is delivered through space – over the course of the school day learners (and teachers) might navigate their way around the school – from classroom to classroom, to the hall for assembly, to the playing fields for physical education, to the music block or the dining hall, design workshop or the art room. They use corridors, foyers and entrance halls as roadways and junctions to facilitate this movement, which in turn is organized by school 'clock' time. These roadways and junctions are also spaces in their own right – for congregating, socializing, exchanging and talking. There are also other spaces in the school, visited less frequently by learners. For example, the head teacher's office, school secretary's office and the staffroom are inhabited by different social actors within the school. There are boundaries between these spaces and other spaces. Some places are out of bounds for children, limited to adults, apart from in particular circumstances. And these 'adult' spaces too will be organized in particular ways, facilitating particular approaches to educational 'work' (Hargreaves and Woods 1984). Thus school spaces are locations for learning and teaching, but also for working, playing and socializing. School spaces will also have patterns and rules. Classrooms may have seating plans, with designated desk space for each child. There are often rules about (not) running in corridors, or (not) entering the staffroom without knocking. Some spaces can also become associated with misbehaviour – the 'naughty' corner or 'naughty' chair in the primary school classroom, or the corridor outside the head teacher's office where 'offenders' might be asked to wait. Informal patterns also emerge. Areas of the playground can become inhabited by, and 'home' to, distinct groups of pupils. For example, school research has consistently shown that boys and their games often dominate the physical space of the playground (Thorne 1993). Equally, the staffroom can also serve as an environment for the creation and maintenance of gendered spaces (Cunnison 1989).

Similar observations could be made about other social policy settings. The point to emphasize is that the places of and for social policy, and how they are spatially arranged, can be important to the ways in which social policy or welfare services are delivered, consumed and experienced. Within this analysis, the physical organization and the symbolic representation of social policy spaces can be considered. This might include the ways in which the spatiality of the setting impacts upon different social actors in different ways – be they practitioners, administrators, managers, clients, consumers – and the ways in which space can be used to facilitate, bind, control, negotiate, regulate, channel and mediate. Such an analysis can take us away from the more obvious institutional arenas, toward a consideration of other spaces of and for social policy. For example, youth work settings (such as youth clubs and drop-in centres) can be reconceptualized as providing young people with the opportunities to carve out a place of their own, and as providing valuable space for association, expression and the exploration of identity (Hall *et al.* 1999). Of course, such settings can also, however, be viewed as space for corralling young people, containing and supervising their activities. The recent physical reorganization of some job centres and social security offices also draws attention to the importance of space. Low desks, comfortable upholstered chairs, carpets and pot plants all provide more pleasant surroundings and an ambience of service, and stand in sharp contrast to plastic 'wipe clean' chairs, high counters and glass screens. These spaces, however, have to serve a multitude of purposes – providing places to work, to wait, to be contained, to consult, to retain self-respect and to be safe.

There are also less formal places and spaces for social policy practice and experience. The home is a location for a considerable amount of welfare provision, for example in the forms of social care, education and health care. Caring for children, the ill and incapacitated, and the elderly all take place within the home. The ways in which the physical space of the home adapts, or fails to adapt, to these welfare needs is one aspect in an exploration of the spatial contexts of care. The home is also the place in which the material and emotional consequences of poverty are most acutely felt; child welfare and protection interventions are carried out; and structural adaptation and care packages are invoked to accommodate disabled or elderly living. The home is also a space to be visited (or invaded) by an entourage of social policy and welfare professionals. Health visitors, district nurses, social workers, occupational therapists, home-school liaison workers and daily carers all bring social welfare 'home'. Equally, the home might also be the place in which the antecedents to social policy intervention may 'live' – for example, increasing mobility difficulties, the disruptive child, child abuse, and domestic violence. The home can be conceptualized as safe haven or place of disruption, abuse or containment. And while that is partially an emotional response to 'home', it is predicated on a physical place of being. Hence the home – as space and place – might be considered a fruitful 'place' for social policy analysis. For example, it could enable an understanding of the identification and explanation of need, of social policy implementation and practice and of social welfare experiences.

There are other informal social policy spaces that could lend themselves to a similar kind of spatial analysis. For example, the transitional spaces that 'accommodate' the homeless, and through which social welfare interventions may or may not take place – doorways, cafés, hostels, bus stations, dock sides or pavements under bridges. These places can become 'sites' for social policy activities, mediated in and through time – for example, soup deliveries by volunteers at dusk, nightly police patrols, weekly visits by outreach workers and teatime queues for and allocations of hostel places. To be homeless also implies a 'home' to have come from or lost, and a transitional status from which one might emerge (Hall 2003). Hence this spatiality of homelessness could also be extended to physical and symbolic connections to past and future 'homes'.

This section has just begun to map out how a sociology of space and place could be used in an analysis of social policy. It is clear that, even at this preliminary level, social policy inhabits formal and informal places and spaces. From this brief exploration it is already possible to consider the ways in which the physical buildings and places of social policy are organized in order to prompt certain kinds of activities and constrain others; the ways in which the range of social policy actors (practitioners, carers, clients, consumers) inhabit different spaces, and have different relationships to the same spaces; and how the home is a multidimensional social policy place and space – where needs are identified, care is given and received, interventions are made and visitations undertaken. A consideration of these, and the ways in which they mediate social policy processes, practices and experiences, is certainly worthy of future work.

Conclusion

There has been relatively little attention paid thus far to the development of a social policy of time and space. And yet, as has been outlined in this chapter, social policy is enacted in and through time and space. The themes that have emerged from sociological analyses of time and space have considerable analytic potential for understanding and making sense of social policy. Temporal and spatial perspectives provide insights into the workings of social policy at a number of different levels, from which the sites, settings and cycles of policy-making might be usefully explored. Equally, our understanding of the implementation, practices, work and lived realities of social policy and social welfare could also be enhanced.

The perspectives of time and space have particular relevance given the dynamic nature of social policy. Policies, practices and provisions are shaped by and in turn help to shape political and social processes. The spaces of social policy are not static but continually shifting and changing – the home takes on greater or lesser importance as a site for welfare provision; community-based mental health teams replace residential psychiatric hospitals; school buildings are redesigned to accommodate more specialist curricula or to appeal to parents as consumers; purpose-built primary health care and community hospital centres become more common and so forth. The spaces for social policy are also shifting in other ways – clients move through different spaces as they are 'processed', admitted, discharged, interviewed, cared for or neglected. Transitional spaces remain – such as the hostel, hospital bed, short stay residential unit or foster home.

The times of and for social policy also embody movement and change – extended lifetimes and differentiated life courses mean that social policy provision and experiences extend and shift. Extended youth demands new approaches to the transitions to adulthood, a place social policy has traditionally inhabited. New social policy 'times' are also implicit in the move towards family-friendly work policies and a greater consideration of the work/life balance, the realization of life-long learning, the commitment to reduce hospital waiting times or in making the legal processes of adoption of children quicker and more straightforward. Hence it is also possible to conceptualize a contemporary analysis in terms of future and changing times, and new spaces of and for social policy.

Further reading

Adam, B. (1995) *Timewatch*. Cambridge: Polity. A sociological exploration of time, as experienced in and through the contexts and institutions of everyday social life. This book challenges and consolidates everyday understandings of time and the temporal, and covers a wide range of topic areas including the body, education, health and the environment.

Gordon, T., Holland J. and Lehelma, E. (2000) *Making Spaces: Citizenship and Difference in Schools*. Basingstoke: Macmillan. This book provides a rich example of a time-space analysis of a particular social policy arena. The book considers the social, physical, temporal and embodied constructions of space within school settings.

Urry, J. (1995) *Consuming Places*. London: Routledge. In this book John Urry considers the sociological treatment of time and space, and the ways in which sociology can contribute to our understanding of place. It is an important contribution to the sociological literature, covering a number of themes, including the consumption of place and space by tourists and others.

chapter

eight

Researching Social Policy

Introduction

The discipline of social policy has a strong research tradition. Indeed, it is hard to think of a discipline that is more empirically based. Social policy is concerned with the consideration *and* evaluation of welfare policies and services; and the ways in which these interrelate to/with consumers, providers and policy-makers. Hence social policy scholars (and practitioners) routinely rely upon the identification, consolidation and analysis of data and evidence as part of their everyday work. Despite this empirical foundation, it is difficult to identify any distinctive methodological contributions that have arisen from within the discipline of social policy in general. There has certainly not been the more widespread attention to social research methods that has occurred in other social science or cognate disciplines, such as education, psychology and sociology. Social research methods *per se* are rarely included as a distinctive category in introductory social policy texts. This is in contrast to (for example) introductory sociological texts, where research strategies and methodological considerations are routinely included. There are not any dedicated social policy research methods texts for students that engage with both research strategies and contemporary methodological debates. This is not to say that there has been a complete absence of methodological attention from within the discipline of social policy. Individual social policy scholars have contributed to edited collections on social research methods (and thus made contributions to methodological debate – see, for example, Finch 1984 and Graham 1984). Within social research methods journals there have been some distinctively social policy contributions (Seymour 2001), and individual research-orientated texts such as *Qualitative Research in Social Work* (Shaw and Gould 2001) have provided a platform for identifying trends in (social policy) research practice.

However, it is fair to say that researching social policy has been a taken-for-granted activity rather than the subject of sustained *critical* attention and innovation.

The teaching of social policy has come under recent scrutiny at both the undergraduate and postgraduate levels. The introduction of subject bench-marking within the UK higher education undergraduate curriculum, and training guidelines for postgraduate students in the UK have both acknowledged that social policy students should have an awareness of strategies for the collection and analysis of social science data (as well as the opportunity to develop research skills). The social policy subject benchmark statements (Quality Assurance Agency (QAA) 2000), for example, state that all students 'should acquire a basic appreciation of quantitative and qualitative research methods and computational skills' (p. 2). Data collection and research skills are thus identified as desirable components of a social policy curriculum. However, social research methods and methodologies are not included as units in their own right in the listings of indicative modules offered by the social policy benchmark document (QAA 2000). Their approach, in so far as research methods are concerned, is thus rather cautious and limited. It does not include the full spectrum of social research methods, nor does it locate the discipline of social policy within wider methodological or epistemological debates. The emphasis is on the acquisition of basic research skills, rather than a more reflective and critical engagement.

The social science postgraduate training guidelines published by the UK Economic and Social Research Council (ESRC 2000a) are aimed at institutions providing doctoral provision. As might be expected they are far more comprehensive with respect to research methods. The main emphasis of these training guidelines is equipping social science postgraduate students with appropriate research skills and understandings. These subject-specific guidelines recognize the distinctive features of social policy research and the desirability for a reflective approach to methodology.

> Students undertaking research in these subjects study and interact with people as individuals and as members of groups, communities and societies. Research training must give students a clear understanding of the ways in which difference and diversity shape research questions, and must equip them with the skills, insights and sensitivity to understand and reflect issues of difference and diversity at every stage of the research process. It may also reflect a concern with engaging with oppression and working in emancipatory ways. The research process itself should generally be reflexive, allowing for adjustment in design and methodology(ies) in the light of emerging understanding.
>
> (ESRC 2000b: 4)

Thus the postgraduate training guidelines for social policy start to map out the distinctiveness of social policy as an empirical subject, and the consequences of this for locating social policy within research strategies and broader methodological debates.

This chapter builds upon these observations by considering some of the relationships between social policy and social research. In particular, the chapter considers the opportunities and implications of the range of social science research strategies, developments and debates for social policy. Sociological approaches to social research form a key reference point, although similar patterns may also be identified across other cognate fields. The chapter has three main aims:

- to address general approaches to research within social policy as an academic discipline;
- to provide an overview of the main research strategies available to the investigator for gathering and analysing data on social policy;
- to locate social policy research within contemporary social research discourses (also see Chapter 9 for a more detailed discussion of contemporary developments within social research).

Social research and the discipline of social policy

Remarkably little attention has been paid to social research methods and methodologies within social policy, despite its empirical basis. The studying of social policy, and hence the academic discipline of social policy, relies upon a critical engagement with various kinds of social science data. As Baldock and his colleagues (1999: xxiii) indicate in the introduction to their social policy text:

> While values and politics may drive the making of social policy, the study of social policy should be informed by evidence. Social research, collecting data about how people live, is central to the traditions of 'social policy' as an academic subject, and it has a long history [. . .] Studying social policy is an excellent way of getting to know about the material world and how people live in it.

Despite this general statement, and a 560-page text that appropriately draws on a wide range of empirical material, this introductory text (Baldock, Manning, Miller and Vickerstaff 1999) does not include any chapter (or part thereof) that deals explicitly with equipping students with the tools to undertake and evaluate social research in their own right. There are no explicit discussions of social research methods, or methodological approaches, and little attention is given to the empirical 'doing' of social policy. This is particularly surprising given the emphasis on evidence, and the balance of the text between social policy as a subject area and as an academic discipline. This paucity of explicit attention to social research methods is not unusual in social policy textbooks more generally. For example, the social policy reader edited by Taylor (1996) had no discussion of methods or methodologies, and Hill's standard text on understanding social policy, now in its seventh edition (Hill 2003), remains service-based, with little attention to the methodological and research underpinnings of the discipline. Alcock, Payne and Sullivan (2004) in their introductory text provide a more critical commentary of the fluid disciplinary boundaries of social policy, and draw on a range of understandings. However, this text still offers little in the way of practical or epistemological social research method advice, or methodological discussion. *The Student's Companion to Social Policy* (Alcock, Erskine and May 2003) is one of the few student-orientated social policy texts that does include research as a social policy skill. There is a section on resources, and within that a useful though rather short introduction to undertaking research projects in social policy (Dean 2003), and a guide to fieldwork placements that has a research-orientated theme (Scott 2003). The chapter by Dean has a brief description of methodological approaches, a listing of data-gathering methods and a short discussion of research ethics. While this chapter is by no means extensive or exhaustive, it does serve as an example of social research being seen as part of the 'curriculum' of social policy.

The methodological discussions that have been increasingly present within social science disciplines, such as education and sociology, have been notably absent from social policy discourses. Recent and more innovative social policy texts have not systematically addressed methodological considerations, controversies or developments. *Rethinking Social Policy* (Lewis, Gewirtz and Clarke 2000), for example, is a volume that challenges conventional social policy approaches, not least by drawing on a range of sociological perspectives and conceptual frameworks (for example around ideas of social identities, the body, emotions, globalization, discourse and time). Such a text would seem an obvious space from which to rehearse and discuss contemporary questions of method and methodology, and yet there are no chapters that explicitly do so.

There appears to be a taken-for-grantedness about the empirical basis of the discipline of social policy, with little critical attention to research skills, or ongoing methodological debate. This may account, at least in part, for the lack of a distinctive social policy contribution to the contemporary research methods discourses. The nature of social policy research may not easily lend itself to methodological reflection. It is possible to characterize a considerable amount of social policy research in terms of evaluation or outcome-based studies. Empirical social policy research is often government initiated, and concerned with the consideration and evaluation of welfare services, systems and policies. This can promote a rather narrow view of the empirical concerns of the discipline, and tends to emphasize the outcomes (rather than the processes) of social research. Indeed, this policy evaluation model of social research can leave little room for more 'basic' research, with a strong disciplinary and theoretical base. Ozga (2000: 1) describes policy research as contested terrain; where conceptualizations and understandings are continually struggled over. Ozga identifies two contrasting approaches to policy research, which she calls the policy analysis project and the social science project. Ozga argues that the first of these dominates the policy research landscape, orientated towards 'finding solutions rather than enlarging understanding' (2000: 40). This is at the expense of a more social science orientated approach, which has the capacity to concentrate more on the social processes of investigation. Ozga (2000: 40) describes this more social scientific approach as being concerned with the advancement of social theory, and orientated towards the academic discipline, rather than 'strategic planning, requirements and possibilities'. This is not to say that social policy scholars have not been involved in a wider social science project, aimed at developing understandings rather than evaluating policy. Research projects have addressed the processes and experiences of social policy, as well as the evaluation of particular strategies and interventions. However, there is a case to be made that as a social science, the discipline of social policy has been slow to develop distinctive methodological approaches, or 'principles of enquiry' (Ozga 2000: 40), and has been relatively silent within contemporary research discourses. A case could certainly be made that the strong empirical base of the discipline of social policy (in terms of a reliance on data and evidence) needs to be complemented by a more explicit engagement with research training, the development of research skills and methodological discourses. The next section of this chapter considers some of the data collection and analytical tools that are potentially at the disposal of social policy students and scholars.

Gathering and analysing data on social policy

Social research methods encompass a wide range of possible strategies and approaches, all of which can be utilized in the study of and for social policy. In this section the main methods are outlined for the collection and analysis of social science data, and examples given on how they might be used as part of a social policy research repertoire. Social policy research can utilize a wide range of research strategies, and it is not the intention here to make critical comparisons between individual methods or methodological approaches. Indeed, prioritizing or valorizing some approaches over others can be disempowering, especially to new researchers. There are, of course, theoretical and methodological considerations that should be borne in mind when 'choosing' between research strategies. Research methods or strategies of inquiry should not be considered in a methodological vacuum, divorced from ways of seeing or understanding the social world. Indeed, a criticism of some approaches to the teaching of social research methods is the presentation of all approaches as though they are part of a 'neutral' tool box with little attention paid to the ways in which methods have developed out of, often long standing, theoretical conceptualizations of the social world (see Chapter 2 of this volume). For example, while the relationships between large-scale quantitative or statistical methods and positivist approaches to social theory are not set in stone, uncritically utilizing quantitative research implies a belief in the ways in which such methods can provide us with valid and reliable data on and about the social world. Equally, qualitative methods such as participant observation and narrative interviewing have emerged out of ethnographic approaches to social anthropology, and have close affinities with symbolic interactionism usually associated with the Chicago School of Sociology. Such methods of social investigation implicitly support particular kinds of understanding about the social world, whereby local experiences and social interactions are considered to be important frames of analysis.

At its simplest, all good social research(ers) should critically engage with a range of perspectives, methodologies, theories and epistemologies as part of a research agenda, alongside particular methods of choice or 'best fit'. Social policy researchers should actively consider all possible methods available, not just the most fashionable or well-known ones. At the same time there is a case to be made that social policy research(ers) could more fruitfully and fully engage with a wider range of methodological and epistemological approaches. What follows is a brief résumé of specific methods of social investigation, and the ways in which these can support social policy research. The methods of investigation are discussed in a general order, beginning with the more positivist or quantitative approaches, and then moving on to those that may considered to be more qualitative or framed within an interactionist paradigm. However, these are not hard and fast categories, and there is inevitably some overlap. While not a specific method for data collection or analysis, the role of action research within social policy research is also discussed. For each method or approach a summary description is given, along with citations to appropriate research methods texts.

Surveys, questionnaires and experiments

The social survey – either by a questionnaire completed by respondents in writing, or discussed with an interviewer – is a common method for the collection of quantitative data sets (and can also be used for the collection of some qualitative data). Surveys and questionnaires are useful ways of gaining quantifiable data on attitudes and opinions, although they are less satisfactory ways of gaining detailed data on lives and experiences. They are especially useful for gaining data from large populations or samples. There are a number of texts that provide advice on using the survey method.

Aldridge and Levine (2001) *Surveying the Social World* is a comprehensive text, suitable for a wide social science audience. May (2001) has an excellent chapter on social surveys (including a balanced critique) in his general text on social research. Oppenheim (1992) and Gillham (2000) both offer good advice on questionnaire design.

Survey methods have been subjected to some criticisms – for example, that they tend to deal with 'surface' rather than 'depth' data; issues of satisfactory sampling frames and poor response rates; and that they are perhaps better at providing descriptions rather than explanations and understandings. All of which mean that we should approach these methods critically and with a clear understanding of what they can and cannot provide. However, these methods do have the advantage of facilitating the collection of large data sets efficiently (in terms of time and other resources), and of providing results that may be generalizable.

Surveys and questionnaires have been well utilized by researchers working in the field of social policy, both historically and in contemporary times. Seebohm Rowntree's social surveys of the working classes of York (Rowntree 1901 and 1941) and Charles Booth's London poverty studies in the late nineteenth and early twentieth centuries (Booth 1901–2) perhaps laid the foundations of what became the empirical study of social policy. There are a number of major social surveys conducted regularly in the UK. For example, the British Household Panel Survey based at the University of Essex and British Social Attitudes Survey conducted by the National Centre for Social Research are both conducted annually (see Berthoud and Gershuny 2000; Jowell *et al.* 2000). The Office for National Statistics is responsible for the continuous General Household Survey (see Maher and Green 2002; Walker *et al.* 2002). All of these collect and analyse aggregate data central to social policy, such as information about demographics, employment and income maintenance, access to welfare services, health experiences and so forth. Examples of social policy projects that have included the collection of survey data include *A Nation of Homeowners* (Saunders 1990), where 450 householders were surveyed in three English towns about home ownership (see Devine and Heath 1999, for a critical commentary); and Wheelock and Jones' (2002) study of informal child care, where working parents were surveyed about their child care arrangements.

Experimental research designs also rely on the collection of quantitative data, but have not been widely used within the social sciences (with the exception of psychology and to a lesser extent educational studies). Experimental designs are concerned with measuring causality; conditions are manipulated and controlled in order to evaluate or assess the impact of one or more variable. It is difficult to undertake experiments in 'natural' settings without the benefit of a laboratory environment. Quasi or natural experiments are more realistic, and certainly easier to marry with social policy research. This is where an experimental approach can be utilized without randomly allocating experimental and control groups. For example, where social interventions or innovations are being introduced anyway, to selected groups at a time, an experimental design can be used to 'test' the 'before and after'. In some ways this kind of approach could be compared with certain kinds of action research, where interventions are put in place and evaluated (action research is discussed later in this chapter). A good critical overview to experiments and quasi experiments within social science can be found in Robson's *Real World Research* (2002). For a discussion of the method-ological, practical and ethical considerations of experimental design in the social sciences, also see De Vaus (2001).

Interviews with individuals

Interviewing is perhaps the most common social science research method. Many of the standard social research methods texts distinguish between different kinds of interviewing in social research, although it is perhaps more helpful to think of these as points along a continuum – from the structured, or standardized interview (most readily associated with survey research) to the focused or in-depth interview (firmly located within a qualitative para-digm), via the semi-structured interview (which navigates between closed and open questions, broadly standardized but allowing for some elaboration from respondents). The most comprehensive text on interviewing is *The Handbook of Interview Research* (Gubrium and Holstein 2001). (More suc-cinct guidance can be found in May 2001.) All kinds of interviewing approaches have and can be used for social policy research, as they enable the collection of different kinds of data about respondents and the social world they occupy. Interviews can generate life and oral histories, narratives, and information about current experiences and opinions.

Qualitative interviews (often multiple interviews with the same respond-ent, each lasting several hours) are a good way of collecting oral history (that is unwritten eyewitness accounts of the past) and life history data. The classic text on collecting oral history in Thompson (1988) and Denzin (1989) also provides a good introduction to the approach. The best account of the position of life histories within social science research is Plummer (2001) (see also Roberts 2001 on biographical research more generally). Qualitative interview data can be valuable in understanding the making and implementation of social policy (for example, in documenting the policy-making process from the perspectives of different social actors, or making sense of the practice of social policy through the life histories of social policy and welfare practitioners). There is an established tradition of collecting life histories from social policy providers (for example, Connell 1985; Sikes, Measor and Woods 1985; Goodson 1992; and Munro 1998 are all examples of projects drawing on the life histories of teachers and educators). Life history approaches can also be used to elicit data with and about the clients of social policy (see Riessman 1994 and 2001 for powerful examples of using a life history approach with social work clients). However, there has been little in the way of systematic attempts to collect life history data to document social policy systems as a whole.

Life history research can be seen as part of a more general 'cluster of approaches which includes narrative research, family stories, oral histories, biographical and autobiographical analyses' (Shaw and Gould 2001: 150). Since the 1990s the collection and analysis of 'stories' have become major research activities, and are part of a research genre that Goodson (1995) calls personal knowledge. They fall within the auspices of the 'narrative' or 'biographical' turn in social science (see Chapter 9). General discussions of the biographical approach to social science research can be found in Roberts (2001) and Chamberlayne *et al.* (2000). Cortazzi (1993) and Reissman (1993) are both excellent introductory texts on the analysis of narratives and stories (also see Silverman 2001 for a general overview). Chapters in some of the general methods handbooks also offer useful, though more complex, discussion of these approaches (for example, Fontana and Frey 2000; Cortazzi 2001; Atkinson 2002; Warren 2002). These approaches offer the potential of enriching our understanding of social policy, by sharing experiences and giving 'voice' to practitioners and clients, as well as to policy-makers. Qualitative interviewing can be an opportunity for genuine collaboration between researcher and researched, and for the giving of voice to otherwise 'invisible' lives. Within the realms of social policy these approaches can be used to study professional groups such as social workers (see Pithouse 1997; Scourfield 2003), other social policy providers such as family and care workers (Finch and Mason 1993; Gunaratnam 2001), or the clients of social policy, such as tenants, patients, the elderly, lone mothers, the marginalized or excluded (see Rojiani 1994; Hey 1999). All stories and narratives do, of course, need to be located, interrogated and analysed within their social contexts (Witherall and Noddings 1991). Not all voices are equally heard. As Becker (1970) argued, the terrain of research involves not only differentiated voices but also stratified voices. Stories and narratives cannot be decontextualized from storylines derived from elsewhere and the dominant messages they may implicitly carry. It is equally important that we are mindful that in gathering stories, we do not 'valorise the subjectivity of the powerless' (Goodson 1995). That is, qualitative or biographical interviewing is concerned with documenting and understanding, but not 'romanticizing' the individual (for further discussion of this, see Chapter 9).

Thus far I have concentrated primarily on qualitative interviewing. Many interviewers, however, are trying to collect data on their respondents current experiences and opinions, and utilize semi-structured interview schedules, with pre-specified questions, to facilitate this. These will often include closed questions, as well as some opportunities for more qualitative discussions. Semi-structured interviews are a primary means of collecting data on the contemporary lives and experiences of social policy actors, and work better for interviewing larger samples. Semi-structured interviews are often used in social policy research, often in combination with other methods, such as a survey or focus group interviews (see, for example, Wheelock and Jones 2002; Pickard, Jacobs and Kirk 2003).

Focus groups and group interviews

Interviews can also be conducted with groups of respondents. Focus groups and group interviews can be used to elicit group opinions and to discover how perspectives are developed. In group interviews, participants are asked to respond (often in turn) to questions from the interviewer. Focus groups are particular forms of group interviews, where the researcher provides a group of respondents with a series of topics or, more often than not, a set of focusing materials or activities – such as photographs, documents, artefacts, vignettes, or sets of variables to discuss or prioritize. A focus group interview is not simply an altercation between researcher's questions and participants' responses. 'Instead, the reliance is on interaction within the group, based on topics supplied by the researcher, who typically takes the role of moderator' (Morgan 1997: 9–10). Hence in focus group formats participants are encouraged to engage in conversation and debate with one another.

Groups can be assembled purely for the purposes of research, or can be a pre-existing group. Sometimes the researcher works with a group over time, regularly collecting their talk; sometimes the study is a one-off. The focus group method is particularly used when the researcher wants to discover how opinions are formed, or gather a variety of views about something complex, not part of everyday immediate experience, or on particularly sensitive topics – where a more general (and distant) discussion may work better then individual interrogation. The main aim of a focus group inter- view is to attempt to understand and document the processes by which views are shared, contrasted and developed. Focus groups have increasingly been used within social research, often in combination with other methods. Bloor *et al.* (2001) provide a good practical guide to conducting focus groups, and analysing focus group data (see also Barbour and Kitzinger 1999). Examples of social policy research that use these methods include Evanson and Spence (2003), who conducted focus group interviews with women as part of a study of women and pensions in Northern Ireland, and East (2002) who undertook group interviews with local residents, voluntary workers and professionals for a study on health initiatives and urban regeneration.

Documents and written data

Written materials can also be used as social science data, and there is a wide range of potential sources, including existing documents and texts generated specifically for the purposes of social research. Prior (2003) and Scott (1990) both provide good overviews to social research using documentary sources; May (2001) also includes a useful critical chapter on documentary research. Documents are, of course, central to processes of social policy formation. Both historical and contemporary documents can be studied and analysed, in order to understand and make sense of social policy development, creation and implementation. Historical accounts of the development of the welfare state and social policy inevitably draw on the analyses of documents (see, for example, Lewis 1992 and Dyhouse 1995). Some aspects of social policy process and practice are particularly well 'documented', for example records of the formal policy formation process and client–professional interactions (although these are not always available for public consumption or research purposes). Documentary materials can be used to explore how welfare organizations, institutions and the everyday work of social policy are managed and reproduced through documentary discourses, articulated via routine correspondence and other records. Examples of 'social policy' documents might include official reports, minutes of meetings, committee reports, policy statements, consultation and briefing papers. Definitions of documents can also be widened to include maps, plans, diagrams, drawings and photographs. People processing professions and organizations (core to social policy) routinely compile documents and records, for example in the production of social work case notes, medical records, school reports, health visitor case records, higher education learning records, and social security case files. These can provide valuable insights into the everyday work of social policy (see Pithouse 1997; Scourfield 2003).

Personal diaries can also be considered as material for social research. These can include diaries and letters kept in the past for private consumption that can be used as a source of historical data (Plummer 2001) and solicited accounts that the researcher has asked people to keep. Written narratives, of various kinds, are valuable sources of social science data, not least because of their storied qualities. Social actors present, represent and contextualize personal knowledge and experiences through stories and narratives. Hence an analysis of written narratives can reveal collective and shared understandings and experience, alongside individual accounts of events and experiences. Clearly the diaries of political figures and social reformers are potentially rich sources of data about social policy campaigns, formation and implementation (see, for example, Benn 2002). Solicited diaries have not been especially well used as a method of social policy investigation, although they offer potential, as a mechanism for mapping the differential experiences of organizations, processes and practices. Coxon (1988) asked gay men to keep diaries of their sexual encounters as part of a project on risk behaviour and HIV/AIDS in the early 1980s; and the students in Mac an Ghaill's study of masculinities and schooling kept diaries as a means of documenting and sharing their life and educational stories (Mac an Ghaill 1994).

Aside from diaries, other forms of writing can be generated and analysed as part of a social science research project. Researchers can ask respondents to write something – letters, stories, essays, and autobiographies. Examples of such 'commissions' include essays and stories written for research teams by children, secondary school pupils and young adults in order to gather data on school days and the transitions to secondary school (Bryan 1980; Delamont 1991; Pugsley, Coffey and Delamont 1996). Haw's (1998) study of the education of Muslim girls in the UK included an analysis of stories written by school pupils about an academically successful Muslim girl. As well as these commissioned writings, there is also potential in utilizing autobiographical accounts of social life, and indeed fiction, in order to explore social policy issues (see, for example, *Benefits: A Novel* by Fairbairns 1979).

Observing the social world

Under the general heading of observation it is possible to distinguish between a number of data gathering approaches. These may be considered as complementary rather than mutually exclusive. They include ethnographic (participant) observation, where the researcher 'learns' about social organizations and settings through direct engagement and participation; systematic observation using pre-specified coding schedules and frameworks; and making a permanent recording of settings and processes (through a range of audio-visual methods). Participant observation and visual methods come firmly under the auspices of qualitative research. Structured observation can be used as a quantitative method, as it can involve quantifying social action and behaviour. There are many excellent sources to observational methods, especially to ethnographic fieldwork. Bailey (1998) is a good basic introduction to conducting observational fieldwork. Hammersley and Atkinson (1995) and Lofland and Lofland (1996) are both standard texts on ethnography and participant observation. May's general text on social research has a good overview of the perspectives and practices of participant observation (May 2001). *The Handbook of Ethnography* (Atkinson *et al.* 2001) and *The Handbook of Qualitative Research* (Denzin and Lincoln 2000) both contain comprehensive discussions on collecting, analysing and theorizing observational data. (For advice on structured observation Robson (2002) has an accessible guide. Bakeman and Gottman (1997) is a more detailed introduction.) There are also a number of excellent sources on using visual methods as a way of collecting social science data. See, for example, Pink (2001) and Banks (2001).

Ethnographic or participant observation has been widely used to study social policy settings. For example, there are ethnographic accounts of social work settings and child care teams (Pithouse 1997; White 2001; Scourfield 2003), homelessness (Hall 2003), and young people, the youth service and youth training (Willis 1977; Bates and Riseborough 1994; Hall *et al.* 1999). There is a long tradition of ethnographic work within educational and medical settings (for example, see Dingwall 1977; Ball 1981; Melia 1987; Bunton 1994; Davies 1994; Mac an Ghaill 1994). These studies have been concerned with documenting and understanding the social (policy) settings through prolonged participation in and observation of everyday events, happenings and practices.

In recent years there has been a level of critical commentary of participant observation methods, and indeed of qualitative research more generally. This has come on the back of a huge growth in the use of qualitative methods within sociology (but also within cognate disciplines such as nursing – see Latimer 2003; Holloway and Wheeler 2003). This critique has emerged primarily from within social anthropology (the natural home of ethnography), and has focused on issues of legitimacy, authority and representation (Atkinson and Coffey 1995). The so-called 'crises' that have resulted are discussed in more detail in Chapter 9, but for now it is important to note that qualitative researchers have become increasingly reflective about their practice. There have also been some lively debates, especially within educational research, about the academic rigour of some qualitative work, and the political stance of the researcher (Ball and Gewirtz 1997; Tooley 1997; Gillborn 1998; Tooley and Darby 1998). Thus, like all other methods of social investigation, ethnographic methods should be used reflexively, critically and with an awareness of their strengths and limitations. Nevertheless, they offer a means of gathering rich data about complex social worlds and social processes.

Large-scale projects using pre-specified observational schedules have also been used to study social policy settings, most notably education (for example, see Galton *et al.* 1999). Like more experimental designs, systematic observation is grounded in a particular approach to social science. There have been various critiques of the positivist paradigm on which such methods are often based (see Gage 1989). More generally, care needs to be taken over the ways in which observational or coding schedules are assembled, and of unexamined assumptions that these might contain. This could, however, be taken to demand simply the same degree of rigour and reflection that should be used in all research approaches.

It is still relatively rare to undertake primary social research based solely on permanent audio-visual recordings. It is relatively usual to audio record interviews, but less common to employ video, photography or multimedia approaches (see the next chapter for more discussion of these approaches). Occasionally social welfare case conferences have been recorded and analysed for research purposes, although there are particularly difficult professional and ethical concerns with this. Brannen (2002) reports on a project that used video in a study of children's conceptions of care. Video recording using simulated clients has also been used, although the data may be less satisfactory that the real thing (Wasoff and Dobash 1998 – see also Fook 2001 on the use of vignettes in social policy research).

Action research

This section on social research methods ends with a brief discussion of action research. Action research is an approach (or set of approaches) for undertaking social research, rather than a specific method of social investigation. There are a range of definitions that encompass action research, and it has had a number of influences. Action research can be associated with collaborative and participatory approaches to social research, feminist research, practitioner and user-led models, and advocacy work. Action research usually entails some kind of intervention or change, together with appropriate monitoring or evaluation. There is often an emphasis on reflexive practice associated with action research (Carr and Kenmis 1986; Noffke and Stevenson 1995), and such research often falls under a general emancipatory research approach, working with social actors in collaborative ways, to give 'voice' and bring about change. The *Handbook of Action Research* (Reason and Bradbury 2000) provides a good overview to the formulation and conduct of a variety of kinds of action research project and strategy.

Action research is an important part of the social policy research repertoire, not least because it provides a mechanism by which practitioners and users can practically engage with the research process. Action research projects can take a number of forms. Some aim to work *with* teachers, or social workers or carers or youth workers, or young people. Others are more explicit in empowering practitioners or users as the front-line researchers in their own right. Practitioner-led research provides the opportunity for professionals to participate as researchers, analysts and indeed catalysts for change. For example teachers-as-researchers, through an action research model, have been responsible for researching their own practice and for enacting change (see Elliott and Sarland 1995; Stronach and MacLure 1997). Equally, social work settings offer the potential for practitioners to research and evaluate their own practice (to consolidate practice or to initiate change). Fook (2001) discusses the process and development of practitioner-led, reflexive social work research practice.

Action research can also have an emancipatory or advocacy dimension, within an evaluation model. Whitmore's research project, which set out to evaluate a drop-in centre for young people, is a good example of this. This project recruited young people as researchers and promoted empowerment through social research (Whitmore and McKee 2000). The young people were involved in all stages of the project – from the research design, through data collection and analysis, to the reporting phases of the research.

The project initiated significant changes to the provision and management of the service, as well as empowering the young people themselves. Whitmore (2001: 98) comments on the potential of this kind of research within social work settings: 'most social workers do not think of research as a place where we can support marginalized groups or influence social institutions. Yet it is one place where we can "make a difference".'

Action research programmes have been subjected to critical assessment. Concerns that have been voiced include the ethics of using action research as a kind of 'natural' experiment to initiate and evaluate change and the actual success of action research to bring about long-term change (many action research projects report little, and/or mainly short-term change). Stronach and MacLure (1997) have also explored the roles of practitioners within the action research process, through an assessment of the 'teachers-as-researchers' project in the UK. This project mapped educational teacher action research, and included life history interviews with key actors of the UK teacher-centred action research movement. Stronach and MacLure highlight the ways in which teacher-researchers occupy a hinterland or border between the academy and the practitioner, or between theory and practice. They refer to action research as a 'boundary dweller' (p. 128), and its project as 'reversing the poles of the old dichotomies', so that practice gets privileged over theory, the practitioner over the researcher, or as 'seeking reconciliation, in which the interests of those who previously lived antagonistically on opposite sides of the boundary will find a new space in which their differences can be resolved or dissolved' (p. 129). Shaw and Gould (2001) address the role of practitioner research within social work, and the possibilities and limitations of this for practice and empowerment. More generally, there has been some critique of the practitioner research movement, with comments ranging from theoretical and methodological naivety through to uncertainties about the capacity of such research to benefit practice or influence policy (Atkinson and Delamont 1993; Hammersley 1993; Bloor 1997). However, it can equally be argued that finding ways of effectively engaging practitioners and clients in research is good practice, even if this does not necessarily result in change.

The aim of this section as a whole has been to heighten awareness of research strategies that can and have been used to pursue social policy research. Issues of method and methodology have been rather peripheral to the discourses of social policy, and have not been seen as central elements of a social policy curriculum. Nevertheless, the empirical basis of the discipline should demand that social policy students and scholars work with/in a variety of approaches and be(come) reflexive researchers. The final section of this chapter engages with some of the contemporary research discourses, and considers the location of social policy within them. It also provides a precursor to the next chapter, where debates about the (re)presentation of social research are addressed.

Feminism, postmodernism and social (policy) research

Social research, as a form of scientific inquiry, has featured within contemporary feminist discourses. Feminist critiques of social research (and indeed of social science more generally) have recognized the importance of gender as an analytical category, and the ways in which gender can impact upon the choice of research programme, research strategy and modes of analysis (Scott 1985). Feminist scholars have argued that the ideologies of gender structure the social relations of research and the patterns of interaction that take place during research (Maynard and Purvis 1993). These arguments can be located within a broader philosophical debate (within and beyond the social sciences), about the nature of knowledge and scientific enquiry (see Harding 1987; Neilsen 1990).

Since the 1970s there has been some re-examination of 'scientific' assumptions that have guided social research and its outcomes. In part this has been concerned with disrupting some of the established dichotomies that have underpinned the nature of 'scientific inquiry' – for example, distinctions between objectivity and subjectivity, reason and emotionality, and science and rhetoric. The intellectual movements of the 1990s, under the auspices of postmodernism and poststructuralism, have contributed to this debate. These movements enable a rethinking of the aims and outcomes of social research and the production of knowledge. They are embedded in an understanding that there are no universal 'truths' to be discovered, and that all knowledge – grounded in human society – is situated, partial, local, temporal and historically specific.

These insights can be potentially disabling for the social research agenda, throwing as they do the objective foundations for knowledge into some doubt. More productively, perhaps, they can also be considered as empowering of new methods, modes and agendas for social research and knowledge creation. Hence they can provide new research and discursive spaces. The opportunities that these insights offer for social policy research have been explored throughout this volume (see, for example, the discussion of feminism and social policy in Chapter 3, and Chapter 6 on social policy and the body). Considering the local, situational and experiential construction of everyday knowledge can promote new understandings – for example, of the ways in which social identity and the body are (re)produced within social work departments (Scourfield 2003); or how educational policies of parental choice are experienced by mothers (David, West and Ribbens 1994); or how 'informal' care constructs gendered inequities *and* identities (Ungerson 1987).

Contemporary critiques of social research have also paid attention to the researcher self and the relationships between researcher and researched (Stanley and Wise 1990). This has enabled social research to be (re)cast as emotional and (auto)biographical work, and indeed for the self to be seen as a legitimate strategy of inquiry (see Chapter 9 for more on autobiography and social research). More generally still, feminist and postmodern discourses have served to discount the myth that social research can ever be 'neutral' or 'hygienic', and to understand the personal and political dimensions of research encounters. Hence such perspectives, and the conversations they have prompted, have contributed to a demystification of social research, and to an understanding that social inquiry is personal, emotional, sensitive, reflexive and situated in cultural contexts. Such a reformulation can be seen as particularly relevant to a social policy research agenda – where, for example, the researcher is personally engaged with social policy and welfare services as client, consumer or practitioner, or where they can personally relate to the experiences that are being recounted, or where vulnerable or marginalized social actors are being interviewed, or where difficult or painful subjects are being researched. It is easy to think of social policy research as being about 'dry' policy processes, and perhaps paying less attention to the ways in which social policy is peopled and experienced.

Thus far I have said little about actual methods or modes of social research in this section. There is no consensus about the applicability (or not) of particular social research methods for feminist or postmodern research praxis. Indeed, postmodern and poststructural engagements with the research process have worked at creating spaces in and between conventional research distinctions. Feminist engagement with research methods in the 1970s drew a distinction between approaches that were quantitative (as hard/masculine) and qualitative (as soft/feminine). However, this distinction artificially divides the strengths and weaknesses of different approaches, and does not engage sufficiently with the processes and praxis of research (Maynard, 1996). Equally limiting, perhaps, is the definition of feminist study as 'by', 'for' and 'about' women (Bowles and Duelli Klein 1983). While such a definition has considerable merit in acknowledging the need for a research space that hears women's voices, enables women to set research agendas, and changes women's lives, it is also problematic. Investigations of gender-power dynamics (Skelton 1998) necessarily demand consideration of men and masculinities as well as women and femininities. Thinking simply in terms of by, for and about women can result in failure to take account of the gender-power dimensions of the research process and praxis. While feminists have increasingly paid attention to issues of epistemology and methodology, Stanley and Wise's (1990) position that no one set of methods or techniques, nor broad category of type of method, should be seen as distinctly feminist is an increasingly agreed position. From this perspective (feminist) research praxis is not about particular methods or techniques, but rather about the methodological framing, outcomes and reflections of research and the research process.

Conclusion

Research strategies and methodological considerations have long been a routine element of sociological academic training and activities. Sociological engagement with research methods can be viewed as dynamic and fluid, rather than fixed or static. The methodological turn in the social sciences has prompted a reconsideration of research approaches and their contributions to the production of knowledge. Quantitative research to some extent laid the foundations of sociological inquiry, and certainly dominated mainstream social research practice until the 1960s. The latter decades of the twentieth century saw a burgeoning of qualitative work – in sociology and in allied disciplines, and an accompanying need for a broader research training. Further shifts are now evident. For example, on the one hand we are seeing experimentation with alternative research genres (see Chapter 9), while on the other hand doubts are currently being raised about the capacity of students and scholars to engage with and undertake rigorous quantitative work. Ironically the 'qualitative' turn in the social sciences may have led to a paucity of good quantitative texts, and a reluctance on the part of many social science students to 'do numbers'. This is really a question of balance, and of ensuring that social science practitioners are well versed in a range of methodological skills. However, the new moral panic about a fear of numbers could result in the re-emphasis of the value of quantitative work, and the repositioning of qualitative methods at the periphery.

There has certainly been a move to increasingly document, codify and teach social research methods across the range of social science disciplines. Social research methods occupy a well-defined space within the knowledge and skills of sociology. It is rare indeed to find a sociology programme that does not have a distinctive research methods element; all major sociology textbooks deal with practical advice on research practice and issues of methodology. Sociological research methods texts have also grown in their own right. Social policy scholars need to become similarly skilled in the range of research approaches, and to appreciate social research methods and knowledges as part of the curriculum, skills and knowledge base of social policy as an academic discipline. Similarly the broader methodological and epistemological debates are ones in which social policy could (and should) engage. There has been a sustained sociological engagement with relationships between social research and (for example) feminism, postmodernism, poststructuralism, and with issues of (for example) reflexivity, biography, validity and representation. These engagements have been more apparent within some circles than others (on the whole qualitative researchers have taken part in these debates more than those working mainly with quantitative approaches), and have been by no means universally embraced – in terms of practice or indeed teaching. Nevertheless it would now be considered unusual to omit such debates from discussions of method, and from methodological commentary.

In conclusion, it could be argued that social policy as a discipline has not systematically and enthusiastically embraced the methodological turn that has been so visible in sociology. This is not an argument that social policy does not engage with social research and the empirical world. On the contrary by its very nature social policy is a discipline with a strong empirical base, and an inherent reliance on collecting and evaluating data of various kinds. However, there is perhaps more to be done, both in recognizing this methodological and empirical base, and in making the research capacity building task a more explicit part of the future development of social policy as a social science discipline.

Further reading

Denscombe, M. (1998) *The Good Research Guide*. Buckingham: Open University Press, and Denscombe, M. (2002) *Ground Rules for Good Research*. Buckingham: Open University Press. Together these texts provide user-friendly guides to conducting small-scale research projects.

Gilbert, N. (ed.) (2001) *Researching Social Life*, 2nd edn. London: Sage. A comprehensive edited collection that takes the reader through research design, ethical concerns, data collection, data analysis and writing. Each chapter has a suggested project task and there are sensible suggestions for further reading.

May, T. (2001) *Social Research*, 3rd edn. Buckingham: Open University Press. This is a good, accessible research methods text that considers the issues, methods and processes associated with the conduct of social scientific research. It offers a good combination of practical advice and engagement with contemporary methodological debate.

chapter

nine

Representing Social Policy

Introduction

Debates over the relationships between social research and postmodernism have become part of the contemporary sociological discourse. In particular, attention has increasingly been paid to the ways in which postmodernism potentially alters the ways in which research is conceived and represented. Stronach and MacLure (1997) have recognized the inherent difficulty in offering a single view of research in the face of postmodern diversity. It is possible to argue that the multiple positionings and 'truths' offered by postmodernism can render all social research problematic, offering a 'kaleidoscope of changing patterns and perspectives that allow us little or no confidence to assume that one interpretation of the social world can claim epistemological superiority over any other' (Porter 2002: 58). However, Stronach and MacLure (1997) suggest that the varied approaches and perspectives that are potentially offered by postmodern perspectives be more positively embraced. It is certainly the case that postmodern approaches do offer a variety of frameworks and resources for rethinking the research process. They also encourage a reflexive approach to issues such as language, power and identity within research endeavours. In attempting to articulate the spaces offered by postmodernism and poststructuralism, Stronach and MacLure (1997) present a number of new ways of thinking about research design, analysis, and representation. They argue that social scientific research needs to address the issues, problems and opportunities put forward by a range of new perspectives, including postmodernism, poststructualism, (post)feminism and postcolonialism/new racial theory.

This chapter explores some of the consequences of these perspectives for social research within social policy. In particular, the chapter focuses on the ways in which the representation of social research has been challenged by contemporary research discourses. As was noted in Chapter 3, social policy as a discipline has sat relatively uneasily with postmodernism and related movements (Taylor Gooby 1994; Carter 1998). Various reasons have been suggested for the caution with which social policy has embraced postmodernist ideas. It is certainly the case that, as a set of ideas postmodernism has been developed outside the borders of social policy, in other (although allied) disciplines (Carter 1998). The various 'textual embodiments' of postmodernism have also been seen by some social policy commentators as being 'too diverse, disparate, incoherent and inconsistent to be of value' to social policy (Gibbins 1998: 31). In this chapter a more positive stance is adopted, allowing these perspectives to be considered as an opportunity for reconceptualizing social policy research. It is possible to draw on the social research debates that have emerged out of general postmodern discourses – for example, around issues of representation, identity, biography – in order to consider alternative or complementary futures for social policy research practice. At a more practical level, social policy researchers should at least be aware of these debates, in order that they can make informed choices about social research praxis.

The chapter is organized around four main themes or sets of issues.

- Firstly, contemporary debates about representation within social research are briefly outlined. This sets a context for the chapter, and highlights the ways in which the products of our research endeavours are both personal and political. These debates have mainly been located within qualitative research (and specifically within social anthropology and to a lesser extent sociology), although they do have a wider relevance to social research more generally.
- Secondly, the so-called 'biographical' turn within sociology is outlined, and the related debates about the self and identity construction explored.
- Thirdly, some of the consequences or outcomes of the debates over representation and the self are discussed. In particular, this section addresses alternative and experimental forms of writing and representation that have emerged over recent years. These 'new' modes are described and examples given (from social policy research where possible).
- Fourthly, the chapter ends with a consideration of the role of new technologies within the research landscape. We have become familiar with the role of computer software in the analysis of research data (both quantitative and qualitative). However, technological innovations such as hypermedia and hypertext applications offer potential new directions and futures for social (policy) research.

Representing research

The writing and representation of social research have become topics for critique and debate over recent years. In general these are issues that have preoccupied the qualitative research community more than those working within quantitative traditions. Some disciplines have also contributed to the dialogue more than others. Social anthropology, and to a lesser extent sociology, have more readily engaged in debate about authorship and authority. Disciplines such as social policy and education have paid significantly less attention to these issues (Coffey 2001).

Debates about writing and representation have revolved around four main themes. Firstly, the art or craft of writing has been identified as an important aspect of the social research process. Attention has increasingly been given to the ways in which researchers-as-authors represent their ideas and data in textual form. This has led to a greater appreciation of the practical or craft skills of research writing, and a recognition of the conventions in which these are embedded. It has encouraged a more self-conscious approach to research writing – both in terms of authorship and in terms of reading (Richardson 1990; Hammersley 1991; Ely *et al.* 1997; Zerubavel 1999; Gilbert 2001). Secondly, the positioning of the self within the research text has been revealed, and become an issue for critical reflection. This has recognized and acknowledged that research texts are authored just like any other texts, and hence can contain within them the life, experiences and positions of the author. This has questioned whether it is possible (or desirable) to adopt the stance of the neutral narrator or silent author of social research (Charmaz and Mitchell 1997). This has also encouraged an exploration of the relationships between (auto)biography, the articulation of the self and research writing in general. Exploring the relationships between the research process, the writing process and the self captures some of the emotional and personal aspects of social research, as well as drawing attention more generally to issues around authorship and authenticity.

Thirdly, the relationships between knowledge, power and (research) texts have been foreshadowed within debates over representation. This recognizes that research writing is actually about the creation (production) and transmission (reproduction) of knowledge. The responsibility of the author to 'translate' data into readable representational (usually textual) formats carries with it implied powers and authority – to decide what is relevant, and how texts will be constructed and stories told. Hence texts are not neutral in themselves, but can be used to exert, confirm, give or take power. Texts can be disempowering or empowering, can exploit or 'give voice' (Hertz 1997). Fourth and last, the writing styles that have conventionally been adopted by social researchers to reproduce, represent and transmit their data have been subjected to critical scrutiny. Some have suggested that these encourage rather thin, one-dimensional accounts (Atkinson 1990), or accounts that only convey a single point of view (of the researcher-as-author). In turn, this has led to some calls for a greater variety of research texts, in order that more justice can be done to complex social worlds and multiple perspectives.

As has already been noted, most of the debate and critique about writing and representation have come from within the auspices of qualitative research. Indeed, there has been little written about writing and representation from scholars working within quantitative traditions. This to some extent reflects the natural science or positivist paradigm within which many quantitative researchers work, but could also be viewed as a reluctance to engage in critical reflection, or perhaps more likely an assumption that the debates going on within qualitative circles have little wider relevance. This is a vexed point. Some of the general issues that are raised, for example about power, authority and authorship, must be addressed by all of those engaged in social research – as practitioners and authors (not least because all research writing is about persuading a readership about the plausibility of the 'story' being told – see Gilbert 2001). Equally, of course, it does social science research no favours to engage in debates about writing, if this is at the expense of a consideration of other important factors, as Flick (1998: 249) notes: 'in favouring the discussion about writing in the research, one must neither give up the discussion about quality in research – and not only that of a good and credible text – nor reduce the emphasis on research practice'. Bearing such a caution in mind, it is still the case that issues of representation have become widely debated, certainly within some parts of the social science research community. The themes that have been outlined thus far can be located within what has sometimes been termed a crisis of representation.

The crisis of representation

The publication of *Writing Culture* (Clifford and Marcus 1986) is conventionally taken as the start of a greater reflexivity in social research writing. This edited collection, the outcome of a research seminar, is built on the earlier work of Geertz (1973 and 1983). The authors in this collection of essays addressed the issue of representation – primarily in qualitative or ethnographic work. This volume served as a reminder that research writing incorporates both politics and poetics (both present in the subtitle to the volume). It acknowledged that all writing is authored and historically and culturally situated (political), and that authors draw upon a range of literary and rhetoric devices ('poetic' conventions). *Writing Culture* fuelled debates over cultural representation and suggested the need for more dialogic, innovative and reflexive approaches to writing. The collection promoted a more self-conscious and critical approach to authoritative research texts, suggesting that researchers' claims to 'textual' authority should be open to question.

Some commentators have suggested that *Writing Culture* was a 'profound rupture' within social research (Denzin and Lincoln 2000). However, others take a more 'evolutionary' approach. Spencer (2001: 443) in an essay on ethnography 'after postmodernism' argues, for example, that *Writing Culture* was an accident waiting to happen: 'many ethnographers in the generation of fieldworkers trained in the late 1970s and early 1980s had simply ceased to believe in the models of scientific and textual authority provided by our disciplinary ancestors'.

This questioning and rethinking of research texts is readily associated with postmodernist and poststructuralist agendas. Indeed, as Denzin and Lincoln (2000) argue, the crisis of representation can be seen alongside other crises confronting contemporary social researchers (for example, crises of legitimation or research practice), all of which are embedded within discourses of postmodernism and poststructuralism. However, there is no need to subscribe wholly to these discourses in order to accept the issues that are highlighted. Many of the contemporary tendencies in social research writing and representation can be seen as developments of earlier perspectives, rather than radical departures from them. Woods (1996), for example, sidelines the 'postmodern turn', perceiving postmodern approaches to research and texts as logical extensions of (social) interactionist practices. Hence, like Spencer, he argues that these developments are transgressive rather than progressive – as an emergent means of expressing research. Others see such developments in much more radical terms, implying much more reflexive, self-conscious research and texts that draw on new literary and conceptual frameworks (for example, of aesthetic understanding), and more complex considerations of authorship and audience.

There have been a number of influences that have contributed both to the claim of crisis within research representation and to new ways of approaching social research writing. The 'rediscovery of rhetoric' has been cited as one such influence (Atkinson and Coffey 1995). This is a wide and diffuse intellectual movement spanning a range of disciplines, within and beyond the social sciences. The Enlightenment, as a major intellectual movement of the seventeenth and eighteenth centuries, saw a separation of rhetoric and science, in the pursuit of 'truth' and a science of society. This implied a clear distinction between two contrastive sets of commitments: on the one hand science, logic, reason, method and evidence; on the other hand art, persuasion, opinion and rhetoric. In their development, the social sciences have attempted to forge affinities with the first set of commitments in order 'to achieve its place amongst the sciences' (Flick 1998: 249). As a consequence of such a distinction, rhetorical forms have been consigned to the margins of legitimate scholarship; and thus there has long been established the desire for social scientists to be armed with a neutral and 'scientific' language, untainted by rhetoric and opinion. The 'rediscovery of rhetoric', and the recognition of rhetorical devices as part of the everyday process of writing, has had a profound impact on the way disciplinary knowledge is conceptualized. For example, scientific accounts have been recast as having rhetorical qualities and features (Law and Williams 1982; Lynch and Woolgar 1990; Lutz and Collins 1993). Moreover, the dichotomy between the 'reality' or 'truthfulness' of the natural scientific world and the narrative accounts of the social world have been problematized. Hence there has been an increasing realization of the rhetorical qualities of all (research) accounts.

The role of research texts in representing the lives and experiences of others has also been subjected to critical scrutiny. For example, Said's (1978) sustained commentary on the orientalizing tendencies of academic representation of the non-Western world makes the case that research texts can be both privileged and privileging. This draws attention to the ways in which some texts reduce *other* people and *other* cultures to what Ardener (1975) refers to as the subjugated and muted (silenced) objects of dominating discourse. The 'observer' (researcher and author) is cast as privileged ('with voice') – able to classify and write the (exotic) characteristics of an (oriental) *other*. The authority of the text is established and maintained through the production of texts of exploitation, description and classification (Marcus 1992). This set of critiques particularly refers to Western treatment of other cultures, and thus can broadly be conceptualized as postcolonial. The critique of postcolonialism is, however, of more general significance than that of race or colour or 'distant' cultures. This is really a set of arguments about the relationships we have with and how we represent *others* – in this case our research participants. Feminist scholars working within the social sciences have raised similar points. The sustained dialogue between feminism and social research has included attention to issues of representation (Jennaway 1990; Wolf 1992; Maynard 1994). The privileged positioning of author has been acknowledged and challenged by feminist theory and research praxis. The feminist critique of social research has also recognized the marginalization of women from many research accounts, and the 'pluralities of power relations' within social research (Harding 1997: 451). Feminist scholarship has thus provided a platform from which to question conventional styles of representation. Feminist epistemology challenges the traditional, masculinist and highly conventional forms of scholarly narratives. Stanley and Wise (1993), for example, locate social research writing within a hegemonic masculine framework.

> Words, sentences, writing styles, ways of presenting arguments, arguments themselves, and criticism, all these are part and parcel of masculinist culture. They are among the artefacts of sexism and their use structures our experience before we can even begin to examine it, because they provide us with how to *think* as well as how to *write*.
>
> (Stanley and Wise 1993: 179, their emphasis)

Thus, it has increasingly been recognized that authors use textual conventions in order to produce written texts, and hence that there is no neutral medium of representation. Conventions of written language are used in the reading and writing of all social research texts. In that sense the formats that academics use are *conventional*; there is no 'natural' way to write about social and cultural life. So, while we can recognize 'standard' accepted ways of writing an academic text or journal article or research report, this should not mask that these are merely drawn from a stock of conventional rhetorical devices (Gilbert 2001; Atkinson, Coffey and Delamont 2003). The authors of academic texts draw on a repertoire of conventional devices in order to construct authoritative, plausible, believable texts. Readers of academic texts also draw on the same stock of literary devices. There are, then, socially shared conventions of reading and writing that exert a major influence on the production and reception of social research; social researchers become accustomed to particular kinds of texts that are conventionally adopted to represent the results of their endeavours. Or to put it more formally, there are particular genres of writing. Van Maanen (1988) identified the common social research genre of literary realism. He characterized the realist approach as implying an impersonal, all but invisible author. This genre presents the 'story' of one (impartial) author whose point of view is the dominant (and often the only) one. It is a familiar genre of authoritative reportage. Such realist writing represents a style and a set of literary devices that are very familiar, overwhelmingly used in the reporting of social research. The point here though is that this is not the only way of (re)presenting the social world. Indeed, it is by no means clear whether this represents the best way to produce accounts of varied and complex social worlds, only that it is conventionally used. Conventional realism treats language as a taken-for-granted resource, and shows little concern for the language of representation itself. Hence the realist approach may actually result in rather *thin* descriptions (Atkinson 1990) that do not do justice to the complexity of cultural forms and social life.

Whether or not one sees this 'crisis' of representation as revolution or evolution; as a result of poststructural discourses or emergent from a wider variety of sources; as a matter for qualitative researchers or for all social researchers, there are a number of elements that can be highlighted. The conventionality of text is recognized and the path laid for alternative representations and textual forms; moreover, the researcher-as-author is made a 'visible' self. Social research texts are also highlighted as potentially privileged and privileging (and conceptualized within wider discourses of power and exploitation).

Social policy as a discipline has not readily engaged with these debates about representation and texts. This may be partly because of the caution with which social policy has (not) embraced postmodernism more generally, or because there is not a distinctive qualitative research community within social policy (even though there is plenty of social policy research that utilizes qualitative approaches). More generally, it could be argued that social policy has not systematically engaged in dialogues about method and methodology, unlike, for example, sociology or social anthropology (see Chapter 8). The issues that are raised through such dialogues are, however, relevant to social policy – as a social science discipline engaged in empirical research. Writing about and representing the social world is part of the craftwork of social policy – and hence social policy scholars, researchers and students are also authors of texts. There has not been any systematic attempt to analyse the literary conventions that social policy authors use to create plausible and readable accounts – of welfare practices, policy processes, professional encounters, the experiences of the social policy system and so forth. Equally, there has been little consideration of the ways in which social policy texts imply particular relations of power and authority. In common with other social science texts, social policy authorship is often silent and distant, yet authoritative. There needs to be a better understanding of how *others* are represented within social policy accounts. Indeed simply by referring to 'lone mothers', or the 'elderly', or the 'disabled', or the 'homeless', or the 'unemployed' there is *othering* at work – 'creating' homogeneous groups to be described, cajoled, worked with and subjected to. We need to ask how women, or black students, or lesbian teachers are represented in social policy texts, and compare these with the representations of welfare professions, students in higher education or voluntary workers. This, then is an argument for having a greater awareness of the ways in which texts (re)present power relations, social groups, everyday experiences and social processes – and for an understanding that there are textual or literary *choices* of how to write about these. Conventional styles or ways of reporting social policy research or data or ideas should not necessarily be regarded as the 'best' or only ways of representing the social (policy) world. Before going on to consider some alternative representational forms, it seems appropriate to consider a related set of issues that have emerged within social science research discourses. Sociology, in particular, has paid increasing attention to the place of the self, identity and (auto)biography within social research. These too raise important questions, and have potential consequences, for the ways in which social (policy) research is written about and represented.

Social research and the (auto)biographical turn

The social sciences in general, and sociology in particular, have increasingly focused on the ways in which self-identity is constructed and negotiated through complex social processes. This has led to what has been called the 'biographical turn' within sociological inquiry and writing. A critical exploration of the links between social science and biography (or identity), and a concern with the ways in which personal narratives and experiences can lead to fruitful data on social processes, are indicative of this approach. There has been an increasing assumption that the personal narrative is able to offer data that are grounded in both biographical experience and social contexts (Atkinson and Silverman 1997). Stanley and Morgan (1993) and others have highlighted the potential significance of biography for sociological inquiry (see Denzin 1989; Erben 1993; Plummer 1995; Ellis and Bochner 1996; Denzin 1997; Plummer 2000; Reed Danahay 2001). Identity and biography have been reconceptualized, as 'work'; as topics for investigation; as research resources; and as analytical tools (Coffey 1999). In so doing it is possible to disrupt conventional analytical distinctions, for example between structure and agency, or the individual and the collective. Hence an individual life (story) can take on a wider significance in the exploration of the social world, as Stanley and Morgan (1993: 2) explain:

> It means rejecting any notion that 'a life' can be understood as a representation of a single life in isolation from networks of interwoven biographies. In spite of the widespread assumption that autobiography is concerned with a single life, in practice it is a very rare autobiography that is not replete with the potted biographies of significant others in the subject's life.

Stanley (1992) has referred to this research approach as the biographizing of social structure, and the structuralizing of biography. She argues that, as well as documenting individual lives and identities, the biographical turn in sociological inquiry provides a strategy for exploring complex histories and biographies, as well as the relationships between structure and agency in contemporary society.

This concern with the biographical within the social sciences has taken two complementary forms;

1. A concern with the identity and biographical work of *others*. This has focused on how individuals and groups negotiate the construction and production of their identities, and the reconstruction and reproduction of their lives through biographical practices. One way in which this has manifested itself is through the increased use of life history/biographical interviews and narratives (see Silverman and Atkinson 1997);
2. The positioning of *autobiography* as part of the social research endeavour – whereby the self has become a legitimate part of research activity, writing and reflection (see, for example, Cotterill and Letherby 1993; Ellis 1995; Ronai 1996; Tillman-Healy 1996; Ellis and Bochner 2000; Reed Danahay 2001). This has encompassed writing by sociologists and others, reflecting on their work and their place within their research and writing, and more personalized, autobiographical accounts of social life.

The latter is a more recent phenomenon, and places the researcher (and their auto/biography) into the actual work and scope of social inquiry (Coffey 1999). This shifts the relations between the research process and the self – from simply making visible the personal experiences and emotions associated with (all) social research (Hammond 1964; Bell and Encel 1978; Roberts 1981; McKeganey and Cunningham-Burley 1987) to positioning the autobiographical as a basis for sociological analysis and understanding in its own right (see, for example, collections by Okely and Callaway 1992; Ellis and Bochner 1996; Wolf 1996; Ellis and Bochner 2002). Thus, so-called 'confessional' accounts (Van Maanen 1988) of what it is like to undertake research have been joined by much more nuanced understandings of the potential relationships between social research, writing and the self. Thus social research and research writing also become mechanisms for 'making sense of who we are and what it is we do' (Agar 1986: xi).

The biographical (and indeed *autobiographical*) turn within sociology has not been adopted universally or uncritically. Some commentators have pointed out that utilizing personal narratives and biographies in social research is potentially problematic (see Atkinson and Silverman 1997; Munro 1998). There is a danger of romanticizing or prioritizing the individual and their stories in biographizing the social. Hence there is a possibility of 'missing' the social contexts and processes, by overly concentrating on the individual and the personal. Thus ways always need to be sought to place personal narratives (back) into their social contexts (Goodson 1992). There has also been discussion about the extent to which, by privileging some biographies, voices and lives (for example, our own), other voices and lives may be ignored. Of course, all social research is partial and situated, but there is still a need to reflect critically upon whose story is being told. For example, there is a danger of a narcissistic preoccupation with one's own voice and life, to the detriment of those we seek to understand. Mykhalovskiy (1997) engages with this argument, and contends that autobiographical sociology *per se* is not necessarily narcissistic or self-indulgent. He suggests instead that autobiography can be productive to the ways we think about the processes of research, and in the reading and writing of research texts. Mykhalovskiy (1997) thus argues that the personal presence in the text can be a source of insightful analysis, reacting against the insularity of academic writing (see Atkinson 1997 and Bochner 2001 for further and divergent views of the place for personal narratives in social science research). Nevertheless commentators such as Munro (1998) suggest that, in embracing the biographical turn, we should remain suspicious of claims of privilege, while welcoming the new insights the approach is able to offer. If we assume that a core component of sociology is to understand individuals in social and cultural context, then the biographical turn is a useful aid to this process, though one that might be approached with caution.

A concern and belief in the personal narrative (or story) as a mechanism for understanding and making sense of social events and processes has not necessarily led to a more general acceptance (or utilization) of biography and autobiography as/in social research. It would certainly be wrong to give the impression that all social research and texts are now teeming with biographical and autobiographical insights. There has, however, been an increasing awareness of the relationships between social research and the self (De Laine 2000; Holstein and Gubrium 2000; Coffey 2002; Skeggs 2002).

Against this backdrop it is difficult to discern an auto/biographical turn within social policy. However, while social policy, as an empirical discipline, may have remained on the periphery of these debates, this is not to say that the auto/biographical turn has no relevance. The construction and maintenance of biographies and identities is central to the processes, practices, and 'people' of social policy. For example, social workers are involved in reconstructing 'identities' for their clients through narrative and case work (Pithouse 1997; Scourfield 2003), 'informal' carers engage in biographical work through their care roles and relationships (Ungerson 1990; Twigg and Adkins 1994; Twigg 2000b), young people engage in identity work through youth work practice and training provision (Bates 1994; Hall *et al.* 1999) and so on. Moreover, a critical engagement with these biographical practices could provide new perspectives – for example, on the role of welfare professionals, the evaluation of services and provision, the (unintended) consequences of welfare practices, or the ways in which the implementation of social policy is negotiated and mediated by and through different lives. The biographical turn has also drawn attention to the role of personal narratives in 'giving voice' to the range of social actors inhabiting complex social worlds. Of course, there are multiple voices present within social policy spheres – not all of which are heard equally within dominant policy discourses. Paying more attention to the biographical experiences of social policy could provide a mechanism by which more silenced voices are 'heard', and dominant discourses disrupted. The 'voices' of social policy include clients, consumers, users, policy-makers, civil servants, welfare professionals and carers (and there are multiple, stratified and differentiated voices within each of these groups) – as well as those who may fall outside its formal auspices – for example, young people not engaged in formal education, training or the labour market (Rees *et al.* 1996).

The role of the autobiographical in social policy research and representations is also one that could be developed. As with all social research, social policy research is a personal, lived experience. Social policy research is not conducted in a social or emotional vacuum. It involves researchers engaging with and in people's lives – sharing their experiences, fears, hopes, concerns and problems. Some of this may be difficult and distressing, some joyous and fulfilling, some repetitive or dull. No matter – all demonstrate an emotional connection to research endeavour. Of course, it is a different matter as to whether these should represented in final research texts. Equally, it is possible to (re)construct social policy research through and in auto-biography. Social policy processes, services and practices affect all our lives, in a myriad of ways. Life times, memories and bodies are all interwoven with/in social policy processes and everyday encounters. For example (and to be autobiographical for a moment), over the course of my lifetime I have been the recipient of unemployment and housing benefit, worked as a volunteer in a day care centre for the elderly and mentally ill, negotiated a care package for a grandparent, lived in a lone parent family, been a member of a tenants' association, helped to run a youth club, worked as a volunteer in woman's refuge, been involved in the training of social workers, been a patient of primary and hospital care, and worked as a secondary school teacher. Hence I have, like everyone else, first-hand experience of a range of social policy spheres, which I could choose to draw upon in undertaking research, or in helping me to make sense of data and biographies that I may be presented with over the course of research. Again there are method-ological choices to be made over how the autobiographical work is incorporated, used and reported upon. But what is not at issue is the autobiographical framing of social policy processes and experiences.

Alternatives and experiments

The debates over representation, and the auto/biographical turn within the social sciences, have prompted the articulation, practice and evaluation of new representational forms. There has been some experimentation, and some moves away from a sole conventional literary type. New formats and sets of textual conventions have been used and adapted by authors across a range of disciplines. Alternative representational forms for the production of scholarly work convey particular analytic and conceptual approaches to data and the production of knowledge. These alternative forms can be viewed as part of an *avant-garde* spirit of experimentation. Equally they can be seen as creative responses to the critiques of social science research writing (some of which have been outlined above). They also reflect a more general postmodernist agenda that questions how research is translated into representations and forms of knowledge production. As was noted earlier in this chapter, most conventional scholarly texts have tended to assume a single dominant voice (of the author) and have been held up as embodying an essentially 'modern' set of assumptions. That is, such texts have been predicated on a discovery of social reality through selective, unproblematic, 'scientific', acts of engagement, inspection and notation. The auspices associated with more postmodern agendas have treated the status of con-ventional texts in different ways – as *representations* of social reality that are more uncertain and problematic in nature. This approach has recognized that all representational conventions are *conventional* – and, to some extent at least, arbitrary. This recognition thus makes it possible to transgress literary boundaries and willingly seek alternative forms of representation. Textual variety becomes welcomed, and even necessary, from such perspectives. There has been the increasing utilization of various 'alternative' approaches to textual representation. These epitomize research diversity and reflect the interpretative/(auto)biographical turns. A number of commentators have argued for texts that are more open, fragmented and messy – both as a mechanism for challenging the conventionality of research writing *and* for allowing for the development of more creative, complex modes of representation (Mulkay 1985). These dynamic approaches to writing and representation have included scripts, poetry, diaries, autobiography, multi-voiced and collaborative texts. Many draw on a dialogic approach to text (Dwyer 1977; Holquist 1990; Allan 1994), and promote a more self-conscious and creative (or aesthetic) approach to writing. Some of these alternative genres also exemplify the relationships between social research and the production and writing of selves and lives (Ely *et al.* 1997).

Dialogic approaches to representation exploit the conventions of naturalistic conversation. Such approaches draw upon the poetical and theatrical qualities of everyday social life in representing social scientific data. For example, scripts have been produced drawing upon and representing interview or observational data. These have aimed to capture multiple voices and perspectives of complex social situations. Using scripts has been seen to be a particularly effective way of re-presenting sensitive or highly emotional settings or events, such as the worlds of dying children (Bluebond-Langer 1990) or the process of abortion decision making (Ellis and Bochner 1992). In some cases these scripts have been performed as theatrical events (Mienczakowski 2001). Poetry has also been used as a way of representing social research data. Richardson (2000) argues that poetry offers a mechanism of capturing the pauses, rhyme and rhythm of everyday life and conversation. The use of auto/biographical writings (such as diaries and personal reflections) has also been extended to social research (Reed Danahay 2001). This has led to a number of research accounts that have explored personal relationships, experiences and lives of authors (researchers) themselves (see Paget 1990 and 1993 on living and dying with cancer; Ellis and Bochner 1996; Bochner and Ellis 2002).

While scripts, dialogues, poetry and similar genres have not been used extensively within social policy research, there are examples that draw upon some of the spaces, themes and experiences of social policy. For example, Mienczakowski (2001) has used performance and theatre to (re)present qualitative data on the experiences of people undergoing detoxification, the experiences of schizophrenic illness (performed in a residential psychiatric setting) and police officers' relationships to the victims of crime. Mienczakowski (2001: 471) argues that, via scripting, 'rehearsals' and performance, researchers may be able to provide 'more accessible and clearer public explanations of research than is frequently the case with traditional, written report texts'. Other relevant examples include Fox (1996) who presents a multi-layered text of the experiences of child sexual abuse (interweaving the voices of survivors, abuser and researcher) and Rath (1999) who uses a mixture of scripts and poetry to (re)tell stories of rape crisis training. These works all have a storied quality to them. Stories more generally can also be used to write about the social (policy) world. For example, England (1994) explores the experiences of Alzheimer carers through fiction and auto/biography; Kolker's essay, written in auto/biographical diary form, presents a personal account of health-care rationing (Kolker 1996); White (2001) also engages in auto/biographical work, researching and writing about the child care social work team of which she was a member; Angrosino (1998) uses creative fiction in his account of a residential care setting.

Collaborative approaches to research writing also offer the potential for innovative representations within social policy. It has become increasingly important to engage potential users of research in the research process. UK research councils and other bodies (such as charities) that fund research explicitly encourage and expect this engagement, and there is no reason why this should not include collaboration on writing as well as reading. Action research, an approach that is often used in social policy inquiry, is well placed to encourage writing collaborations between academics and welfare practitioners, users and clients. Indeed in some empirical areas where there is a tradition of action research, there have been fruitful research collaborations between practitioners and researcher. For example, educational research has often fostered joint projects between teachers and researchers, although these have not always culminated in collaborative writing projects (see Haw 1998 as an example of innovative collaborative writing in education). Promoting the 'voice' of the user within social policy research could also foster collaborative writing endeavours, although projects to date have rarely included the joint production of texts as part of the agenda (Pithouse and Williamson 1997; Evans and Fisher 1999).

Despite these examples, there is little sign of a wide engagement with innovative and creative texts within social policy research. However, it should also be noted that alternative genres of representation are also not widely used within the sociological research community. Experimental social science texts remain confined to rather small networks of researchers. A relatively small number of peer-reviewed journals explicitly encourage and publish contributions that are in unconventional forms. There are a few research groupings (mainly though not exclusively in North American) and associated edited collections of papers that actively promote alternative and experimental texts. Monographs that reflect new forms of representation are still rather few and far between, mostly restricted to the lists of a small number of publishing houses. In other words, there has not been a major revolution or paradigm shift in the representation of social research.

However, creative approaches to the production of research texts can aid and promote a reflexive and self-conscious approach to textual production and the creation of knowledge. Sparkes (1995) has argued that alternative writing genres can create opportunities for more realistic pictures of events to be presented. Moreover he suggests that they can also be used blur the power boundaries between researcher and researched. This is not, however, a universally agreed view, even by those who have engaged in and practised different modes of representation. Lather (1991), for example, has argued that alternative representative forms do not necessarily remove the issue of power from the production of research, but may shift it somewhat. The so-called crisis of representation and its aftermath was, in part at least, a critique of the monologic, authorial voice of the researcher-as-author. New writing formats (such as poetry scripts or fiction) disrupt this and provide opportunities for more messy and multi-vocal texts. However, turning social science data into poetry or drama also re-emphasises the individual researcher as a writer or author (or poet or playwright). If a life-history, for example, is to be re-presented as a poem, or if a series of social encounters is to be re-constructed into a drama, then the 'voices' that might inhabit that work are still pressed into service to serve the author's own interests and are re-presented at the author's own choosing. So there is a balance to be struck between representing the social world in collaborative, sensitive and indeed innovative ways, and ensuring that research accounts do not just become a vehicle for literary experimentation (for its own sake), poor poetry, bad plays or autobiographical 'therapy'.

The aim of this section has not been to suggest that all social (policy) researchers should experiment with alternative writing genres, but they should certainly be aware of their possibilities and limitations. In so far as there is a message here for social policy scholars it is that they should be (more) mindful of the conventionality of the texts that they produce and of the messages that are conveyed through their texts. Alternative styles of writing are partly a response to a genuine concern about authority and authorship within the social sciences, and this is something with which social policy must engage. Thinking more creatively about writing does not fully address these concerns. However, it does serve to make explicit the authorship of social research. It can also be a liberating experience and open up new opportunities for representing complex and polyvocal social (policy) worlds.

Hypermedia and social research

In the twenty-first century it would be an omission to discuss the representation of social research without including something on the technological possibilities. Technological advancement offers the potential to rethink social research *and* representation. Computer software has long been used for the analysis of quantitative data, and is increasingly utilized for the analysis of qualitative data (Weitzman 2000; Fielding 2001). As well as helping with the tasks of data management and data analysis, it is also possible to conceptualize contemporary technology in terms of its representative potential for the social researcher. Computer and information technology offer ways of increasing the representational diversity and flexibility available for the production of research texts (Dicks *et al.* 2004). The use of hypertext applications, for example, increases the ways in which research data can be presented (on the page or 'screen'), and the ways in which those data can be read (or 'navigated'). Hypertext enables several 'texts' to be stored and accessed at any one time. This lends itself to multi-layered texts and to the simultaneous representation of different documents and accounts. Hence, hypertext applications can support a much more complex and messy representation of texts than, for example, the conventional written scholarly monograph or journal article. Hypertext is also an interactive medium. This means that the reader can potentially navigate his or her own path through the texts that are presented, choosing which 'links ' to follow and hence the order of the pages or 'screens'. Varieties of data and analyses can thus be presented to the 'reader'. This means that readers can see how analyses are derived from the data, and indeed 'write' their own interpretations. This thus presents the opportunity to make social research analyses more transparent. Hypermedia applications expand these possibilities further, by adding non-textual possibilities of representing – such as moving images, sound and pictures. Hypermedia can allow a more complex authoring and reading environment to be created. Social research data are increasingly collected through a variety of modes – such as video, film, photography, audio recording and graphics (Ball and Smith 2001; Banks 2001; Pink 2001). Hypermedia is a way of being able to retain this variety in the 'writing' and representation of those data, by allowing 'texts' to be authored in multi-media.

The use of hypertext and hypermedia applications for the representation of social research is still relatively new (Dicks and Mason 1998), and has thus far not been exploited by social policy researchers. Dey (1993) particularly welcomed the use of hypertext for the management, retrieval and analysis of (qualitative) data, but did not really discuss or illustrate the use of a hypertext/hypermedia strategy for the writing, reading and representation of research more generally. One of the most exciting possibilities of hypertext and hypermedia software may lay precisely in its capacities to support new forms of representation. These forms of technological advancement are capable of adding to the debates and innovations about the representation of social research. Representational innovation such as that offered by computer technology removes the focus solely on the conventional written text, thus contributing to a more creative approach to social research and the production of knowledge. Hypermedia and hypertext strategies could well extend the possibilities for multi-voiced, multi-visual, multi-authored texts. They also have the capacity to challenge power relations between authors, readers and users of social research, and can certainly contribute to a more self-conscious approach to representing the social world. Fielding (2001) suggests that hypertext raises 'intriguing possibilities' for social research, allowing for different and varied readings of social research 'texts'. However, he adds a caveat that may well have implications for the future use of hypertext within social policy research. He argues that these new applications may have less appeal in areas of applied research, where 'policy makers may feel that researchers are already too equivocal, and regard the invitation to "make their own sense of the data" as an abdication of responsibility rather than an opportunity to celebrate the postmodern turn' (Fielding 2001: 463).

Conclusion

This chapter has provided an overview of some of the contemporary debates within social science research, particularly those relating to issues of representation. Sociological work has increasingly engaged with these debates. It would be wrong to suggest that there has been a wide scale adoption of alternative representational genre, nevertheless the relationships between sociology and autobiography continue to be explored (Plummer 2001). Sociological authors are becoming increasingly aware of their authoring practices; and sociological research practice is beginning to work with/in technological frames for data collection, analysis and representation. There are a few examples of auto/biographical social policy practice, and some innovative social science texts that draw broadly on social policy topics and themes. However, as a discipline, social policy has not yet systematically engaged with these debates, innovations and developments. While representation and voice may be implicitly a routine part of social policy practice, the debates over authorship, writing and the representation of research and selves are not yet part of the scholarly agenda of social policy. The social science concern with representation is a response not only to critique from within the disciplines. It also addresses more general questions – for example, about the nature of evidence, the authority of the researcher and the text, ethical and political stances, the possibilities for generalization, and the role of the self in the research process. These are all questions that should concern researchers working in social policy. Thus if we are to enhance the research capacity of social policy there needs to be a more critical engagement with these questions.

Further reading

Becker, H. (1986) *Writing for Social Scientists*. Chicago: Chicago University Press. A wonderful book that shares the agonies and ecstasies of social scientific writing – with cartoons, jokes and anecdotes.

Ellis, C. and Bochner, A.P. (eds) (1996) *Composing Ethnography*. Walnut Creek, CA: Altamira. A collection of innovative 'writings', which illustrate the opportunities for social scientists to engage in a wide range of representational work. The pieces include poetry, scripts, multi-voiced texts, autobiography and photographic essays.

Richardson, L. (1990) *Writing Strategies: Reaching Diverse Audiences*. Newbury Park, CA: Sage. Explores how the same data can be crafted into different texts for different audiences. Provides a good example of the relationship between analysis, writing and the production of knowledge.

References

Abbott, P. and Wallace, C. (2000) *An Introduction to Sociology: Feminist Perspectives*. London: Routledge.

Adam, B. (1990) *Time and Social Theory*. Oxford: Polity.

Adam, B. (1992) There is more to time in education than calendars and clocks, in M. Morrison (ed.) *Managing Time for Education*, CEDAR working papers series, Coventry: University of Warwick.

Adam, B. (1995) *Timewatch*. Cambridge: Polity.

Advisory Group on Citizenship (1998) *Education for Citizenship and the Teaching of Democracy in Schools*. London: Qualifications and Curriculum Authority.

Agar, M. (1986) Foreword to T.L. Whithead and M.E. Conway (eds) *Self, Sex and Gender in Cross Cultural Fieldwork*. Urbana, IL: University of Illinois Press.

Ahmed, B. (1992) *Black Perspectives in Social Work*. Birmingham: Venture Press.

Alcock, C., Payne, S. and Sullivan, M. (2004) *Introducing Social Policy*. Harlow: Pearson Education.

Alcock, P., Erskine, A. and May, M. (eds) (2003) *The Student's Companion to Social Policy*. Oxford: Blackwell.

Aldridge, A. and Levine, K. (2001) *Surveying the Social World: Principles and Practice in Survey Research*. Buckingham: Open University Press.

Allan, S. (1994) 'When discourse is torn from reality': Bakhtin and the principle of chronlogoplicity, *Time and Society*, 3: 193–218.

Andrews, G. (ed.) (1991) *Citizenship*. London: Lawrence and Wishart.

Angrosino, M. (1998) *Opportunity House: Ethnographic Stories of Mental Retardation*. Walnut Creek, CA: Altamira.

Annandale, E. and Hunt, K. (2000) *Gender Inequalities in Health*. Buckingham: Open University Press.

Arber, S. and Ginn, J. (eds) (1995) *Connecting Gender and Ageing: A Sociological Approach*. Buckingham: Open University Press.

Ardener, S. (ed.) (1975) *Perceiving Women*. London: J.M. Dent.

Arnot, M., David, M. and Weiner, G. (1999) *Closing the Gender Gap*. Cambridge: Polity.

Atkinson, P.A. (1990) *The Ethnographic Imagination*. London: Routledge.

Atkinson, P.A. (1997) Narrative turn or blind alley?, *Qualitative Health Research*, 7: 325–44.

Atkinson, P.A. and Coffey, A. (1995) Realism and its discontents: on the crisis of cultural representation in ethnographic texts, in B. Adam and S. Allan (eds), *Theorizing Culture: An Interdisciplinary Critique after Post-Modernism*. London: UCL Press.

Atkinson, P., Coffey, A., Delamont, S., Lofland, J. and Lofland, L. (eds) (2001) *Handbook of Ethnography*. London: Sage.

Atkinson, P., Coffey, A. and Delamont, S. (2003) *Key Themes in Qualitative Research*. Walnut Creek, CA: Altamira.

Atkinson, P. and Delamont, S. (1993) Bread and dreams or bread and circuses: A critique of case study research in evaluation, in M. Hammersley (ed.) *Controversies in the Classroom*. Milton Keynes: Open University Press.

Atkinson, P. and Housley, W. (2003) *Interactionism*. London: Sage.

Atkinson, P.A. and D. Silverman (1997) Kundera's *Immortality*: the interview society and the invention of the self, *Qualitative Inquiry*, 3: 304–25.

Atkinson, R. (2002) The life story interview, in J.F. Gubrium and J.A. Holstein (eds) *Handbook of Interview Research*. Thousand Oaks, CA: Sage.

Bacchi, C.L. (1996) *The Politics of Affirmative Action*. London: Sage.

Bailey, C.A. (1998) *A Guide to Field Research*. Thousand Oaks, CA: Pine Forge.

Baines, C.T., Evans P.M. and Neysmith, S.M. (eds) (1998) *Women's Caring: Feminist Perspectives on Social Welfare*. Oxford: Oxford University Press.

Bakeman, R. and Gottman, J.M. (1997) *Observing Interaction: An Introduction to Sequential Analysis*. Cambridge: Cambridge University Press.

Balbo, L. (1987) Crazy quilts, in A.S. Sassoon, (ed.) *Women and the State*. London: Hutchinson.

Baldock, J., Manning, N., Miller, S. and Vickerstaff, S. (eds) (1999) *Social Policy*. Oxford: Oxford University Press.

Baldwin, S. and Twigg, J. (1991) Women and community care; reflections on a debate, in M. MacLean and D. Groves (eds) *Women's Issues in Social Policy*. London: Routledge.

Ball, M. and Smith, G. (2001) Technologies of realism? Ethnographic uses of photography and film, in P. Atkinson, A. Coffey, S. Delamont, J. Lofland and L. Lofland (eds) *Handbook of Ethnography*. London: Sage.

Ball, S.J. (1981) *Beachside Comprehensive*. Cambridge: Cambridge University Press.

Ball, S.J. and Gewirtz, S. (1997) A rejoinder to Tooley's 'On school and social class', *British Journal of Sociology of Education*, 18(4): 575–86.

Banks, M. (2001) *Visual Methods in Social Research*. London: Sage.

Banks, O. (1981) *Faces of Feminism*. Oxford: Martin Robertson.

Barbalet, J.M. (1988) *Citizenship*. Milton Keynes: Open University Press.

Barbour, R.S. and Kitzinger, J. (1999) *Developing Focus Group Research: Politics, Theory and Practice*. London: Sage.

Bates, I. (1990) No bleeding, whining minnies: the role of YTS in class and gender reproduction, *British Journal of Education and Work*, 3: 91–110.

Bates, I. (1993) A job which is 'right for me'?, in I. Bates and G. Riseborough (eds) *Youth and Inequality*. Buckingham: Open University Press.

Bates, I. and Riseborough, G. (1994) *Youth and Inequality*. Buckingham: Open University Press.

Bauman, Z. (1993) *Postmodern Ethics*. Oxford: Basil Blackwell.

Beck, J. (1996) Citizenship education: problems and possibilities, *Curriculum Studies*, 4 (3): 349–66.

Beck, U. (1992) *Risk Society*. London: Sage.

Beck, U. (1994) The reinvention of politics: towards a theory of reflexive modernization, in U. Beck, A. Giddens and S. Lash (eds), *Reflexive Modernization*. Cambridge: Polity Press.

Becker, H.S. (1970) *Sociological Work*. Chicago: Aldine.

Bell, A., Nicholls, D., Parker, B. and Williamson, H. (1994) *Planning for a Sufficient Youth Service*. Coventry: Sufficiency Working Group.

Bell, C. and Encel, S. (eds) (1978) *Inside the Whale*. Oxford: Pergamon.

Benn, T. (2002) *Free at Last: Diaries 1991–2001*. London: Arrow.

Bennett, C. (2000) Equal opportunities strategies: ways of developing feminist embodiment as a physical reality in bureaucracies, in L. McKie and N. Watson (eds) *Organizing Bodies: Policy, Institutions and Work*. Basingstoke: Macmillan.

Bernstein, B. (2003) *Class, Codes and Control*. London: Routledge.

Berthoud, R. and Gershuny, J. (eds) (2000) *Seven Years in the Lives of British Families: Evidence on the Dynamics of Social Change from the British Household Panel Survey*. Bristol: Policy Press.

Bett, M. (1995) *Great Britain Independent Review of Higher Education Pay and Conditions*. London: HMSO.

Billington, R., Hockey, J. and Strawbridge, S. (1998) *Exploring Self and Society*. London: Macmillan.

Bilton, T., Bonnett, K., Jones, P., Skinner, D., Stanworth, M. and Webster, A. (1996) *Introductory Sociology*. Basingstoke: Macmillan.

Blakemore, K. and Boneham, M. (1994) *Age, Race and Ethnicity*. Buckingham: Open University Press.

Blakemore, K. and Drake, R.F. (1996) *Understanding Equal Opportunity Policies*. London: Prentice Hall.

Bloor, M. (1997) Addressing social problems through qualitative research, in D. Silverman (ed.) *Qualitative Research*. London: Sage.

Bloor, M. Frankland, J., Thomas, M. and Robson, K. (2000) *Focus Groups in Social Research*. London: Sage.

Bluebond-Langer, M. (1980) *The Private Worlds of Dying Children*. Princeton, NJ: Princeton University Press.

Bochner, A. and Ellis, C. (eds) (2002) *Ethnographically Speaking*. Walnut Creek, CA: Altamira.

Booth, C. (1901–2) *Life and Labour of the People of London*. London: Macmillan.

Boston Women's Health Collective (1973) *Our Bodies, Ourselves*. Harmondsworth: Penguin.

Boulton, P. and Coldron, J. (1998) Why women say 'stuff it' to promotion, *Gender and Education*, 10(2): 149–62.

Bourdieu, P. (1990) *In Other Words: Essays Towards a Reflexive Sociology* (translated by M. Adamson). Cambridge: Polity.

Bowles, G. and Duelli Klein, R. (eds) (1983) *Theories of Women's Studies*. London: Routledge and Kegan Paul.

Bown, L. (1999) Beyond the degree: men and women at the decision-making levels in British higher education, *Gender and Education*, 11(1): 5–26.

Bradshaw, J. and Sainsbury, R. (eds) (2000) *Experiencing Poverty*. Aldershot: Ashgate.

Brain, K. (1998) *In Pursuit of Parenthood: Experiences of IVF*. London: Bloomsbury.

Brannen, J. (2002) The use of video in research dissemination: Children as experts on their own family lives, *International Journal of Social Research Methodology*, 5(2): 173–80.

Brewis, J. (1999) How does it feel? Women managers, embodiment and changing public sector cultures, in S. Whitehead and R. Moodley (eds) *Transforming Managers: Gendering Change in the Public Sector*. London: Taylor and Francis.

Brewis, J. (2000) 'When a body meets a body . . .': Experiencing the female body at work, in L. McKie and N. Watson (eds) *Organizing Bodies: Policy, Institutions and Work*. Basingstoke: Macmillan.

Brodribb, S. (1992) *Nothing Mat(t)ers: A Feminist Critique of Postmodernism*. Melbourne: Spinifex Press.

Brown, P., Halsey, A.H., Lauder, H. and Wells, A. Stuart (1997) The transformation of education and society: an introduction, in A.H. Halsey, H. Lauder, P. Brown and A. Stuart Wells (eds) *Education: Culture, Economy, Society*. Oxford: Oxford University Press.

Bryan, K. (1980) Pupil perceptions of transfer, in A. Hargreaves and L. Tickle (eds) *Middle Schools*. London: Harper Row.

Bulmer, M. and Rees, A.M. (eds) (1996) *Citizenship Today*. London: UCL Press.

Bunton, R. (1994) Reproducing psychiatry, in A. Coffey and P. Atkinson (eds) *Occupational Socialization and Working Lives*. Avebury: Ashgate.

Bury, M. (1995) The body in question, *Medical Sociology News*, 21(1): 36–48.

Butler, I. and Williamson, H. (eds) (1994) *Children Speak: Children, Trauma and Social Work*. Harlow: NSPCC/Longman.

Butler, V. (1998) Bodies on display: Experiences from the fetish club field, in J. Richardson and A. Shaw (eds) *The Body in Qualitative Research*. Aldershot: Ashgate.

Bynner, J., Chisholm, L. and Furlong, A. (eds) (1997) *Youth, Citizenship and Social Change in a European Context*. Aldershot: Ashgate.

Byrne, D. (1999) *Social Exclusion*. Buckingham: Open University Press.

Bystydzienski, J. (ed.) (1992) *Women Transforming Politics*. Bloomington: Indiana University Press.

Canaan, J. and Griffin, C. (1990) The new men's studies: Part of the problem or part of the solution?, in J. Hearn and D. Morgan (eds) *Men, Masculinities and Social Theory*. London: Unwin Hyman.

Carabine, J. (1996) A straight playing field or queering the pitch? Centring sexuality in social policy, *Feminist Review*, 54: 31–64.

Carlson, J. (2004) Contemporary theoretical perspectives, in C. Alcock, S. Payne and M. Sullivan (eds) *Introducing Social Policy* (revised edition). London: Prentice Hall.

Carr, W. and Kemmis, S. (eds) (1986) *Becoming Critical: Education, Knowledge and Action Research*. London: Falmer.

Carter, J. (ed.) (1998) *Postmodernity and the Fragmentation of Welfare*. London: Routledge.

Chamberlayne, P., Bornat, J. and Wengraf, T. (2000) *The Turn to Biographical Methods in Social Science*. London: Routledge.

Charles, N. (2000) *Feminism, the State and Social Policy*. London: Macmillan.

Charmaz, K. and Mitchell, R.G. Jr (1997) The myth of silent authorship: Self, substance and style in ethnographic writing, in R. Hertz (ed.) *Reflexivity and Voice*. Thousand Oaks, CA: Sage.

Citizenship Advisory Group (1998) *Report of the Advisory Group on Education for Citizenship and the Teaching of Democracy in Schools*. London: Qualifications and Curriculum Authority.

Clarke, G. (1996) Conformimg and contesting with (a) difference: How lesbian students and teachers manage their identities, *International Studies in Sociology of Education*, 6(2): 191–210.

Clarke, P. (1996) *Deep Citizenship*. London: Pluto Press.

Clifford, J. and Marcus, G. (eds) (1986) *Writing Culture: The Poetics and Politics of Ethnography*. Berkeley, CA: University of California Press.

Coffey, A. (1999) *The Ethnographic Self*. London: Sage.

Coffey, A. (2001) *Education and Social Change*. Buckingham: Open University Press.

Coffey, A. (2002) Ethnography and self: Reflections and representations, in T. May (ed.) *Qualitative Research in Action*. London: Sage.

Coffey, A. and Delamont, S. (2000) *Feminism and the Classroom Teacher*. London: Routledge/Falmer.

Coffield, F. (ed.) (1999) *Why's the Beer Always Stronger Up North? Studies of Lifelong Learning in Europe*. Bristol: The Policy Press.

Commission on Citizenship (1990) *Encouraging Citizenship*. London: HMSO.

Connell, R.W. (1985) *Teachers Work*. Sydney: Allen and Unwin.

Connell, R.W. (1992) Citizenship, social justice and the curriculum, *International Studies in Sociology of Education*, 2(2): 133–46.

Corea, G. (1985) *The Mother Machine*. London: The Women's Press.

Cortazzi, M. (1993) *Narrative Analysis*. London: Falmer.

Cortazzi, M. (2001) *Narrative Analysis in Ethnography*, in P. Atkinson, A. Coffey, S. Delamont, J. Lofland and L. Lofland (eds) *Handbook of Ethnography*. London: Sage.

Cotterill, P. and Letherby, G. (1993) Weaving stories: Personal auto/biographies in feminist research, *Sociology*, 27 (1): 67–80.

Coxon, T. (1988) Something sensational, *The Sociological Review*, 36(2): 353–67.

Craib, I. (1997) *Classical Social Theory*. Oxford: Oxford University Press.

Craig, J. (1997) Population review, *Population Trends*, 88: 5–12.

Crang, M., Crang, P. and May, J. (eds) (1999) *Virtual Geographies: Bodies, Space and Relations*. London: Routledge.

Cranny-Francis, A., Waring, W., Stavropoulos, P. and Kirkby, J. (2003) *Gender Studies*. London: Palgrave Macmillan.

Crompton, R. and Sanderson, K. (1990) *Gendered Jobs and Social Change*. London: Unwin Hyman.

Cunnison, S. (1989) Gender joking in the staffroom, in S. Acker (ed.) *Teachers, Gender and Careers*. London: Falmer.

Dahrendorf, R. (1996) Citizenship and social class, in M. Bulmer and A.M. Rees (eds) *Citizenship Today*. London: UCL Press.

Dale, J. and Foster, P. (1986) *Feminists and State Welfare*. London: Routledge and Kegan Paul.

Dalley, G. (1988) *Ideologies of Caring*. Basingstoke: Macmillan.

David, M., West, A. and Ribbens, J. (1994) *Mother's Intuition?: Choosing Second-ary Schools*. London: Falmer Press.

Davies, R.M. (1994) Novices and experts: Initial encounters in midwifery, in A. Coffey and P. Atkinson (eds) *Occupational Socialization and Working Lives*. Avebury: Ashgate.

De Laine, M. (2000) *Fieldwork, Participation and Practice*. Thousand Oaks, CA: Sage.

De Vaus, D. (2001) *Research Design in Social Research*. London: Sage.

Dean, H. (2000) Introduction: Towards an embodied account of welfare, in K. Ellis and H. Dean (eds) *Social Policy and the Body*. Basingstoke: Macmillan.

Dean, H. (2003) Doing projects in social policy, in P. Alcock, A. Erskine, and M. May, (eds) (2003) *The Student's Companion to Social Policy*. Oxford: Blackwell.

Deegan, M.J. (1988) *Jane Addams and the Men of the Chicago School*. New Brunswick, NJ: Transaction Press.

Delamont, S. (1991) The hit list and other horror stories, *The Sociological Review*, 39 (1): 238–59.

Delamont, S. (2003) *Feminist Sociology*. London: Sage.

Denzin, N.K.(1989) *Interpretive Biography*. Newbury Park, CA: Sage.

Denzin, N.K. (1997) *Interpretive Ethnography*. Thousand Oaks, CA: Sage.

Denzin, N.K. and Lincoln, Y.S. (eds) (2000) *Handbook of Qualitative Research*, 2nd edn. Thousand Oaks, CA: Sage.

Devine, F. and Heath, S. (1999) *Sociological Research Methods in Context*. London: Macmillan.

Dey, I. (1993) *Qualitative Data Analysis*. London: Routledge.

DfEE (1998) *School Standards and Framework Act*. London: Department for Education and Employment.

DFES (2002) *Statistics for Education: Teachers, England and Wales*. Department for Education and Skills, London: HMSO.

Dicks, B. and Mason, B. (1998) Hypermedia and Ethnography, *Sociological Research Online*, 3 (3), http://www.socresonline.org.uk/socresonline/3/3/3.html

Dicks, B., Mason, B., Coffey, A. and Atkinson, P. (2004, forthcoming) *Hypermedia for Ethnography*. London: Sage.

Dingwall, R. (1977) *The Social Organisation of Health Visitor Training*. London: Croom Helm.

Doogan, K. (1988) Falling off the treadmill – the causes of youth homelessness, in G. Bramley, K. Doogan, P. Leather, A. Murie and E. Watson (eds), *Homelessness and the London Housing Market*. Bristol: University of Bristol, School for Advanced Urban Studies.

Douglas, M. (1966) *Purity and Danger*. London: Routledge and Kegan Paul.

Drake, R.F. (1998) Housing and older people, in A. Symonds and A. Kelly (eds) *The Social Construction of Community Care*. London: Macmillan.

Drake, R.F. (2001) *The Principles of Social Policy*. London: Palgrave.

Dwyer, K. (1977) On the dialogic of fieldwork, *Dialectical Anthropology*, 2: 143–51.

Dyhouse, C. (1995) *No Distinction of Sex? Women in British Universities 1870–1939*. London: UCL.

Eadie, J. (2001) Boys talk: Social theory and its discontents, *Sociology*, 35(2): 575–82.

East, L. (2002) Regenerating health in communities: Voices from the inner city, *Critical Social Policy*, 22(2): 147.

Elliott, J. and Sarland, C. (1995) A study of 'teachers as researchers' in the context of award-bearing courses and research degrees, *British Educational Research Journal*, 21(3): 371–86.

Ellis, C. (1995) *Final Negotiations: A Story of Love, Loss and Chronic Illness*. Philadelphia: Temple University Press.

Ellis, C. (1996) Maternal connections, in C. Ellis and A.P. Bochner (eds) *Composing Ethnography*. Walnut Creek, CA: Altamira.

Ellis, C. and Bochner, A.P. (1992) Telling and performing personal stories: The constraints of choice in abortion, in C. Ellis and M.G. Flaherty (eds) *Investigating Subjectivity: Research on Lived Experience*. Newbury Park, CA: Sage.

Ellis, C. and Bochner, A.P. (1996) *Composing Ethnography*. Walnut Creek, CA: Altamira.

Ellis, C. and Bochner, A.P. (2000) Autoethnography, personal narrative, reflexivity: researcher as subject, in N.K. Denzin and Y.S. Lincoln (eds) *Handbook of Qualitative Research*, 2nd edn. Thousand Oaks, CA: Sage.

Ely, M., Vinz, R., Downing, M. and Anzul, M. (1997) *On Writing Qualitative Research*. London: Falmer.

England, S.E. (1994) Modelling theory from fiction and autobiography, in C.K. Riessman (ed.) *Qualitative Studies in Social Work Research*. Thousand Oaks, CA: Sage.

Epstein, D. and Johnson, R. (1998) *Schooling Sexualities*. Buckingham: Open University Press.

Epstein, D., Elwood, J., Hey, V. and Maw, J. (eds) (1998) *Failing Boys?* Buckingham: Open University Press.

Equal Opportunities Commission (Equal Pay Task Force) (2001) *Just Pay*. Manchester: EOC.

Erben, M. (1993) The problem of other lives: Social perspectives on written biography, *Sociology*, 27(1): 15–26.

Esmail, A. and Everington, S. (1997) Asian doctors are still being discriminated against, *British Medical Journal*, 314: 1619.

Esmail, A., Everington, S. and Doyle, H. (1998) Racial discrimination in the allocation of distinction awards, *British Medical Journal*, 316: 193–5.

Esping Anderson, G. (1990) *The Three Worlds of Welfare Capitalism*. Cambridge: Polity.

ESRC (2000a) *Postgraduate Training Guidelines*. Swindon: Economic and Social Research Council.

ESRC (2000b) *Postgraduate Training Guidelines: Social Policy, Social Work and Health Studies*. Economic and Social Research Council, http://www.esrc.ac.uk/ersccontent/postgradfunding/2000_Guidelines_f13.asp

European Commission (1996) *Teaching and Learning: Towards the Learning*

Society. Luxembourg: Office for Official Publications of the European Communities.

Evans, C. and Fisher, M. (1999) Collaborative evaluation with service users, in I. Shaw and J. Lishman (eds) *Evaluation and Social Work Practice*. London: Sage.

Evans, K. (1995) Competence and citizenship: Towards a complementary model for times of critical social change, *British Journal of Education and Work*, 8(2): 14–27.

Evans, M. (1993) Reading lives: How the personal might be social, *Sociology*, 27(1): 5–14.

Evans, M. (2003) *Gender and Social Theory*. Buckingham: Open University Press.

Evanson, E. and Spence, L. (2003) Women and pensions: Time for a rethink, *Social Policy and Administration*, 37(3): 253–70.

Fairbairns, Z. (1979) *Benefits: A Novel*. London: Virago.

Farish, M., McPake, J., Powney, J. and Weiner, G. (1995) *Equal Opportunities in Colleges and Universities*. Buckingham: SRHE and Open University Press.

Faulks, K. (1998) *Citizenship in Modern Britain*. Edinburgh: University of Edinburgh Press.

Featherstone, M. (1982) The body in consumer culture, *Theory, Culture and Society*, 1(1): 18–33.

Featherstone, M. and Turner, B. (1995) Body and society: An introduction, *Body and Society*, 1(1): 1–12.

Fielding, N. (2001) Computer applications in qualitative research, in P. Atkinson, A. Coffey, S. Delamont, J. Lofland and L. Lofland (eds) *Handbook of Ethnography*. London: Sage.

Finch, J. (1984) 'Its great to have someone to talk to': The ethics and politics on interviewing women, in C. Bell and H. Roberts (eds) *Social Researching: Politics, Problems, Practice*. London: Routledge and Kegan Paul.

Finch, J. (1991) Feminist research and social policy, in M. MacLean and D. Groves (eds) *Women's Issues in Social Policy*. London: Routledge.

Finch, J. and Groves, M. (eds) (1983) *A Labour of Love: Women, Work, and Caring*. London: Routledge and Kegan Paul.

Finch, J. and Mason, J. (1993) *Negotiating Family Responsibilities*. London: Tavistock/ Routledge.

Finlayson, L.R. and Nazroo, J.Y. (1997) *Gender Inequalities in Nursing Careers*. London: Policy Studies Institute.

Firestone, S. (1971) *The Dialectic of Sex*. London: Women's Press.

Flanders, N.A. (1970) *Analysing Teaching Behaviour*. New York: Addison Wesley.

Flax, J. (1993) The end of innocence, in J. Butler and J.W. Scott (eds) *Feminists Theorize the Political*. New York: Routledge.

Flick, U. (1998) *An Introduction to Qualitative Research*. London: Sage.

Fogelman, K. (1997) Citizenship education, in J. Bynner, L. Chisholm and A. Furlong (eds) *Youth, Citizenship and Social Change in a European Context*. Aldershot: Ashgate.

Fontana, A. and Frey, J.A. (2000) The interview: From structured questions to negotiated text, in N.K. Denzin and Y.S. Lincoln (eds) *Handbook of Qualitative Research*, 2nd edn. Thousand Oaks, CA: Sage.

Fook, J. (2001) Identifying expert social work: Qualitative practitioner research, in

I. Shaw and N. Gould (eds) *Qualitative Research in Social Work*. London: Sage.

Fordham, S. (1996) *Blacked Out: Dilemmas of Race, Identity and Success at Capital High*. Chicago: University of Chicago Press.

Foucault, M. (1974) *The Archaeology of Knowledge*. London: Tavistock.

Foucault, M. (1977) *Discipline and Punish*. Harmondsworth: Allen Lane.

Foucault, M. (1979) *The History of Sexuality: Volume 1*. London: Allen Lane.

Foucault, M. (1982) The subject and power, in H.L. Dreyfus and P. Rabinov (eds) *Michel Foucault: Beyond Structuralism and Hermeneutics*. Brighton: Harvester Wheatsheaf.

Fox Genovese, E. (1986) The claims of a common culture, *Salmagundi*, 72 (Fall): 134–51.

Fox, K.V. (1996) Silent voices: A subversive reading of child sexual abuse, in C. Ellis and A.P. Bochner (eds) *Composing Ethnography: Alternative Forms of Qualitative Writing*. Walnut Creek, CA: Altamira.

France, A. (1996) Youth and citizenship in the 1990s, *Youth and Policy*, 53: 28–43.

Francis, B. (1999) *Boys, Girls and Achievement*. London: Routledge/Falmer.

Frank, A.W. (1990) Bringing bodies back, in *Theory, Culture and Society*, 7(1): 131–62.

Frank, A.W. (1991) For a sociology of the body, in M. Featherstone, M. Hepworth and B.S. Turner (eds) *The Body: Social Process and Cultural Theory*. London: Sage.

Fulcher, J. and Scott, J. (2003) *Sociology*, 2nd edn. Oxford: Oxford University Press.

Furlong, A. and Cartmel, F. (1997) *Young People and Social Change*. Buckingham: Open University Press.

Gage, N. (1989) The paradigm wars and its aftermath, *Educational Researcher*, 18 (7): 4–10.

Galton, M., Hargreaves, L., Comber, C. and Wall, D. (1999) *Inside the Primary Classroom: 20 Years On*. London: Routledge.

Garber, L. (eds) (1994) *Tilting the Tower: Lesbians, Teaching, Queer Subjects*. New York: Routledge.

Gamarnikow, E., Morgan, D., Purvis, J. and Taylorson, D. (eds) (1983) *The Public and the Private*. Aldershot: Gower.

Gazdar, C. (1997) Service is 'dreadful', *Community Care*, 26 June: 7.

Geertz, C. (1973) *The Interpretation of Cultures*. New York: Basic Books.

Geertz, C. (1983) *Local Knowledge: Further Essays in Interpretive Anthropology*. New York: Basic Books.

George, V. and Wilding, P. (1994) *Welfare and Ideology*. London: Harvester Wheatsheaf.

Gibbins, J.R. (1998) Postmodernism, poststructuralism and social policy, in J. Carter (ed.) *Postmodernity and the Fragmentation of Welfare*. London: Routledge.

Giddens, A. (1990) *The Consequences of Modernity*. Cambridge: Polity Press.

Giddens, A. (1994) *Beyond Left and Right: The Future of Radical Politics*. Cambridge: Polity Press.

Giddens, A. (1996) T.H. Marshall, the state and democracy, in M. Bulmer and A.M. Rees (eds), *Citizenship Today*. London: UCL Press.

Giddens, A. (1997) *Sociology*, 3rd edn. Cambridge: Polity.

Giddens, A. (1998) *The Third Way*. Cambridge: Polity.

Gilbert, N. (2001) Writing about social research, in N. Gilbert (ed.) *Researching Social Life*. London: Sage.

Gillborn, D. (1992) Citzenship, 'race' and the hidden curriculum, *International Studies in Sociology of Education*, 2(1): 57–73.

Gillborn, D. (1998) Racism and the politics of qualitative research: learning from controversy and critique, in P. Connolly and B. Troyna (eds) *Researching Racism in Education: Politics, Theory and Practice*. Buckingham: Open University Press.

Gillham, B. (2000) *Developing a Questionnaire*. London: Continuum.

Gittens, D. (1993) *The Family in Question*, 2nd edn. London: Macmillan.

Glendinning and J. Millar (eds) (1992) *Women and Poverty in Britain: the 1990s*. London: Harvester Wheatsheaf.

Goffman, E. (1959) *The Presentation of Self in Everyday Life*. Harmondsworth: Penguin.

Goffman, E. (1963) *Behavior in Public Places*. New York: Free Press.

Goffman, E. (1968) *Asylums*. Harmondsworth: Penguin.

Goodson, I.F. (1995) The story so far: personal knowledge and the political, *International Journal of Qualitative Studies in Education*, 8: 89–98.

Goodson, I.F. (ed.) (1992) *Studying Teachers' Lives*. London: Routledge.

Gordon, T. (1986) *Democracy in One School: Progressive Education and Restructuring*. Lewes: Falmer.

Gordon, T. (1992) Citizens and others: Gender, democracy and education, *International Studies in Sociology of Education*, 2(1): 43–56.

Gordon, T., Holland, J. and Lehelma, E. (2000a) *Making Spaces: Citizenship and Difference in Schools*. Basingstoke: Macmillan.

Gordon, T., Holland, J. and Lehelma, E. (2000b) Moving bodies/still bodies: Embodiment and agency in schools, in L. McKie and N. Watson (eds) *Organizing Bodies: Policy, Institutions and Work*. Basingstoke: Macmillan.

Graham, H. (1984) Surveying through stories, in C. Bell and H. Roberts (eds) *Social Researching: Politics, Problems, Practice*. London: Routledge and Kegan Paul.

Graham, H. (1992) Budgeting for health: mothers in low income households, in C. Glendenning and J. Millar (eds) *Women and Poverty in Britain*. London: Harvester Wheatsheaf.

Gregory, J. (1999) Revisiting the sex equality laws, in S. Walby (ed.) *New Agendas for Women*. London: Macmillan.

Gubrium, J.F. and Holstein, J.A. (eds) (2002) *Handbook of Interview Research*. Thousand Oaks, CA: Sage.

Gunaratnam, Y. (2001) Eating into multiculturalism, *Critical Social Policy*, 21(3): 287.

Gurney, C.M. (2000) Accommodating bodies: The organization of corporeal dirt in the embodied home, in L. McKie and N. Watson (eds) *Organizing Bodies: Policy, Institutions and Work*. Basingstoke: Macmillan.

Hague, G. and Malos, E. (1993) *Domestic Violence*. Cheltenham: New Clarion Press.

Hakim, C. (1979) *Occupational Segregation*. Department of Employment: Research Paper 9. London: Department of Employment.

Halford, S., Savage, M. and Witz, A. (1997) *Gender, Careers and Organisations*. Basingstoke: Macmillan.

Hall, S. and Held, D. (1989) Citizens and citizenship, in S. Hall and M. Jacques (eds) *New Times*. London: Lawrence and Wishart.

Hall, T. (2003) *Better Times Than This: Youth Homelessness in Britain*. London: Pluto Press.

Hall, T., Coffey, A. and Williamson, H. (1999) Self, space and place: Youth identities and citizenship, *British Journal of Sociology of Education*, 20(4): 501–13.

Hall, T., Williamson, H. and Coffey, A. (1998) Conceptualizing citizenship: Young people and the transition to adulthood, *Journal of Education Policy*, 13(3): 301–15.

Hall, T., Williamson, H. and Coffey, A. (2000) Young people, citizenship and the third way: A role for the youth service, *Journal of Youth Studies*, 3(4): 461–72.

Hallett, C. (ed.) (1996) *Women and Social Policy*. London: Prentice Hall.

Hallett, C. and Prout, A. (eds) (2003) *Hearing the Voices of Children; Social Policy for a New Century*. New York: Routledge.

Hammersley, M. (1991) *Reading Ethnographic Research*. London: Longman.

Hammersley, M. (1993) On practitioner ethnography, in M. Hammersley (ed.) *Controversies in the Classroom*. Milton Keynes: Open University Press.

Hammersley, M. and Atkinson, P. (1995) *Ethnography*. London: Routledge.

Hammond, P.E. (ed.) (1964) *Sociologists at Work*. New York: Basic Books.

Haraway, D. (1997) *Modest_Witness@Second_Millennium.FemaleMan (c)_Meets_OncoMouse (tm): Feminism and Technoscience*. London: Routledge.

Harber, C. and Meighan, R. (eds) (1989) *The Democratic School: Educational Management and the Practice of Democracy*. Derby: Education Now.

Harding, S. (ed.) (1987) *Feminism and Methodology*. Milton Keynes: Open University Press.

Hargreaves, A. and Woods, P. (eds) (1984) *Classrooms and Staffrooms*. Milton Keynes: Open University Press.

Harrison, M.L. (1991) Citizenship, consumption and rights: A comment on B.S. Turner's theory of citizenship, *Sociology*, 25(2): 209–13.

Harvey, D. (1973) *Social Justice and the City*. London: Arnold.

Hastrup, K. (1992) *A Passage to Anthropology*. London: Routledge.

Haw, K. (with Shah, S. and Hanifa, M.) (1998) *Educating Muslim Girls: Shifting Discourses*. Buckingham: Open University Press.

Hay, C. (1996) *Re-stating Social and Political Change*. Buckingham: Open University Press.

Hayek, F.A. (1960) *The Constitution of Liberty*. London: Routledge and Kegan Paul.

Hearn, J. (1987) *Gender of Oppression*. London: Wheatsheaf.

Hearn, J. and Morgan, D. (eds) (1990) *Men, Masculinities and Social Theory*. London: Unwin Hyman.

Hertz, R. (ed.) (1997) *Reflexivity and Voice*. Thousand Oaks, CA: Sage.

Hey, V. (1999) Frail elderly people: Difficult questions and awkward answers, in S. Hood, B. Mayall and S. Oliver (eds) *Critical Issues in Social Research*. Buckingham: Open University Press.

Hill, M. (2003) *Understanding Social Policy*. Oxford: Blackwell.

Hobsbawm, E. (1995) *Age of Extremes*. London: Abacus.

Hochschild, A.R. (1983) *The Managed Heart*. Berkeley: University of California Press.
Hochschild, A.R. (2003) *The Commercialization of Intimate Life*. Berkeley: University of California Press.
Holloway, I and Wheeler, W. (2003) *Qualitative Research in Nursing*. Oxford: Blackwell.
Holquist, M. (1990) *Dialogism*. London: Routledge.
Holstein, J.A. and Gubrium, J.F. (1999) *The Self We Live By*. Oxford: Oxford University Press.
hooks, b. (1982) *Ain't I a Woman? Black Women and Feminism*. London: Pluto.
Howson, A. and Inglis, D. (2000) The body in sociology: Tensions inside and outside sociological thought, *The Sociological Review*, 49(3): 297–317.
Humm, M. (ed.) (1992) *Feminisms*. New York: Harvester Wheatsheaf.
Hutson, S. and Jenkins, R. (1989) *Taking the Strain: Families, Unemployment and the Transition to Adulthood*. Milton Keynes: Open University Press.
Iganski, P. and Mason, D. (2002) *Ethnicity, Equality of Opportunity and the British National Health Service*. Aldershot: Ashgate.
Jackson, S. (1997) Women, marriage and family relationships, in V. Robinson and D. Richardson (eds) *Introducing Women's Studies*, 2nd edn. London: Macmillan.
Jackson, S. and Moores, S. (eds) (1995) *The Politics of Domestic Consumption*. Hemel Hempstead: Prentice Hall.
Jamieson, A., Harper S. and Victor, C. (eds) (1997) *Critical Approaches to Ageing and Later Life*. Buckingham: Open University Press.
Jeffs, T. and Smith, M. (1996) *Informal Education*. Derby: Education Now.
Jenkins, R. (1990) Dimensions of adulthood in Britain: Long-term unemployment and mental handicap, in P. Spencer (ed.) *Anthropology and the Riddle of the Sphinx*. London: Routledge.
Jennaway, M. (1990) Paradigms, postmodern epistemologies and paradox: The place of feminism in anthroplogy, *Anthropological Forum*, 6(2): 167–89.
Jones, G. (1995) *Leaving Home*. Buckingham: Open University Press.
Jones, G. and Wallace, C. (1992) *Youth, Family and Citizenship*. Buckingham: Open University Press.
Jowell, R. et al. (2000) *British Social Attitudes*. London: Sage.
Junor, B. (1995) *Greenham Common Women's Peace Camp: A History of Non-Violent Resistance, 1984–1995*. London: Working Press.
Kandola, R. and Fullerton, J. (1994) *Managing the Mosaic – Diversity in Action*. London: Institute of Personnel and Development.
Kolker, A. (1996) Thrown overboard: the human costs of health care rationing, in C. Ellis and A.P. Bochner (eds) *Composing Ethnography: Alternative Forms of Qualitative Writing*. Walnut Creek, CA: Altamira.
Land, H. (1991) Time to care, in M. MacLean and D. Groves (eds) *Women's Issues in Social Policy*. London: Routledge.
Lash, S. and Urry, J. (1994) *Economies of Signs and Space*. London: Sage.
Lather, P. (1991) *Getting Smart: Feminist Research and Pedagogy With/in the Postmodern*. London: Routledge.
Latimer, J. (ed.) (2003) *Advanced Qualitative Research for Nursing*. Oxford: Blackwell.

Lavalette, M. and Pratt, A. (eds) (2001) *Social Policy: A Conceptual and Theoretical Introduction*, 2nd edn. London: Sage.

Law, J. and Williams, R.J. (1982) Putting the facts together: A case study of scientific persuasion, *Social Studies of Science*, 12: 535–58.

Lawler, J. (ed.) (1997) *The Body in Nursing*. Melbourne: Churchill Livingstone.

Lee Treweek, G. (1998) Women, resistance and care: An ethnographical study of nursing auxillary work, *Work, Employment and Society*, 11(1): 47–63.

Lewis, G. (2000) Introduction: Expanding the social policy imaginary, in G. Lewis, S. Gewirtz and J. Clarke (eds) *Rethinking Social Policy*. London: Sage.

Lewis, G., Hughes, G. and Saraga, E. (2000) The body of social policy: Social policy and the body, in L. McKie and N. Watson (eds) *Organizing Bodies*. Basingstoke: Macmillan.

Lewis, J. (1992a) Gender and the development of welfare regimes, *Journal of European Social Policy*, 2(3): 159–73.

Lewis, J. (1992b) *Women in Britain since 1945*. Oxford: Blackwell.

Liddington, J. and Norris, J. (2000) *One Hand Tied Behind Us: The Rise of the Women's Suffrage Movement*. London: Rivers Oram Press.

Lingard, B. and Douglas, P. (1999) *Men Engaging Feminisms*. Buckingham: Open University Press.

Lister, R. (1997) *Citizenship: Feminist Perspectives*. London: Macmillan.

Lister, R. (2000) Gender and the analysis of social policy, in G. Lewis, S. Gewirtz and J. Clarke (eds) *Rethinking Social Policy*. London: Sage.

Lofland, J. and Lofland, L. (1995) *Analysing Social Settings*, 3rd edn. Belmont, CA: Wadsworth.

Lovenduski, J. (1997) Gender politics: A breakthrough for women?, in P. Norris and N. Gavin, (eds) *Britain Votes 1997*. Oxford: Oxford University Press.

Lull, J. (1995) *Media, Communication, Culture: A Global Approach*. Cambridge: Polity.

Lutz, C.A. and Collins, J.L. (1993) *Reading National Geographic*. Chicago: University of Chicago Press.

Lynch, M. and Woolgar, S. (eds) (1990) *Representation in Scientific Practice*. Cambridge, MA: MIT Press.

Lyotard, J.F. (1992) *The Postmodern Condition*. Manchester: Manchester University Press.

Mac an Ghaill, M. (1994) *The Making of Men*. Buckingham: Open University Press.

Mac an Ghaill, M. (1999) *Contemporary Racisms and Ethnicities*. Buckingham: Open University Press.

MacDonald, R. (ed.) (1997) *Youth, the 'Underclass' and Social Exclusion*. London: Routledge.

Macionis, J.J. and Plummer, K. (2002) *Sociology: A Global Introduction*, 2nd edn. London: Prentice Hall.

Maclean, M. and Groves, D. (1991) *Women's Issues and Social Policy*. London: Routledge.

Madood, T. and Bethoud, R. (1997) *Ethnic Minorities in Britain*, 4th edn. London: Policy Studies Institute.

Maher, J. and Green, H. (2002) *Carers 2000: Results from the Carers Module of the General Household Survey 2000*. London: HMSO.

Mama, A. (1996) *The Hidden Struggle*. London: Whiting and Birch.

Manning, N. (1999) The politics of welfare, in J. Baldock, N. Manning, S. Miller and S. Vickerstaff, (eds) *Social Policy*. Oxford: Oxford University Press.

Marcus, J. (1992) *A World of Difference*. London: Zed.

Markham, A. (1998) *Life Online: Researching Real Experiences in Virtual Space*. Walnut Creek, CA: Altamira.

Marshall, T.H. (1950) *Citizenship and Social Class and Other Essays*. Cambridge: Cambridge University Press.

Mason, D. (2000) *Race and Ethnicity in Modern Britain*, 2nd edn. Oxford: Oxford University Press.

Massey, D. (1984) *Spatial Divisions of Labour*. London: Macmillan.

Massey, D. (1994) *Space, Place and Gender*. Cambridge: Polity Press.

May, T. (2001) *Social Research*. Buckingham: Open University Press.

Maynard, M. (1996) *Feminist Social Research*. London: UCL.

Maynard, M. (1998) Women's studies, in S. Jackson and J. Jones (eds) *Contemporary Feminist Theories*. Edinburgh: Edinburgh University Press.

Maynard, M. and Purvis, J. (1993) *Researching Women's Lives From a Feminist Perspective*. London: Taylor and Francis.

McBeth, M. (2004) Traditional theories of welfare, in C. Alcock, S. Payne and M. Sullivan, *Introducing Social Policy*, revised edition. London: Prentice Hall.

McCrudden, C. (1996) *Mainstreaming Fairness?* Belfast: C.A.J. Maynard.

McKeganey, N. and Cunningham Burley, S. (1987) *Enter the Sociologist*. Aldershot: Avebury.

McKie, L., Bowlby, S. and Gregory, S. (eds) (1999) *Gender, Power and the Household*. Basingstoke: Macmillan.

Measor, L. and Sikes, P. (1992) *Gender and Schools*. London: Cassell.

Measor, L. and Woods, P. (1994) *Changing Schools: Pupil Perspectives on Transfer to a Comprehensive*. Milton Keynes: Open University Press.

Melia, K. (1987) *Learning and Working*. London: Tavistock.

Mienczakowski, J. (2001) Ethnodrama: Performed research – limitations and potential, in P. Atkinson, A. Coffey, S. Delamont, J. Lofland and L. Lofland (eds) *Handbook of Ethnography*. London: Sage.

Mill, J.S. (1869) [1948] *On Liberty, Representative Government, the Representation of Women*. London: Oxford University Press.

Millar, J. and Glendinning, V. (1992) It all really starts in the family: Gender divisions and poverty, in C. Glendinning and J. Millar (eds) *Women and Poverty in Britain: the 1990s*. London: Harvester Wheatsheaf.

Mills, C. Wright (1959) *The Sociological Imagination*. New York: Oxford University Press.

Monaghan, L. (2001) *Bodybuilding, Drugs and Risk*. London: Routledge.

Morgan, D.L. (1997) *Focus Groups as Qualitative Research*, 2nd edn. Thousand Oaks, CA: Sage.

Morrow, V. and Richards, M. (1996) *Transitions to Adulthood: A Family Matter?* York: Joseph Rowntree Foundation.

Mulkay, M. (1985) *The World and the Word: Explorations in the Form of Sociological Analysis*. London: Allen and Unwin.

Munro, P. (1998) *Subject to Fiction: Women Teachers' Life History Narratives and the Cultural Politics of Resistance*. Buckingham: Open University Press.

Murcott, A. (ed.) (1983) *The Sociology of Food and Eating.* Aldershot: Gower.

Murray, C. (1990) *The Emerging British Underclass.* London: Institute of Economic Affairs.

Murray, C. (1994) *Underclass: The Crisis Deepens.* London: Institute of Economic Affairs.

Mykhalovskiy, E. (1997) Reconsidering 'table talk': Critical thoughts on the relationship between sociology, autobiography and self-indulgence, in R. Hertz (ed.) *Reflexivity and Voice.* Thousand Oaks, CA: Sage.

National Assembly for Wales (2001) *The Learning Country.* Cardiff: National Assembly for Wales.

National Curriculum Council (1990) *Curriculum Guidance 8: Education for Citizenship.* London: NCC.

Neilsen, J.M. (1990) *Feminist Research Methods.* Boulder, CO: Westview Press.

Nettleton, S. (1995) *The Sociology of Health and Illness.* Cambridge: Polity Press.

Nicholson, L.J. (ed.) (1990) *Feminism/ Postfeminism.* London: Routledge.

Noffke, S.E. and Stevenson, R.B. (eds) (1995) *Educational Action Research.* New York: Teachers College Press.

O'Brien, M. and Penna, S. (1998) *Theorizing Welfare.* London: Sage.

Oakley, A. (1974) *The Sociology of Housework.* London: Martin Robertson.

Okely, J. and Callaway, H. (eds) (1992) *Anthropology and Autobiography.* London: Routledge.

Olesen, V. (2000) Feminisms and qualitative research at and into the Millennium, in N.K. Denzin and Y.S. Lincoln (eds) *Handbook of Qualitative Research*, 2nd edn. Thousand Oaks, CA: Sage.

Oliver, M. and Barnes, C. (1996) *Disabled People and Social Policy.* London: Longman.

OPCS (1995) *Young People's Participation in the Youth Service.* London: Department of Education.

Oppenheim, A.N. (1992) *Questionnaire Design, Interviewing and Attitude Measurement.* London: Punter.

Osler, A. and Vincent, K. (2003) *Girls and Exclusion.* London: Routledge/Falmer.

Ozga, J. (2000) *Policy Research in Educational Settings: Contested Terrain.* Buckingham: Open University Press.

Paetcher, C. (1998) *Educating the Other.* London: Falmer.

Paget, M.A. (1990) Performing the text, *Journal of Contemporary Ethnography*, 19: 136–55.

Paget, M.A. (1993) *A Complex Sorrow: Reflections on Cancer and an Abbreviated Life.* Philadelphia: Temple University Press.

Pahl, J. (1989) *Money and Marriage.* London: Macmillan.

Pahl, J. (1990) Household spending, personal spending and the control of money in marriage, *Sociology*, 24(1): 119–38.

Parker, G. and Lawton, D. (1994) *Different Types of Care, Different Types of Carer.* London: HMSO.

Pascall, G. (1986) *Social Policy: A Feminist Analysis.* London: Tavistock.

Pateman, C. (1988) *The Sexual Contract.* Oxford: Blackwell.

Pickard, S., Jacobs, S. and Kirk, S. (2003) Challenging professional roles: Lay carers' involvement in health care community, *Social Policy and Administration*, 37(1): 82–9.

Pierson, C. (1998) *Beyond the Welfare State*, 2nd edn. Cambridge: Cambridge University Press.

Pilcher, J. (1995) *Age and Generation in Modern Britain*. Oxford: Oxford University Press.

Pilcher, J. (1999) *Women in Contemporary Britain*. London: Routledge.

Pink, S. (2001) *Doing Visual Ethnography*. London: Sage.

Pinker, R. (1971) *Social Theory and Social Policy*. London: Heinemann.

Pithouse, A. (1997) *Social Work: The Social Organisation of an Invisible Trade*, 2nd edn. Aldershot: Ashgate.

Pithouse, A. and Williamson, H. (eds) (1997) *Engaging the User in Welfare Services*. Birmingham: Venture.

Place, B. (2000) Constructing the bodies of ill children in the intensive care unit, in A. Prout (ed.) *The Body, Childhood and Society*. Basingstoke: Macmillan.

Plummer, K. (1995) *Telling Sexual Stories*. London: Routledge.

Plummer, K. (2001) *Documents of Life 2*. London: Sage.

Popay, J., Hearn, J. and Edwards, J. (1998) *Men, Gender Divisions and Welfare*. London: Routledge.

Popay, J., Thomas, C., Williams, G., Bennett, S., Gatrell, A. and Bostock, L. (2003) A proper place to live: Health inequalities, agency and the normative dimensions of space, *Social Science and Medicine*, 57(1): 55–69.

Porter, S. (2002) Critical realist ethnography, in T. May (ed.) *Qualitative Research in Action*. London: Sage.

Pringle, R. and Watson, S. (1992) Fathers, brothers, mates: The fraternal state in Australia, in S. Watson (ed.) *Playing the State*. London: Verso.

Prior, L. (2003) *Using Documents in Social Research*. London: Sage.

Pugsley, L., Coffey, A. and Delamont, S. (1996) Daps, dykes, five mile hikes, *Sport, Education and Society*, 1(2): 133–46.

Puwer, N. (1997) Gender and politic elites: Women in the House of Commons, *Sociology Review*, 7(2): 2–6.

QAA (2000) *Subject Benchmark Statements*. Gloucester: Quality Assurance Agency for Higher Education.

Quinney, R. (1996) Once my father travelled west to California, in C. Ellis and A.P. Bochner (eds) *Composing Ethnography: Alternative Forms of Qualitative Writing*. Walnut Creek, CA: Altamira.

Raphael Reed, L. (1999) Troubling boys and disturbing discourses on masculinity and schooling, *Gender and Education*, 11(1): 93–110.

Rath, J. (2001) Representing feminist educational research with/in the postmodern, *Gender and Education*, 13(2): 117–36.

Rawls, J. (1972) *A Theory of Justice*. Cambridge, Mass: Harvard University Press.

Raymond, J. (1993) *Women as Wombs: Reproductive Technologies and the Battle over Women's Freedom*. San Francisco: Harper.

Reason, P. and Bradbury, H. (2000) *The Handbook of Action Research*. London: Sage.

Reed-Danahay, D. (2001) Autobiography, intimacy and ethnography, in P. Atkinson, A. Coffey, S. Delamont, J. Lofland and L. Lofland (eds) *Handbook of Ethnography*. London: Sage.

Rees, A.M. (1996) T.H. Marshall and the progress of citizenship, in M. Bulmer and A.M. Rees (eds) *Citizenship Today*. London: UCL Press.

Rees, G., Williamson, H. and Istance, D. (1996) 'Status Zero': A study of jobless school-leavers in South Wales, *Research Papers in Education*, 11(2): 219–35.

Rees, T. (1990) *Women and the Labour Market*. London: Routledge.

Rees, T. (1998) *Mainstreaming Equality in the European Union*. London: Routledge.

Richardson, L. (2000) Writing: A method of inquiry, in N.K. Denzin, and Y.S. Lincoln, (eds) *Handbook of Qualitative Research*, Thousand Oaks, CA: Sage.

Riddell, S. and Salisbury, J. (2000) Introduction, in J. Salisbury and S. Riddell (eds) *Gender, Policy and Educational Change*. London: Routledge.

Riessman, C. (1993) *Narrative Analysis*. Newbury Park, CA: Sage.

Riessman, C. (1994a) Making sense of marital violence, in C. Riessman (ed.) *Qualitative Studies in Social Work Research*. Thousand Oaks, CA: Sage.

Riessman, C. (ed.) (1994b) *Qualitative Studies in Social Work Research*. Thousand Oaks, CA: Sage.

Riska, E. and Wegar, K. (eds) (1993) *Gender, Work and Medicine: Women and the Medical Division of Labour*. London: Sage.

Roberts, B. (2001) *Biographical Research*. Buckingham: Open University Press.

Roberts, H. (1981) *Doing Feminist Research*. London: Routledge and Kegan Paul.

Robson, C. (2002) *Real World Research*. Oxford: Blackwell.

Roche, M. (1992) *Rethinking Citizenship*. Cambridge: Polity Press.

Rojiani, R. (1994) Disparities in the social construction of long-term care, in C.K. Riessman (ed.) *Qualitative Studies in Social Work Research*. Thousand Oaks, CA: Sage.

Ronai, C.R. (1996) 'My mother is mentally retarded', in C. Ellis and A.P. Bochner (eds) *Composing Ethnography: Alternative Forms of Qualitative Writing*. Walnut Creek, CA: Altamira Press.

Roth, J. (1963) *Timetables*. Indianapolis: Bobbs-Merrill.

Rowntree, S. (1901) *Poverty: A Study of Town Life*. London: Longmans Green.

Rowntree, S. (1941) *Poverty and Progress*. London: Longmans Green.

Rubery, J. and Humphries, J. (1995) *The Economics of Equal Opportunities*. Manchester: EOC.

Said, E. (1978) *Orientalism*. London: Routledge and Kegan Paul.

Sainsbury, D. (1994) *Gendering Welfare States*. London: Sage.

Saunders, P. (1990) *A Nation of Home Owners*. London: Unwin Hyman.

Scott, D. (2003) Fieldwork placements and the social policy curriculum, in P. Alcock, A. Erskine, and M. May (eds) *The Student's Companion to Social Policy*. Oxford: Blackwell.

Scott, J. (1990) *A Matter of Record*. Cambridge: Polity.

Scott, S. (1985) Feminist research and qualitative methods, in R.G. Burgess (ed.) *Issues in Educational Research: Qualitative Methods*. London: Falmer.

Scott, S. and Morgan, D. (1993) *Body Matters*. London: Falmer.

Scourfield, J. (2000) The rediscovery of child neglect. *The Sociological Review*, 48(3): 365–82.

Scourfield, J. (2003) *Gender and Child Protection*. Basingstoke: Palgrave Macmillan.

Scourfield, J. and Coffey, A. (2002) Understanding gendered practice in child protection, *Qualitative Social Work*, 1(3): 319–40.

Scourfield, J. and Drakeford, M. (2002) New Labour and the 'problem of men', *Critical Social Policy*, 22(4): 615–36.

Seymour, W.S. (2001) In the flesh or online? Exploring qualitative research methodologies, *Qualitative Research*, 1(2): 147–68.

Shakespeare, T. (ed.) (1998) *The Disability Reader*. London: Cassell.

Shakespeare, T. (2000) The social relations of care, in G. Lewis, S. Gewirtz and J. Clarke (eds) *Rethinking Social Policy*. London: Sage.

Shaw, I. and Gould, N. (eds) (2001) *Qualitative Research in Social Work*. London: Sage.

Shilling, C. (1993) *The Body and Social Theory*. London: Sage.

Sikes, P., Measor, L. and Woods, P. (1985) *Teacher Careers*. Milton Keynes: Open University Press.

Silverman, D. (2001) *Interpreting Qualitative Data*, 2nd edn. London: Sage.

Skeggs, B. (2002) Techniques for telling the reflexive self, in T. May (ed.) *Qualitative Research in Action*. London: Sage.

Skelton, C. (1998) Feminism and research into masculinities and schooling, *Gender and Education*, 10(2): 217–28.

Skidelsky, R. and Raymond, K. (1998) *Education Action Zones: The Conditions of Success*. London: Social Market Foundation.

Smaje, C. (1995) *Health, 'Race' and Ethnicity: Making Sense of the Evidence*. London: King's Fund Institute.

Smith, L.M., Dwyer, D.C., Prunty, J.J. and Kleine, P.F. (1988) *Innovation and Change in Schooling*. New York: Falmer.

Snitow, A. (1990) A gender diary, in M. Hirsch and E. Fox Keller (eds) *Conflict in Feminism*. London: Routledge.

Somerville, J. (2000) *Feminism and the Family*. London: Macmillan.

Sparkes, A. (1994) Silence, self and invisibility as a beginning teacher: A life story of a lesbian experience, *British Journal of Sociology of Education*, 15(1): 93–118.

Sparkes, A. (1995) Writing people: Reflections on the dual crises of representation and legitimation in qualitative inquiry, *Quest*, 47(2): 158–95.

Spencer, J. (2001) Ethnography after postmodernism in P. Atkinson, A. Coffey, S. Delamont, J. Lofland and L. Lofland (eds) *Handbook of Ethnography*. London: Sage.

Stanley, L. (1992) *The Auto/biographical I: Theory and Practice of Feminist Auto/biography*. Manchester: University of Manchester Press.

Stanley, L. (1993) On auto/biographies in sociology, *Sociology*, 27(1): 41–52.

Stanley, L. (ed.) (1997) *Knowing Feminisms*. London: Sage.

Stanley, L. and Morgan, D. (1993) Editorial introduction, *Sociology*, 27(1): 1–4.

Stanley, L. and Wise, S. (1990) Method, methodology and epistemology in feminist research processes, in L. Stanley (ed.) *Feminist Praxis*. London: Routledge.

Stanley, L. and Wise, S. (1993) *Breaking Out Again: Feminist Ontology and Epistemology*. London: Routledge.

Stanworth, M. (ed.) (1987) *Reproductive Technologies: Gender, Motherhood and Medicine*. Cambridge: Polity/Blackwell.

Stronach, I. and MacLure, M. (1997) *Educational Research Undone: The Postmodern Embrace*. Buckingham: Open University Press.

Tawney, R.H. (1964) *Equality*. London: Allen and Unwin.

Taylor, D. (1996) *Critical Social Policy: A Reader*. London: Sage.

Taylor Gooby, P. (1994) Postmodernism and social policy: A great leap backwards, *Journal of Social Policy*, 23(3): 385–404.

Taylor Gooby, P. (1999) The future of social policy, in J. Baldock, N. Manning, S. Miller and S. Vickerstaff (eds) *Social Policy*. Oxford: Oxford University Press.

Thompson, P. (1998) *The Voice of the Past*. Oxford: Oxford University Press.

Thorne, B. (1993) *Gender Play*. New Brunswick, NJ: Rutgers.

Tillman-Healy, L.M. (1996) A secret life in a culture of thinness: Reflections on body, food and bulimia, in C. Ellis and A.P. Bochner (eds) *Composing Ethnography: Alternative Forms of Qualitative Writing*. Walnut Creek, CA: Altamira.

Tooley, J. (1997) On school choice and social class: A response to Ball, Bowe and Gewirtz, *British Journal of Sociology of Education*, 18(2): 217–30.

Tooley, J. and Darby, D. (1998) *Educational Research: A Critique*. London: Office for Standards in Education.

Townsend, P. (1975) *Sociology and Social Policy*. London: Allen Lane.

Turner, B. (1984) *The Body and Society*. Oxford: Basil Blackwell.

Turner, B.S. (1986) *Citizenship and Capitalism*. London: Allen and Unwin.

Turner, B.S. (1990) Outline of a theory of citizenship, *Sociology*, 24(2): 189–217.

Turner, B.S. (1994) Postmodern culture/modern citizens, in B. van Steenbergen (ed.), *The Condition of Citizenship*. London: Sage.

Twigg, J. (2000a) Social policy and the body, in G. Lewis, S. Gewirtz and J. Clarke (eds) *Rethinking Social Policy*. London: Sage.

Twigg, J. (2000b) *Bathing: The Body and Community Care*. London: Routledge.

Twigg, J. (2002) The body in social policy: Mapping a territory, *Journal of Social Policy*, 31(3): 421–39.

Ungerson, C. (ed.) (1985) *Women and Social Policy*. Basingstoke: Macmillan.

Ungerson, C. (1987) *Policy is Personal: Sex, Gender and Informal Care*. London: Tavistock.

Urry, J. (1995) *Consuming Places*. London: Routledge.

Van Every, J. (1995) *Heterosexual Women Changing the Family: Refusing to be a Wife!* London: Taylor and Francis.

Van Maanen, J. (1988) *Tales of the Field: On Writing Ethnography*. Chicago: University of Chicago Press.

Van Steenbergen, B. (ed.) (1994) *The Condition of Citizenship*. London: Sage.

Vincent, J. (1995) *Inequality and Old Age*. London: UCL Press.

Walby, S. (1986) *Patriarchy at Work*. Cambridge: Polity.

Walby, S. (1990) *Theorizing Patriarchy*. Oxford: Basil Blackwell.

Walby, S. (ed.) (1999) *New Agendas for Women*. London: Macmillan.

Walker, A. (2002) *Living in Britain: Results from the 2001 General Household Survey*. London: HMSO.

Wardhaugh, J. (1999) The unaccommodated woman: Home, homelessness and identity, *The Sociological Review*, 47(1): 91–109.

Warren, C. (2002) Qualitative interviewing, in J.F. Gubrium and J.A. Holstein (eds) *Handbook of Interview Research*. Thousand Oaks, CA: Sage.

Wasoff, F. and Dobash, R.E. (1996) *The Simulated Client: A Method for Studying Professionals Working with Clients*. Aldershot: Avebury.

Watson, S. (2000) Foucault and the study of social policy, in G. Lewis, S. Gewirtz and J. Clarke (eds) *Rethinking Social Policy*. London: Sage.

Weiner, G. (1986) Feminist education and equal opportunities, *British Journal of Sociology of Education*, 7(3): 265–74.

Weiner, G. (1994) *Feminisms in Education*. Milton Keynes: Open University Press.

Weitzman, E. (2000) Software and qualitative research, in N.K. Denzin, and Y.S. Lincoln, (eds) *Handbook of Qualitative Research*, 2nd edn. Thousand Oaks, CA: Sage.

Wheelock, J. and Jones, K. (2002) 'Grandparents are the next best thing': Informal childcare for working parents in urban Britain, *Journal of Social Policy*, 31: 441–63.

Whelehan, I. (1995) *Modern Feminist Thought*. Edinburgh: Edinburgh University Press.

White, S. (2001) Auto-ethnography as reflexive inquiry: The research act as self-surveillance, in I. Shaw and N. Gould (eds) *Qualitative Research in Social Work*. London: Sage.

Whitmore, E. (2001) 'People listened to what we had to say': Reflections on an emancipatory qualitative evaluation, in I. Shaw and N. Gould (eds) *Qualitative Research in Social Work*. London: Sage.

Whitmore, E. and Mckee, L. (2000) Six street youth who could, in P. Reason and H. Bradbury (eds) *The Handbook of Action Research*. London: Sage.

Whyte, J. (1986) *Girls into Science and Technology: The Story of a Project*. London: Routledge and Kegan Paul.

Whyte, J., Deem, R., Kant, L. and Cruickshank, M. (eds) (1988) *Girl-Friendly Schooling*. London: Methuen.

Wilensky, H. (1975) *The Welfare State and Equality*. Berkeley and LA: University of California Press.

Williams, F. (1989) *Social Policy: A Critical Introduction*. Cambridge: Polity Press.

Williams, F. (1997) Feminism and social policy, in V. Robinson and D. Richardson (eds) *Introducing Women's Studies*. Basingstoke: Macmillan.

Williamson, H. (1997a) Status Zero youth and the 'underclass': Some considerations, in R. MacDonald (ed.) *Youth, the 'Underclass' and Social Exclusion*. London: Routledge.

Williamson, H. (1997b) Youth work and citizenship, in J. Bynner, L. Chisholm and A. Furlong (eds) *Youth Citizenship and Social Change in a European Context*. Aldershot: Ashgate.

Willis, P. (1977) *Learning to Labour*. Farnborough: Saxon House.

Willis, P. (1984) Youth unemployment: thinking the unthinkable, *Youth and Policy*, 2: 17–24.

Wilson, E. (1977) *Women and the Welfare State*. London: Tavistock.

Wilton, T. (1995) *Lesbian Studies: Setting an Agenda*. London: Routledge.

Wirth, L. (1938) Urbanism as a way of life, *American Journal of Sociology*, 44(1): 1–24.

Wise, S. and Stanley, L. (2003) Looking back and looking forward: Some recent feminist sociology reviewed, *Sociological Research Online*, 8(3), http://www.socresonline.org.uk/8/3/wise.html

Witherall, K. and Noddings, N. (eds) (1991) *Narrative and Dialogue in Education*. New York: Teachers College Press.

Witz, A. (1992) *Professions and Patriarchy*. London: Routledge.

Wolf, D.L. (1996) Situating feminist dilemmas in fieldwork, in D.L. Wolf (ed.) *Feminist Dilemmas in Fieldwork*. Boulder, CO: Westview.

Wolf, M. (1992) *A Thrice Told Tale: Feminism, Postmodernism and Ethnographic Responsibility*. Stanford, CA: Stanford University Press.

Women and Equality Unit (2003) *Delivering on Gender Equality*. London: Department of Trade and Industry.

Woods, P. (1996) *Researching the Art of Teaching: Ethnography for Educational Use*. London: Routledge.

Wollstonecraft, M. (1792) [1975] *A Vindication of the Rights of Women*. Harmondsworth: Penguin.

Wright, C., Weekes, D. and McGlaughlin, A. (2000) *Race, Class and Gender in Exclusion in School*. London: Falmer.

Wringe, C. (1992) The ambiguities of education for active citizenship, *Journal of Philosophy of Education*, 26(1): 29–38.

Young, A. (1990) *Femininity in Dissent*. London: Routledge.

Young, B. (1993) Feminism and masculinism: A backlash response, in T. Haddad (ed.) *Men and Masculinities: A Critical Anthology*. Toronto: Canadian Scholars Press.

Zerubavel, E. (1979) *Patterns of Time in Hospital Life: A Sociological Perspective*. Chicago: University of Chicago Press.

Zerubavel, E. (1999) *The Clockwork Muse*. Cambridge, Mass: Harvard University Press.

Index